BORDER CONTROL AND NEW TECHNOLOGIES
Addressing Integrated Impact Assessment

This book is based on the research project PERSONA (*Privacy, ethical, regulatory and social no-gate crossing point solutions acceptance*; 2018-21) and constitutes its Deliverable D5.3. This project has received funding from the European Union's Horizon 2020 research and innovation programme under grant agreement No. 787123. The contents are the sole responsibility of the authors and can in no way be taken to reflect the views of the European Union or of any of the beneficiaries of the aforementioned grant agreement.

Significant effort has been made to ensure the correctness and accuracy of the information provided in this textbook. This textbook does not constitute professional or legal advice. However, neither the publisher, nor the editors, nor the authors accept any liability whatsoever with regard to the information herein provided.

Every effort has been made to identify and credit copyright holders and, should the need be, obtain their permission for the use of copyrighted material. We would be pleased to rectify any omissions in subsequent editions, if any, should they be drawn to our attention.

The GPRC label (Guaranteed Peer Review Content) was developed by the Flemish organization Boek.be and is assigned to publications which are in compliance with the academic standards required by the VABB (Vlaams Academisch Bibliografisch Bestand).

This work is licensed under the Creative Commons Attribution-NonCommercial 4.0 International License. To view a copy of this license, visit http://creativecommons.org/licenses/by-nc/4.0/.

DOI: 10.46944/9789461171375

Cover Image: Gunnar Andersen, *Gradient 1:2:3*, Statens Museum for Kunst, Cophenhagen.
Cover design: Peer De Maeyer
Typesetting: Crius Group, Hulshout

© 2021 Uitgeverij ASP (Academic and Scientific Publishers nv)

Keizerslaan 34
1000 Brussel
Tel. +32 (0)2 289 26 56
Fax +32 (0)2 289 26 59
E-mail info@aspeditions.be
www.aspeditions.be

ISBN 978 94 6117 085 9 (Print)
ISBN 978 94 6117 137 5 (ePDF)
ISBN 978 94 6117 193 1 (epub)
NUR 820, 980
Legal deposit D/2021/11.161/004

BORDER CONTROL AND NEW TECHNOLOGIES

Addressing Integrated Impact Assessment

Edited by
J. Peter Burgess and Dariusz Kloza

ASP

Table of contents

List of abbreviations 11
Glossary 15

1	**Introduction**	27
	J. Peter BURGESS and Dariusz KLOZA	
2	**The concept of impact assessment**	31
	Dariusz KLOZA, Niels VAN DIJK, Simone CASIRAGHI, Sergi VAZQUEZ MAYMIR and Alessia TANAS	
2.1	Introduction	31
2.2	Impact assessment	32
	2.2.1 Overview	32
	2.2.2 History	33
	2.2.3 The benefits of impact assessment	34
	2.2.4 The drawbacks of impact assessment	35
	2.2.5 Integration of evaluation techniques	36
2.3	The framework for impact assessment	37
2.4	A generic method for impact assessment	39
3	**Privacy**	49
	Nikolaos IOANNIDIS	
3.1	Introduction	49
	3.1.1 Definition of privacy	49
	3.1.2 Historical development of the right to privacy in Western legal systems	49
	3.1.3 The importance of the right to privacy in society	50
	3.1.4 The importance of the right to privacy in the PERSONA benchmark	51
	3.1.5 Relevant regulatory instruments and actors involved	52
3.2	The contents of (the right to) privacy	54
	3.2.1 Legal conceptualisations	54
	3.2.2 Theoretical conceptualisations	56

4	**Personal data protection**	61
	Nikolaos IOANNIDIS	
4.1	Introduction	61
	4.1.1 Definition and development of the right to personal data protection	61
	4.1.2 The importance of data protection in society	62
	4.1.3 The role of data protection in the benchmark	62
	4.1.4 List of relevant regulatory instruments and systems	63
	4.1.5 Connection with other fundamental rights	65
4.2	Key concepts and actors	65
	4.2.1 Personal data and data subject	65
	4.2.2 Data controller	66
	4.2.3 Data processor	66
	4.2.4 Data protection authorities	67
4.3	Principles of EU data protection law	67
	4.3.1 Lawfulness, fairness, transparency	67
	4.3.2 Purpose limitation	68
	4.3.3 Data minimisation	69
	4.3.4 Data accuracy	69
	4.3.5 Storage limitation	69
4.4	Legal requirements	70
	4.4.1 Lawfulness of processing	70
	4.4.2 Accountability and compliance	71
	4.4.3 Data transfers	73
4.5	Data subject rights	74
	4.5.1 Right to be informed	74
	4.5.2 Right of access by the data subject	75
	4.5.3 Right to rectification	75
	4.5.4 Right to erasure ('right to be forgotten')	75
	4.5.5 Right to restriction of processing	75
	4.5.6 Right to data portability	76
	4.5.7 Right to object	76
	4.5.8 Right not to be subject to automated decision-making, including profiling	76
	4.5.9 Data subject rights in border control	76
5	**Ethics and border control technologies**	81
	Simone CASIRAGHI, *J. Peter* BURGESS *and Kristoffer* LIDÉN	
5.1	Introduction	81
	5.1.1 Definition of ethics	81
	5.1.2 The importance of ethics for society	82
	5.1.3 The role of ethics in the benchmark	82

		5.1.4	Historical development of applied ethics	83
		5.1.5	The profile for assessing ethics	84
		5.1.6	Literature overview	85
	5.2	Ethical arguments and fallacies		86
		5.2.1	Ethics and technology arguments	86
		5.2.2	Normative ethics	88
		5.2.3	Types of ethical fallacies	91

6 Social acceptance and border control technologies 99
Simone CASIRAGHI, *J. Peter* BURGESS *and Kristoffer* LIDÉN

6.1	Introduction			99
	6.1.1	Definition of the social acceptance		99
	6.1.2	The importance of social acceptance for society		100
	6.1.3	The role of social acceptance in the benchmark		101
	6.1.4	Historical development of social acceptance		102
	6.1.5	The profile needed for assessing social acceptance		103
	6.1.6	Literature overview		103
6.2	Social acceptance concepts and misconceptions			105
	6.2.1	What social acceptance is about		105
	6.2.2	What social acceptance is *not* about		109

7 Border management law in the European Union 117
Alessandra CALVI

7.1	Introduction		117
	7.1.1	The concept of border management	117
	7.1.2	How border management laws and policies affect fundamental rights: the case of EU large-scale databases and their interoperability	119
	7.1.3	How border control technologies affect fundamental rights	121
7.2	The historical development of border management law in the EU		122
7.3	Legal and regulatory instruments governing border management in the EU		124
7.4	Actors involved in border management in the EU		125
7.5	Legal requirements enshrining data protection, privacy and ethics in EU border management law		126
	7.5.1	An introduction to the built-in safeguards system of EU border management law	126
	7.5.2	Summary of the data protection, privacy and ethics requirements of the EU border control system	127

| 8 | A tailored method for the process of integrated impact assessment on border control technologies in the European Union and the Schengen Area | 143 |

Nikolaos IOANNIDIS, *Simone* CASIRAGHI, *Alessandra* CALVI *and Dariusz* KLOZA

Introduction	143
Overview of the method	145
PHASE I: PREPARATION OF THE ASSESSMENT PROCESS	146
Step 1: Screening (threshold analysis)	146
Step 2: Scoping	147
Step 3: Planning and Preparation	149
PHASE II: ASSESSMENT	151
Step 4: Systematic (detailed) description of the initiative	151
Step 5: Appraisal of Impacts	151
Step 6: Recommendations	155
PHASE III: EX POST (EVENTUAL) STEPS	157
Step 7: Prior Consultation with a Supervisory Authority	157
Step 8: Revisiting	158
ONGOING PHASE	158
Step A: Stakeholder involvement	158
Step B: Quality control	159
Step C: Documentation	160

Annexes 161

Annex 1: A template for a report from the process of integrated impact assessment on border control technologies in the European Union and the Schengen Area 163

Nikolaos IOANNIDIS, *Simone* CASIRAGHI, *Alessandra* CALVI *and Dariusz* KLOZA

Phase I: preparation of the assessment process	165
Phase II: Assessment	185
Phase III: *Ex post* (eventual) steps	209

Annex 2: Inventory of stakeholder involvement techniques 219

Simone CASIRAGHI

Annex 3: Inventory of appraisal techniques 229

Nikolaos IOANNIDIS

3.1	Introduction	229
3.2	Appraisal techniques explicitly required by the General Data Protection Regulation	230

	3.3	Supplementary appraisal techniques compatible with the General Data Protection Regulation	234
	3.4	Standalone evaluation techniques	238
	3.5	Technology ranking techniques	248

Annex 4: Inventory of relevant EU legal and regulatory instruments for border management 251

Alessandra CALVI

	4.1	Primary law	251
	4.2	Secondary law	251

List of abbreviations

ADDS	Automated Deception Detection System
AFIS	Automated Fingerprint Identification System
AFSJ	Area of Freedom, Security and Justice
AI	Artificial Intelligence
API	Advanced Passenger Information
BMS	Biometric Matching Service
CBA	Cost-Benefit Analysis
CFR	Charter of Fundamental Rights of the European Union
CIR	Common Identity Repository
CJEU	Court of Justice of the European Union
CoE	Council of Europe
DG	Directorate-General
DG JUST	Directorate-General for Justice and Consumers
DG HOME	Directorate-General for Migration and Home Affairs
DPA	Data Protection Authority
DPIA	Data Protection Impact Assessment
DPO	Data Protection Officer
EASO	European Asylum Support Office
EC	European Commission
ECHR	European Convention for Human Rights
ECRIS-TCN	European Criminal Records Information System for Third Country Nationals
ECtHR	European Court of Human Rights
EDPB	European Data Protection Board
EDPS	European Data Protection Supervisor
EDRi	European Digital Rights
EEA	European Economic Area
EES	Entry-Exit System
EIA	Environmental Impact Assessment
ELSI	Ethical, Social and Legal Implications of emerging technologies
ESP	European search portal
eTA	ethical Technology Assessment
ETIAS	European Travel Information and Authorisation System

EU	European Union
EUDPR	European Institutions Data Protection Regulation (Regulation 1725/2018)
eu-LISA	European Union Agency for the Operational Management of Large-Scale IT Systems in the Area of Freedom, Security and Justice
Eurodac	European Asylum Dactyloscopy Database
Europol	European Union Agency for Law Enforcement Cooperation
Eurosur	European Border Surveillance System
FRA	European Union Agency for Fundamental Rights
Frontex	European Border and Coast Guard Agency
GDPR	General Data Protection Regulation
IA	Impact Assessment
ICAO	International Civil Aviation Organisation
ICCPR	International Covenant on Civil and Political Rights
ICESCR	International Covenant on Economic, Social and Cultural Rights
ICO	Information Commissioner's Office [United Kingdom]
Interpol	International Criminal Police Organization
IOM	International Organization for Migration
ISO	International Organization for Standardization
IS	Information System
IT	Information Technology
LED	Law Enforcement Directive (Directive 2016/680)
LFR	Live Facial Recognition Technology
MID	Multiple Identity Detector
NEST	New and Emerging Science and Technologies
NIST	National Institute of Standards and Technology
NGO	Non-Governmental Organisation
PbD	Privacy by Design
PIA	Privacy Impact Assessment
PIU	Passenger Information Unit
PNR	Passenger Name Record
R&I	Research and Innovation
REC	Research Ethics Committees
RFID	Radio-Frequency Identification
RIA	Regulatory Impact Assessment
RRI	Responsible Research and Innovation
SA	Supervisory Authority
SBC	Schengen Borders Code
SCGs	Supervision Coordination Groups
SIS	Schengen Information System
SLTD	Stolen and Lost Travel Documents
SWOT	Strengths, Weaknesses, Opportunities and Threats Analysis

List of abbreviations

TA	Technology Assessment
TAM	Technology Acceptance Model
TEU	Treaty on the European Union
TFEU	Treaty on the Functioning of the European Union
UDHR	Universal Declaration of Human Rights
UK	United Kingdom of Great Britain and Northern Ireland
UN	United Nations
US	United States of America
UTAUT	Unified Theory of Acceptance and Use of Technology
VIS	Visa Information System

Glossary

Evaluation techniques[1]

Assessor the actor who performs an assessment process, be it in-house (internal) or outsourced (external).

Benchmark a societal concern or concerns (that is, a matter or matters of interest or importance) that is/are in a need of governance and management, including its/their protection and promotion.

Framework an "essential supporting structure"[2] or organisational arrangement for an evaluation technique, which defines and describes the conditions and principles thereof.

Impact assessment an evaluation technique used to analyse the possible consequences of an initiative for a relevant societal concern or concerns, if this initiative could present danger to these concerns, with a view to supporting an informed decision on whether to deploy the initiative and under what conditions, and constitutes – in the first place – a means to protect those concerns.[3]

Likelihood a "chance of something happening […], whether defined, measured or determined objectively or subjectively, qualitatively or quantitatively, and described using general terms or mathematically (such as a probability or a frequency over a given time period)."[4]

Method a "particular procedure for accomplishing or approaching something",[5] organising the practice of impact assessment and defining the consecutive or iterative steps to be undertaken in order to carry out the assessment process; a method corresponds to a framework, and can be seen as a practical reflection of it.

Template a practical aid for the assessor, taking the form of a schema to be completed following the given method and, upon completion, serving as a final report stemming from the assessment process.[6]

Probability a "measure of the chance of occurrence expressed as a number between 0 and 1, where 0 is impossibility and 1 is absolute certainty".[7]

Risk	an "effect of uncertainty on objectives. [...] An effect is a deviation from the expected. It can be positive, negative or both, and can address, create or result in opportunities and threats."[8]
Severity	the "magnitude of the damage, harm, etc."[9]

Privacy and personal data protection

Accountability	a twofold legal obligation for the data controller to take appropriate and effective measures to implement data protection principles, and to demonstrate, upon request, that appropriate and effective measures have been taken, thus providing evidence thereof.[10]
Consent	any freely given, specific, informed and unambiguous indication of the data subject's wishes by which they, through a statement or clear affirmative action, signify agreement to the processing of personal data relating to themselves.[11]
Data controller	the natural or legal person, public authority, agency or other body that, alone or jointly with others, determines the purposes and means of the processing of personal data.[12]
Data processor	a natural or legal person, public authority, agency or other body that processes personal data on behalf of the controller.[13]
Data subject	an identifiable natural person, that is, one who can be identified, directly or indirectly, in particular by reference to an identifier such as a name, an identification number, location data, an online identifier, or to one or more factors specific to the physical, physiological, genetic, mental, economic, cultural or social identity of that natural person.[14]
Directive	a legislative act of the EU, which sets out a goal that all EU Member States must achieve, while allowing the individual countries to devise their own laws on how to reach these goals.[15]
Data protection impact assessment	a type of impact assessment; in the EU, a legal obligation of the data controller, prior to the processing, to carry out an assessment of the impacts of the envisaged processing operations on the protection of personal data, where a type of processing in particular using new technologies, and taking into account the nature, scope, context and purposes of the processing, is likely to result in a high risk to the rights and freedoms of natural persons (data subjects).[16]

Glossary

Personal data	any information relating to an identified or identifiable natural person (data subject).[17]
Processing of personal data	any operation or set of operations performed on personal data or on sets of personal data, whether or not by automated means, such as collection, recording, organisation, structuring, storage, adaptation or alteration, retrieval, consultation, use, disclosure by transmission, dissemination or otherwise making available, alignment or combination, restriction, erasure or destruction.[18]
Profiling	any form of automated processing of personal data consisting of the use of personal data to evaluate certain personal aspects relating to a natural person, in particular to analyse or predict aspects concerning that natural person's performance at work, economic situation, health, personal preferences, interests, reliability, behaviour, location or movements.[19]
Recommendation	a non-binding legislative act of the EU, which enables the EU institutions to express a view to EU Member States, and in some cases, to individuals.[20]
Regulation	a legislative act of the EU, binding in its entirety and directly applicable within all EU Member States.[21]
Security of processing	a legal obligation of the data controller and the data processor to implement appropriate technical and organisational measures to ensure a level of security of personal data appropriate to the risk, taking into account the state of the art, the costs of implementation and the nature, scope, context and purposes of processing, as well as the varying likelihood and severity of risks for the rights and freedoms of natural persons.[22]
Special categories of personal data	personal data revealing racial or ethnic origin, political opinions, religious or philosophical beliefs, or trade union membership, and the processing of genetic data, biometric data for the purpose of uniquely identifying a natural person, data concerning health, or data concerning a natural person's sex life or sexual orientation.[23]
Supervisory authority (data protection authority)	a relevant public body (that is, an independent regulatory agency) empowered to perform specific functions in the field of personal data protection;[24] its roles usually include: ombudsmen, consultants, negotiators, auditors, educators, policy advisers, and enforcers.[25]

Ethics and social acceptance

Anticipatory methods techniques of governance that aim to anticipate possible future consequences by tackling impacts of technologies before they materialise and by influencing future decision-making.[26]

Applied ethics the practical application of normative theories to concrete controversial cases by performing rigorous philosophical reasoning to solve dilemmas or guide decision-making; the most established forms of applied ethics are currently bioethics, business ethics, computer ethics and environmental ethics; emerging fields are robo-ethics, big data ethics and artificial intelligence (AI) ethics.

Consequentialism a set of theories stating that actions are right or wrong only on the basis of their outcomes (that is, consequences); in other words, among the possible actions available, one chooses the option that maximises the expected outcomes.

Deficit model "the orthodox assumption [...] found amongst most policy-makers and scientists that the general public lack[s] sufficient knowledge and understanding of basic science and technology";[27] this lack of knowledge, in turn, produces scepticism or hostility towards science and technology.

Deontology a set of theories that defines rules on the basis of fundamental moral principles, rather than the consequences of an action; an action is morally right if it conforms to certain duties, rights, prohibitions, or responsibilities, and/or if the actor has certain intentions, regardless of the consequences of such an action; roughly, the definition of duty precedes that of what counts as "good".

Descriptive ethics a form of empirical research describing existing norms or ways to discuss moral issues;[28] it describes people's beliefs about morality (which can originate from traditions, habits, education or personal attitudes) at a given time in a given place, as a form of sociological, ethnographical or (neuro)psychological inquiry; examples of descriptive ethics come from neuroscience, where moral thoughts and emotions are described in terms of the neural circuits that are activated when people engage in moral thinking.[29]

Distributive justice	a set of theories based on the idea of "fairness in distribution" or "what is deserved"; an action is therefore morally wrong whenever some benefit to which a person is entitled is denied (without any compelling reason) or whenever there is an unequal distribution of benefits and burdens.
Ethics	a branch of philosophy that deals, roughly, with a rational and practical reflection on what is good or bad and right or wrong; "ethics" is a synonym for moral philosophy.
Engagement model	the theoretical account in which individuals are not only "instructed" but also involved in a dialogue with scientists and policy makers;[30] the idea is that participation is moved "upstream"[31] by taking the lay knowledge of the citizens seriously and possibly achieving a two-way dialogue between them and scientists.
Function creep	the deployment of a specific initiative (for example, a border control technology) for the purpose for which it was not originally intended.[32]
Metaethics	the study of a wide range of metaphysical, epistemological or psychological presuppositions related to moral language, thought and practice, regardless of particular substantive debates about morality; for example, in a debate on the validity of ethical principles, the European Commission (EC) has been supportive of an idea of a global framework for ethics of Artificial Intelligence (AI) that goes beyond particularities, and which could possibly become globally applicable.[33]
Normative ethics	the study of the criteria or principles that one should follow to act morally; of the consequences that one should take into account when making a decision that is morally laden; or, more generally, of the type of life one should live to be fulfilled or serve as an example to others; in the technology discourse, an exemplary debate is that of self-driving cars with reference to the famous trolley dilemma;[34] the basic idea is that an autonomous car will have to face moral dilemmas and therefore take morally charged decisions; the outcome of these decisions would – crucially – depend on the normative theory that the programmer would "inscribe" in the software.
Principles	in ethics, propositions that provide general or abstract guidance for action, typically formulated in sentences such as "You should (not) do X" or "You should respect Y".

Rules	in ethics, indications of what individuals ought (not) to or are (not) allowed to do in a given situation.
Social acceptance	"the fact that a new technology is accepted – or merely tolerated – by a community";[35] to accept, in turn, refers to the act of receiving something that is offered, of giving an affirmative reply to it, and accommodating to it with approval.[36]
Stakeholder	"someone who holds a stake (interest) in something, regardless of whether or not he or she is aware of this and of whether the interest is articulated directly or not".[37]
Values	indications of the extent to which someone cares about an object or action, for example dignity, solidarity or equality.[38]

Border management

Border checks	checks carried out at border crossing points to ensure that persons, including their means of transport and the objects in their possession, may be authorised to enter the territory of a state or authorised to leave it.[39]
Border control	activity carried out at a border, exclusively in response to an intention to cross or the act of crossing that border, regardless of any other consideration, consisting of both border checks and border surveillance.[40]
Border crossing points	crossing points authorised by the competent authorities for the crossing of (external) borders.[41]
Border guard	a public official assigned, in accordance with national law, to a border crossing point, along a border, or in the immediate vicinity of that border, who carries out border control tasks, in accordance with law.[42]
Border surveillance	the activity of surveillance of borders between border crossing points and the surveillance of border crossing points outside the fixed opening hours, with the aim of preventing persons from circumventing border checks;[43] in a broader – but not strictly legal – sense, other activities happening before the border that target individuals and groups (for example, monitoring of sea corridors and of social media to identify migration routes) can be considered border surveillance.[44]

Glossary

Dual-use items items, including software and technology, which can be used for both civil and military purposes, including all goods that can be used for both non-explosive purposes and that can assist in any way in the manufacture of nuclear weapons or other nuclear explosive devices.[45]

ECRIS-TCN the European Criminal Records Information System for Third Country Nationals, the EU's large-scale database that will supplement the existing EU criminal records database (ECRIS) on non-EU nationals convicted in the European Union; based on a centralised hit/no-hit system, it will allow Member States' authorities to identify which other Member States hold criminal records on the third-country nationals or stateless persons being checked, so that they can then use the existing ECRIS system to address requests for conviction information only to the identified Member States.[46]

EES the Entry-Exit System, the EU's large-scale database that will electronically register the time and place of entry and exit of third-country nationals, both those who require a visa and those who are visa-exempt, admitted for a short stay, as well as those refused entry.[47]

EU large-scale databases the Schengen Information System II (SIS II), the European Dactyloscopy (Eurodac), the Visa Information System (VIS), the Entry-Exit Systems (EES), the European Criminal Records Information System for Third Country Nationals (ECRIS-TCN) and the European Travel Information and Authorisation System (ETIAS).

Eurodac the European Dactyloscopy, the EU's large-scale database for the storage of fingerprints of asylum seekers and irregular migrants aged 14 and over, which enables Member States to compare the fingerprints of asylum applicants in order to see whether they have previously applied for asylum or entered the EU irregularly via another Member State, to determine the responsibility for examining an asylum application; since July 2015, Eurodac has also been used for law enforcement purposes by Member State law enforcement authorities and Europol.[48]

ETIAS	the European Travel Information and Authorisation System, a pre-travel authorisation system for visa-exempt travellers, the key function of which is to verify if a third-country national meets entry requirements before travelling to the Schengen area, enabling pre-travel assessment of irregular migration risks, and security or public health risk checks; Member States' designated authorities and Europol will be able to consult data stored in the ETIAS Central System for the purposes of the prevention, detection and investigation of terrorist offences or of other serious criminal offences.[49]
Europol	the European Union Agency for Law Enforcement Cooperation, a European agency established with a view to supporting cooperation among law enforcement authorities in the Union.[50]
External borders	in the Schengen Area, Member States' land borders, including river and lake borders, sea borders and their airports, river ports, seaports and lake ports, which are not internal borders.[51]
Externalisation of (European) border control	a range of processes whereby the EU and its Member States complement policies to control migration across their territorial boundaries with initiatives that realise such control extra-territorially and through countries and organs other than their own.[52]
Internal borders	in the Schengen Area, borders *exclusively* involving the territories of Member States of the EU; for example common land borders, including river and lake borders; airports for internal flights; sea, river and lake ports for regular internal ferry connections.[53]
Interoperability	the ability of information technology (IT) systems and of the business processes they support to exchange data and to enable the sharing of information and knowledge.[54]
Interpol	the International Criminal Police Organisation, an inter-governmental organisation with 194 Member Countries, that ensures and promotes mutual assistance between the criminal police authorities of its members.[55]
Privatisation of border control	any measure by a state that delegates the implementation of border management to a private actor.[56]

Glossary

SIS the Schengen Information System, the EU's large-scale database aimed at ensuring a high level of security and facilitating the free movement of people within the Schengen Area through three areas of cooperation: border control, law enforcement and vehicle registration; it contains alerts on persons who may have been involved in a serious crime or may not have the right to enter or stay in the Schengen Area; on missing persons, in particular children; on certain property, such as banknotes, aircraft, boats, cars, vans, containers, firearms and identity documents, that may have been stolen, misappropriated or lost;[57] new functionalities are being implemented in different stages, with a requirement for the work to be completed by 2021.[58]

Smart Borders in the EU, automated systems to speed up and facilitate the border check procedure of the majority of travellers, and to hinder and stop those immigrants that poses a threat to the security of the EU through their status as irregular immigrants, criminals or terrorists.

VIS the Visa Information System, the EU's large-scale database that supports Member States' consular authorities in the management of applications for short-stay visas to visit or to transit through the Schengen Area; it enables the exchange of visa information and the matching of biometric data to verify the authenticity of a visa;[59] the VIS supports the fight against fraud and facilitates checks within the territory of the Member States, assisting in the identification of any person who may not or may no longer fulfil the conditions for entry to, stay in, or residence on the territory of the Member States; as ancillary objectives, the VIS supports the asylum applications process and contributes to the prevention of threats to internal security.[60]

Endnotes

1. Unless specified otherwise, definitions in this sub-section are taken from: Dariusz Kloza et al., "Data Protection Impact Assessment in the European Union: Developing a Template for a Report from the Assessment Process," d.pia.lab Policy Brief (Brussels: VUB, 2020) 1–2, https://doi.org/10.31228/osf.io/7qrfp.
2. Oxford Dictionary of English, https://www.lexico.com/.
3. Dariusz Kloza et al., "Towards a Method for Data Protection Impact Assessment: Making Sense of GDPR Requirements," d.pia.lab Policy Brief (Brussels: VUB, 2019), 1, https://doi.org/10.31228/osf.io/es8bm.
4. International Organization for Standardization (ISO), *Risk management – Guidelines*, ISO 31000:2018, § 3.7.
5. Oxford Dictionary of English.
6. Kloza et al., "Data Protection Impact Assessment in the European Union: Developing a Template for a Report from the Assessment Process."
7. ISO, *Risk management — Vocabulary*, ISO Guide 73:2009, § 3.6.1.4.
8. ISO 31000:2018, § 3.1.
9. Society for Risk Analysis, "Society for Risk Analysis Glossary," 2015, 6.
10. General Data Protection Regulation, Article 5(2). See also Article 29 Working Party, *Opinion 3/2010 on the Principle of Accountability*, Brussels 2010, https://ec.europa.eu/justice/article-29/documentation/opinion-recommendation/files/2010/wp173_en.pdf; Joseph Alhadeff, Brendan van Alsenoy, and Jos Dumortier, "The Accountability Principle in Data Protection Regulation: Origin, Development and Future Directions," in *Managing Privacy through Accountability*, ed. Daniel Guagnin et al. (London: Palgrave Macmillan, 2012), 49–82, https://doi.org/10.1057/9781137032225_4.
11. General Data Protection Regulation, Article 4(11).
12. General Data Protection Regulation, Article 4(7).
13. General Data Protection Regulation, Article 4(8).
14. General Data Protection Regulation, Article 4(1).
15. Klaus-Dieter Borchardt, *The ABC of EU Law* (Luxembourg: Publications Office of the European Union, 2016).
16. General Data Protection Regulation, Article 35(1).
17. General Data Protection Regulation, Article 4(1).
18. General Data Protection Regulation, Article 4(2).
19. General Data Protection Regulation, Article 4(4).
20. Borchardt.
21. Borchardt.
22. General Data Protection Regulation, Article 32(1).
23. General Data Protection Regulation, Article 9(1).
24. Dariusz Kloza and Anna Mościbroda, "Making the Case for Enhanced Enforcement Cooperation between Data Protection Authorities: Insights from Competition Law," *International Data Privacy Law* 4, no. 2 (2014): 121, https://doi.org/10.1093/idpl/ipu010.
25. Colin J. Bennett and Charles D. Raab, *The Governance of Privacy: Policy Instruments in Global Perspective* (Cambridge, Massachusetts: MIT Press, 2006).
26. Philip Brey, "Anticipatory Ethics for Emerging Technologies," *NanoEthics* 6, no. 1 (2012): 1–13, https://doi.org/10.1007/s11569-012-0141-7.
27. Rob Flynn, "Risk and the Public Acceptance of New Technologies," in *Risk and the Public Acceptance of New Technologies*, ed. Rob Flynn and Paul Bellaby (London: Palgrave Macmillan UK, 2007), 10, https://doi.org/10.1057/9780230591288.

28. Tsjalling Swierstra, "Introduction to the Ethics of New and Emerging Science and Technology," in *Handbook of Digital Games and Entertainment Technologies* (2015): 1–25, https://doi.org/10.1007/978-981-4560-52-8_33-1.
29. Joshua D. Greene et al., "An FMRI Investigation of Emotional Engagement in Moral Judgment," *Science* 293, no. 5537 (2001): 2105–8, https://doi.org/10.1126/science.1062872; Antonio Damasio, *Descartes' Error: Emotion, Rationality and the Human Brain* (New York: Putnam, 1994).
30. Alan Irwin and Brian Wynne, "Introduction," in *Misunderstanding Science?*, ed. Alan Irwin and Brian Wynne (Cambridge: Cambridge University Press, 1996), 1–18, https://doi.org/10.1017/CBO9780511563737.001.
31. James Wilsdon and Rebecca Willis, *See-Through Science: Why Public Engagement Needs to Move Upstream* (London: Demos, 2004).
32. Bert-Jaap Koops, "The concept of function creep," *Law, Innovation and Technology* 13, no. 1 (2021): 29-56, https://doi.org/10.1080/17579961.2021.1898299.
33. European Commission, *Building Trust in Human Centric Artificial Intelligence*, Brussels, 2019, COM(2019)168.
34. Edmond Awad et al., "The Moral Machine Experiment," *Nature* 563, no. 7729 (2018): 59–64, https://doi.org/10.1038/s41586-018-0637-6.
35. Behnam Taebi, "Bridging the Gap between Social Acceptance and Ethical Acceptability," *Risk Analysis* 37, no. 10 (2017): 1817–27, https://doi.org/10.1111/risa.12734.
36. Susana Batel, Patrick Devine-Wright and Torvald Tangeland, "Social Acceptance of Low Carbon Energy and Associated Infrastructures: A Critical Discussion," *Energy Policy* 58 (2013): 2, https://doi.org/10.1016/j.enpol.2013.03.018.
37. Kloza et al., "Towards a Method for Data Protection Impact Assessment: Making Sense of GDPR Requirements."
38. J. Peter Burgess et al., "Towards a Digital Ethics" (Brussels: European Data Protection Supervisor, 2018).
39. Article 2(11) Regulation (EU) 2016/399 of the European Parliament and of the Council of 9 March 2016 on a Union Code on the rules governing the movement of persons across borders (Schengen Borders Code), OJ L 77, 23.3.2016, p. 1–52.
40. Article 2(10) Schengen Borders Code.
41. Article 2(8) Schengen Borders Code.
42. Article 2(14) Schengen Borders Code.
43. Article 2(12) Schengen Borders Code.
44. Petra Molnar, EDRi and the Refugee Law Lab, "Technological Testing Grounds – Migration Management Experiments and Reflections from the Ground Up," 2020.
45. Article 1, Council Regulation (EC) No 428/2009 of 5 May 2009 setting up a Community regime for the control of exports, transfer, brokering and transit of dual-use items, OJ L 134, 29.5.2009, p. 1–269.
46. eu-LISA, "ECRIS-TCN European Criminal Records Information System-Third Country Nationals," 2019, https://doi.org/10.2857/499149.
47. Udo Bux, "Management of the External Borders," *Fact Sheets on the European Union*, 2019, 1–5.
48. eu-LISA, "Eurodac-2019 Annual Report" (2020), https://doi.org/10.2857/157463.
49. Gloria González Fuster, "Artificial Intelligence and Law Enforcement. Impact on Fundamental Rights" (Brussels, 2020).
50. Regulation (EU) 2016/794 of the European Parliament and of the Council of 11 May 2016 on the European Union Agency for Law Enforcement Cooperation (Europol) and replacing and repealing Council Decisions 2009/371/JHA, 2009/934/JHA, 2009/935/JHA, 2009/936/JHA and 2009/968/JHA, OJ L 135, 24.5.2016, p. 53–114.

51. Article 2(2) Schengen Borders Code.
52. Violeta Moreno-Lax and Martin Lemberg-Pedersen, "Border-Induced Displacement: The Ethical and Legal Implications of Distance-Creation through Externalization," *QIL, Zoom-In* 56 (2019): 5–33.
53. Article 2(1) Schengen Borders Code.
54. European Commission, Communication on improved effectiveness, enhanced interoperability and synergies among European databases in the area of Justice and Home Affairs, Brussels, 2005, COM(2005) 597 final.
55. Article 2, Constitution of the International Criminal Police Organization INTERPOL, 13 June 1956, I/CONS/GA/1956 (2008).
56. Frank Mc Namara, "Externalised and Privatised Procedures of EU Migration Control and Border Management – A Study of EU Member State Control and Legal Responsibility" (European University Institute, 2017).
57. eu-LISA, "Report on the Technical Functioning of Central SIS II and the Communication Infrastructure , Including the Security Thereof and the Bilateral and Multilateral Exchange of Supplementary Information between Member States" (2015), https://doi.org/10.2857/567010.
58. Bux, "Management of the External Borders."
59. Teresa Quintel, "Connecting Personal Data of Third Country Nationals: Interoperability of EU Databases in the Light of the CJEU's Case Law on Data Retention," *University of Luxembourg Law Working Paper* 2 (2018).
60. eu-LISA, "Report on the VIS 1 Report on the Technical Functioning of the Visa Information System (VIS)," 2020, https://doi.org/10.2857/66661.

1 Introduction

J. Peter Burgess* and Dariusz Kloza**
* *École normale supérieure, Paris and Vrije Universiteit Brussel.*
  E-mail: james.peter.burgess@ens.pls.eu.
** *Vrije Universiteit Brussel. E-mail: dariusz.kloza@vub.be.*

This book is occasioned by the convergence of two political occurrences.

The first is the unprecedented rise in global migration. According to the International Organization for Migration's (IOM) *2020 World Migration Report*, 272 million people, or roughly 3.5% of the world's population, are migrants.[1] The IOM – as well as other commentators – notes that migration has taken a particularly serious turn in recent years, in part as a result of armed conflict (for example, in Syria, Yemen, the Central African Republic, the Democratic Republic of the Congo and South Sudan), economic and/or political instability, and, increasingly, climate change.[2] This multi-year global evolution and its ill-fated transformation into various forms of identity politics has led to the transformation of migration from its traditional status as a humanitarian challenge to its new incarnation as a *security* problem.[3] Moreover, the particularity of this new security challenge is that it does not prioritise the more-or-less plainly visible security crisis in which migrants find themselves, but rather the cultural and, in part, societal security of the recipient states. This has strengthened the politically unavoidable hypothesis that solving the problem of migration is workable only through addressal of the issue of securing state borders.

The second occurrence is less concrete and less visible, but nonetheless impacts the first in important ways. It involves the growing expectation of immediacy in politics, the demand for quicker political decision-making and implementation, especially in the face of a perceived danger. Together with the rise of the notion of risk at the end of the last century, and the actuarial impulse brought about by the growing global influence of New Public Management (an organisational strategy according to which public affairs should be governed in accordance with private business models) and the rise of anticipatory politics, such as the precautionary principle developed in the field of environmental studies, it has become a political necessity to foresee and pre-calibrate political processes and the impacts they will have upon individuals and societies.

This double challenge forms the political, social and technological motivation for the development of evaluation techniques and other tools that are used to govern the development and application of new initiatives, including – in this context – border technologies, in order to assess their possible impact on societal values such as human rights, including – again, particularly in this context – the rights to privacy and personal data protection.

This book takes a particular interest in new border technologies for two reasons. First, such technologies are deployed in environments characterised by a complex interaction between societal values and technological constraints. In other words, border technologies, having the ambition of allowing for 'seamless' or 'contactless' passage through state borders, are increasingly utilised at borders with the aim of improving the flow of travellers and facilitating border checks. Experience has shown, however, that their use often conflicts with societal values. Second, on the macro-political level, such border technologies are often a focus of highly contentious debates about identity, sovereignty, security, national and European values, resilience, risk, and the fragility of life itself.

As a result, there is a growing need to accommodate two requirements: the deployment of new border technologies and the respect for relevant societal values.

As a tool by which to help clarify issues within this complex debate, this book proposes a concept of impact assessment. Alongside the myriad evaluation techniques also available, this tool will aid the anticipation of and critical reflection on the possible future consequences of envisaged border management initiatives, and contribute to more sound decisions being made about their use.

To that end, this book offers a number of novel aspects. Aiming at comprehensiveness and provision of the most robust advice for decision making, it adapts the method of impact assessment to the on-the-ground realities and needs of border technologies by integrating at least four societal concerns triggered by these technologies, namely: privacy, personal data protection, ethics and social acceptance. It offers the option of adding further concerns and adjusting them to local contexts. It furthermore allows for the integration of this four-part impact assessment with other evaluation techniques, for example regulatory impact assessment (RIA).[4]

* * *

The book is organised into eight Chapters and four Annexes. Chapter 2 proposes an overall introduction to the concept of impact assessment. As the appraisal of consequences of initiatives for individuals and society requires a certain degree of suppleness for the reading and interpreting of social values, Chapters 3-7 describe the components of the benchmark used for integrated impact assessment. In this context, these components are the notions of privacy, personal data protection, ethics and social acceptance. Chapter 8 then presents a tailored method for integrated impact assessment of border control technologies, supplemented by methodological indications aimed at supporting assessors and other border management actors.

These Chapters are followed by four Annexes containing supplementary information and aids for users of the book. These include, in Annex 1, a tailored template for a report from the process of integrated impact assessment of border control technologies. Annexes 2-4 provide more specific, detail-oriented information intended to help impact assessors in carrying out assessment processes. These include analytic inventories of stakeholder involvement techniques (Annex 2), a list of concrete assessment methods (Annex 3) and, finally, an inventory of relevant border management legislation applicable in the European Union and the Schengen Area (Annex 4). The Chapters and Annexes are preceded by a glossary of key terms used throughout the book. In parallel, the book includes copious references to academic and professional sources, the majority of which are available in open access format.

In summary, this book constitutes a textbook on the use of integrated impact assessment. It is addressed to anyone involved in the 'supply chain' of border management and, in particular, to assessors and those in charge of decision-making pertaining to new border technologies. It focuses on the European Union and the Schengen Area, notwithstanding a possibility for adaptation and use elsewhere in the world.

The book reflects the law and practice as they stood on 31 March 2021.

* * *

During the creation of this book, we received with gratitude help from – in alphabetical order – Simone Casiraghi, Athena Christofi, Diana Dimitrova, Konstantinos Kakavoulis, Ioulia Konstantinou, Inge Lindsaar, Giulio Mancini, Petra Molnar, Anna Mościbroda, Annet Steenbergen and Eckhard Szimba. We also thank the two anonymous reviewers who have contributed to ensuring the scientific quality and integrity of this book in accordance with the Guaranteed Peer-Review Content (GPRC) scheme.[5]

This book constitutes the main output of the research project PERSONA (*Privacy, ethical, regulatory and social no-gate crossing point solutions acceptance*; 2018-21),[6] funded by the European Union under its Horizon 2020 programme.

Paris – Brussels
April 2021

Endnotes

1. *World Migration Report 2020* (Geneva: International Organization for Migration, 2019), 1–2, https://publications.iom.int/books/world-migration-report-2020.
2. Elżbieta Kużelewska, Amy Weatherburn, and Dariusz Kloza, "Introduction: Asking Big Questions: Migrants Ante Portas and What to Do with Them?," in *Irregular Migration as a Challenge for Democracy*, ed. Elżbieta Kużelewska, Amy Weatherburn, and Dariusz Kloza (Cambridge: Intersentia, 2018), xiii–xlvii, http://intersentia.com/en/pdf/viewer/item/id/9781780686226_0/.
3. J. Peter Burgess and Serge Gutwirth, eds., *A Threat Against Europe?: Security, Migration and Integration* (Brussels: VUBPress, 2011).
4. Anne Meuwese, *Impact Assessment in EU Lawmaking* (Alphen aan den Rijn: Kluwer Law International, 2008).
5. Cf. https://www.gprc.be/en/content/what-gprc.
6. Grant Agreement No. 787123. Cf. http://www.persona-project.eu.

2 The concept of impact assessment[1]

Dariusz KLOZA,* Niels VAN DIJK,** Simone CASIRAGHI,*** Sergi VAZQUEZ MAYMIR**** and Alessia TANAS*****

* Vrije Universiteit Brussel. E-mail: dariusz.kloza@vub.be.
** Vrije Universiteit Brussel, E-mail: niels.Van.Dijk@vub.be.
*** Vrije Universiteit Brussel. E-mail: simone.casiraghi@vub.be.
**** Vrije Universiteit Brussel, E-mail: sergi.Vazquez.Maymir@vub.be.
***** Vrije Universiteit Brussel, E-mail: Alessia.Tanas@vub.be.

2.1 Introduction

This Chapter introduces the concept of impact assessment, and thus lays down a foundation for the present textbook on integrated impact assessment for border control technologies. It intends to offer, in an accessible way, an overview of the said concept, eventually aiming to constitute a reference work for anybody interested in the topic.[2]

The Chapter is structured as follows: After the present introduction, it outlines the concept of impact assessment, namely its definition, terminology, and historical development, as well as its merits and drawbacks, ultimately exploring the possibility of integrating multiple evaluation techniques (Section 2.2). In Section 2.3, it offers 16 principles and conditions that apply to both the theory and practice of impact assessment (namely, the framework) and, in Section 2.4, it defines and describes, in a general manner, the consecutive or iterative steps to be undertaken in order to carry out an assessment process of any type and in any area of practice (namely, the method). This Chapter is to be read in conjunction with Chapter 8 and Annex 1, offering a tailored method and template, respectively, for a report arising from the process of integrated impact assessment for border control technologies.

This Chapter builds on the work of Vrije Universiteit Brussel's (VUB's) Brussels Laboratory for Data Protection & Privacy Impact Assessments (d.pia.lab)[3] and, wherever necessary, revises and updates it. However, nothing in this Chapter is to be considered 'final', as the concept of impact assessment is a 'living instrument', constantly necessitating a reflection on the most recent stage(s) of its development.

2.2 Impact assessment

2.2.1 Overview

Generally speaking, impact assessment is an evaluation technique used to analyse the possible consequences of an initiative for a relevant societal concern or concerns (that is, a matter, or matters, of interest or importance), to determine whether this initiative could present danger to these societal concerns, with a view to supporting an informed decision on whether to deploy the initiative and under what conditions, and constitutes – in the first place – a means by which to protect those societal concerns.[4]

Analogous to the structure of risk management,[5] the architecture of impact assessment typically consists of three main elements: framework, method and template. A *framework* constitutes an 'essential supporting structure'[6] or organisational arrangement for something, which, in this context, defines and describes the conditions and principles of impact assessment. A *method* is a 'particular procedure for accomplishing or approaching something'.[7] It organises the practice of impact assessment and defines the consecutive or iterative steps to be undertaken in order to carry out the assessment process. A method corresponds to a framework and can be seen as a practical reflection of it. Finally, a *template* is a practical aid for the assessor. It takes the form of a schema to be completed following the given method. It structures the assessment process, guides the assessor through the process and, upon completion, serves as a final *report* from the process. It documents all the activities undertaken within a given assessment process, clarifies the extent of compliance with the law, and provides evidence as to the quality of the assessment process.[8]

This architecture is often supplemented by aids such as *guidelines* (handbooks, manuals), *knowledge bases* (for example, inventories of possible risks and corresponding countermeasures), and *software* to aid assessors in the assessment process by automating parts thereof;[9] all such aids vary significantly in their quality and applicability.

The *assessor* is the actor who performs an assessment process, be it in-house (internal) or outsourced (external). The assessment process frequently necessitates expertise from more than a single domain, and hence is to be considered a collaborative activity. The team of assessors remains professionally independent from the leadership of a sponsoring organisation throughout the assessment process.

Finally, a *benchmark* is a societal concern or concerns that is/are in a need of governance and management, including protection and promotion, for example privacy and personal data protection.

2.2.2 History

While some rudimentary anticipation of consequences has perhaps always been present in any form of decision-making, impact assessment and similar evaluation techniques formalised such anticipation of consequences as they grew out of the emergence of new and – at the time – poorly understood dangers to individual and collective societal concerns. These dangers were typically framed as uncertainty and risk,[10] and it was understood to be in the interest of society to reduce them. For example, technology assessment (TA) emerged in 1960s in the United States, initially as a tool used by scientific committees to respond – largely, by advising policy makers on policy alternatives – to increasing public concerns relating to the negative social consequences of discoveries and inventions. TA was subsequently institutionalised as a means to ensure product safety, and gradually came to encompass a broader spectrum of issues relating to society and technology.[11] In parallel, environmental impact assessment (EIA) surfaced as a response to the gradual degradation of the natural environment.[12] These developments have aided the spread of evaluation techniques as a practice worldwide, and have resulted in the proliferation, and sometimes institutionalisation, of impact assessment in areas of practice ranging from healthcare,[13] regulation (governance),[14] ethics[15] and surveillance practices[16] to privacy[17] and personal data protection. New types and areas of practice of impact assessment may well also emerge in the future.

Nevertheless, some 50 years after the emergence of the first types of impact assessment, this evaluation technique still failed to stand out as a clear-cut practice. Only in certain areas had it taken hold, such as TA, EIA or regulatory impact assessment (RIA), while in other areas it remains under development, for example in the areas of 'social' impact assessment[18] or human rights impact assessment.[19]

The emergence and proliferation of privacy impact assessment (PIA) and – subsequently – data protection impact assessment (DPIA) is frequently attributed to four main factors, namely: (1) the development of science and technology, and their growing intrusiveness into individual lives and social fabric,[20] (2) the increasing importance of the processing of personal data for contemporary economies, national security, scientific research, technological development and inter-personal relationships, among others,[21] (3) the process of globalisation and (4) the negative experiences stemming from the use and misuse of personal data in the past, in both public and private sectors, and the growing awareness of all of these.[22]

Based on the experience of evaluation techniques in other areas of practice, it was expected that PIA and DPIA would become powerful vehicles for compliance with, and enforcement of, privacy and personal data protection law.[23] PIA – and later DPIA – emerged in the 1990s and became institutionalised in different forms and at various levels of compulsion, first in common law jurisdictions, such as New Zealand, Australia, Canada and the United States. In Europe, the earliest policy for PIA was developed in the United Kingdom in 2007.[24]

The European Union (EU) has thus far put in place two sector-specific voluntary PIA policies: the first for radio-frequency identification (RFID) applications (2009),[25] and the second for intelligent energy networks ('smart grids'; 2012-14).[26] In a parallel development, the most recent 'better regulation' package (2017) advances privacy and personal data protection as just two of the many societal concerns under assessment in the processes of EU law- and policy-making; the other being (all other) fundamental rights, environmental and economic concerns.[27]

After the entry into force of the GDPR (2016),[28] the Police and Criminal Justice Data Protection Directive (2016),[29] and Regulation 2018/1725 on the protection of personal data processed by EU institutions, bodies, offices and agencies (2018),[30] a mandatory policy for impact assessment was progressively introduced across the EU in the area of personal data protection. (By virtue of the European Economic Area (EEA) Agreement, the GDPR is likewise applicable in Norway, Iceland and Liechtenstein.)[31] In addition, the ePrivacy Regulation, proposed in 2017 and expected to be passed into law in 2021, if adopted in its current wording, would also require a process of DPIA to be conducted in specific situations.[32]

This proliferation of mandatory policies for impact assessment in the areas of privacy and personal data protection is also observed beyond the EU. The Council of Europe's recently finalised modernisation of 'Convention 108' (2018)[33] introduced a similar requirement; the importance of the said Convention lies in the fact that it is open for signature *also* by non-Member States of the Council of Europe, hence influencing global standard setting.[34] At the same time, various policies for PIA and DPIA, or – simply – for risk appraisal in the areas of privacy and personal data protection, have been introduced recently in Serbia (2018)[35] and Switzerland (2020),[36] and – beyond Europe – in Israel, Japan, South Africa and South Korea, among other states. In addition, a number of international organisations, such as the International Committee of the Red Cross,[37] have introduced a requirement for such an assessment process into their by-laws.

2.2.3 The benefits of impact assessment

The benefit of impact assessment lies predominantly in its parallel contribution to informed decision-making and to the protection and promotion of societal concerns.

The former category, namely informed decision-making, usually attracts sponsoring organisations, as it brings with it benefits associated with a switch to anticipatory thinking. This permits those organisations to reflect on the consequences of their envisaged initiatives as well as on the means to – at least – minimise, or sometimes even avoid, negative and unintended consequences before they occur ('early warning'), leading to gains both in terms of resources and public trust.

Impact assessment can also ease compliance with legal and otherwise regulatory requirements (such as technical standards); for example, PIA 'can be an excellent entry point for applying the principles of Privacy by Design'.[38] Being a 'best-efforts obligation', impact assessment constitutes evidence of due diligence, which can potentially limit or even exclude legal liability.[39] In parallel, impact assessment allows sponsoring organisations to explain themselves to regulatory authorities (that is, to give account of) as to how they have acquitted themselves of certain responsibilities (that is, accountability) often facilitating part(s) of the work of such authorities. Eventually, impact assessment, if conducted in a transparent manner, may increase public confidence by showing that a sponsoring organisation takes societal concerns seriously. In addition, the private sector might be particularly interested in using impact assessment to demonstrate corporate social responsibility.

The latter category, namely protection and promotion of societal concerns, is usually attractive for public authorities because a requirement to conduct the assessment process helps them in fulfilling their mission to offer practical and efficient protection of relevant societal concerns (for example, certain human rights, such as privacy or personal data protection) for the benefit of the individual and society at large. For individuals and social groups, impact assessment is a means to voice their concerns (primarily through stakeholder involvement), which contributes to procedural justice.[40] Impact assessment seeks to accommodate diverse interests and consequently contributes to the drawing of a 'thin red line' between legitimate yet seemingly competing interests, for example national security and the protection of personal data (for instance, in DPIA), or the competitiveness of national economy and environmental protection (for instance, in EIA). In comparison with other protection tools, impact assessment may provide a wider scope in this regard than, for example, compliance checks, which can often be reduced to mere 'tick-box' exercises.

2.2.4 The drawbacks of impact assessment

Critics of impact assessment have argued that it unnecessarily burdens sponsoring organisations, adding to an already-overgrown bureaucracy, causing unnecessary expenditure and delays in decision-making, or even slowing the deployment of an initiative in question. It is thus no surprise that there is a recurrent wish for the process of impact assessment to be quick, simple and cheap.[41] Opponents underline the complexity of the assessment process in practice, the difficulties it brings, the lack of practical experience, and minimal or non-existent guidance and oversight. They further question its added value over other evaluation techniques, for example, compliance checks, as well as its efficacy, pointing out the broad discretion often afforded as to whether and how an assessment process should be conducted.

Impact assessment is often criticised for contributing to achieving only the minimum necessary compliance with regulatory requirements, with the least amount of effort, or instrumentally, in order to legitimise intrusive initiatives. Some sponsoring organisations are criticised for focusing on assessment processes in an abstract fashion, instead of using them as a means to address the consequences of a given envisaged initiative. Such organisations often confuse impact assessment with auditing. They incorrectly consider the consequences as being applicable only to themselves (for example, reputational or financial risks), rather than assessing the consequences for individuals and the public at large. Ultimately, impact assessment is often performed too late, that is, when the design of an initiative can no longer be meaningfully influenced. Critics further suggest that when impact assessment is compulsory, it represents a regulatory requirement too narrow in scope, allowing significantly dangerous initiatives to escape scrutiny. When an assessment process has been performed, it usually lacks transparency, that is, the process as a whole is opaque, hard for the layperson to understand (for example, due to a high level of technical complexity) and final results (in particular, the report including recommendations) are difficult, if not impossible, to find. It is often also criticised for failing to involve stakeholders, or giving them limited scope, therefore making their participation meaningless.

All in all, impact assessment is first and foremost an aid for decision-making. It is no 'silver bullet' solution: the quality of advice, and hence protection and promotion it can offer, depends on the way it is used, on the support it receives from public authorities, and, in the long run, on the oversight exercised by regulatory authorities and courts of law alike. Impact assessment does not come without difficulties, yet with straightforward application and clear methods, supported by guidance, advice and oversight, impact assessment can ultimately contribute to a more robust protection and promotion of societal concerns.[42]

2.2.5 Integration of evaluation techniques

Following the principles of the relevance of the benchmark and its adaptiveness (cf. *infra*), each assessment process is tailored (adapted) to the needs and reality of the initiative under assessment. In this regard, experience has shown that multiple types and areas of impact assessment – and, more broadly, evaluation techniques – can be integrated within a single assessment process. For example, the processes of PIA and DPIA might be combined if an envisaged initiative touches upon both societal concerns of privacy and personal data.

Such integration of evaluation techniques can be beneficial for at least three reasons: (1) since 'everything is inherently interconnected',[43] integration might render a more complete picture for decision-makers, (2) it leads to greater efficiency, i.e. a maximisation of productivity with minimum wasted effort or expense, and (3) it allows for inclusion of aspects not required in legally mandated evaluation techniques.[44] Such integration bears fruit on the condition that the integrated method, and in particular its benchmark, is internally coherent and not contradictory. In other words, integration of diverse types and areas of practice of impact assessment leads to an outcome that is greater than the sum of its parts.

However, while integration may contribute to efficiency, it could also lead to the subordination of certain elements of the benchmark, particularly 'those that are supposed to have their status raised in decision making through specific assessment instruments',[45] an outcome that is not desired. For example, the process of human rights impact assessment is intended to deal with the entirety of human rights, yet largely at the expense of the attention normally given to each human right were they to be assessed individually.

2.3 The framework for impact assessment

The framework for impact assessment sets foundations for both the theory and practice of impact assessment. It consists of 16 conditions and principles applicable to any type or area of practice of impact assessment.

Building on a comparative analysis and critical appraisal of multiple frameworks for impact assessment, these conditions and principles are:[46]

1. *Systematic process.* Impact assessment is a systematic process undertaken in accordance with an appropriate method and conducted in a timely manner. It starts early in the lifecycle of a single initiative, or a limited number of similar initiatives (for example, a proposed technology or a piece of legislation), prior to deployment. It continues throughout the development life-cycle and beyond as the society changes, dangers evolve and knowledge grows. It is revisited when needed, thus continuously influencing the design of the initiative under assessment.
2. *Relevant benchmark.* The assessment process analyses the possible future consequences of deploying a given initiative, or a set of similar initiatives, against the relevant societal concerns, both individual and collective, commensurate with its type (for example, DPIA pertains to the protection of individuals whenever their personal data are being processed and EIA pertains to the natural and human environment). Threshold analysis (scoping, context establishment, etc.) and stakeholder involvement help in determining and maintaining a list of such concerns. Whenever necessary, multiple types of impact assessment are performed for a given initiative, possibly in an integrated manner.
3. *Rational requirement.* Not all initiatives require an assessment process. Such a need is therefore determined by factors such as the nature, scope, context and purpose of the initiative under assessment, the number and types of individuals affected, etc. Impact assessment is, however, to be considered compulsory at least for initiatives capable of causing severe negative consequences to relevant societal concerns.
4. *Appropriate method.* There is no 'silver bullet' method for performing the assessment process. What matters is the choice of an appropriate assessment method allowing for the most comprehensive understanding of possible future consequences of the envisaged initiative.
5. *Recommendations.* The assessment process not only identifies, describes and analyses possible future consequences – positive or negative, intended or unintended – of an initiative under assessment, but also identifies, describes, analyses and prioritises possible solutions (recommendations) to address these consequences.
6. *Best efforts endeavour.* Impact assessment constitutes a 'best efforts obligation'. Since it is impossible to reduce negative consequences in absolute terms (as it is to maximise positive ones), sponsoring organisations react to them to the best of their abilities, depending upon the state-of-the-art and, to a reasonable extent, available resources.

7. *Assessor's competence.* The assessment process requires the assessor, or team of assessors, to have sufficient knowledge and know-how, corresponding to the type and area of practice of impact assessment at stake, for successful completion of the process.
8. *Assessor's professional independence.* The independence of the assessor – be they external or in-house – is ensured: they do not seek nor accept any instruction, avoid any conflict of interest, avoid any (personal) bias, and have sufficient resources (namely: time, money, workforce, knowledge and know-how, premises, and infrastructure) at their disposal.
9. *Documentation and transparency.* The assessment process is documented in writing or other permanent form, and is made available for unrestricted public access. The public at large is informed about the assessment process, its terms of reference, in particular the method, and its progress. Both draft and final assessment reports are easily accessible. Such access is granted without prejudice to state secrets, trade secrets, personal data or otherwise privileged information.
10. *Deliberativeness.* The assessment process is deliberative in the sense that it involves the participation of stakeholders. External stakeholders, be they individuals or civil society organisations affecting, affected, concerned by or merely interested in the initiative under assessment, or the public at large, are identified and meaningfully informed about it, their voices are actively sought and duly taken into consideration (namely through a process of consultation and – possibly – co-decision). Information given and sought is robust, accurate and inclusive. Individuals and/or their representatives have effective means of challenge, for example, in a court of law or similar tribunal, should they be denied involvement or should their views be ignored. In parallel, anyone within the sponsoring organisation (that is, internal stakeholders) is to participate in the assessment process under the same conditions. Exceptions to stakeholder involvement, if justified, are interpreted narrowly.
11. *Accountability.* The sponsoring organisation is accountable for the assessment process. Decision-makers within such an organisation choose, among other things, the method of assessment and assessors that will conduct it. They eventually approve the final assessment report and, in a subsequent process, may monitor the implementation of proposed solutions (recommendations). An external entity (for example, a regulatory authority or an auditing body) scrutinises the quality of the assessment process; the selection criteria are transparent. Therefore, a sponsoring organisation is able to demonstrate the satisfactoriness of the undertaken assessment process. However, in situations where an assessment process is made compulsory by law (for example, in DPIA in the EU, when there is a likelihood of a high risk to the rights and freedoms of data subjects), non-compliance and malpractice are proportionately sanctioned.
12. *Simplicity.* The assessment process is simple, that is, not unduly burdensome. The method serves those who use it, and is therefore structured, coherent, easily understan-

dable, and avoids prescriptiveness, over-complication and abuse of resources. There is however an inherent trade-off between the simplicity of use and the technical sophistication and accuracy of the assessment.
13. *Adaptiveness*. Impact assessment is adaptive to the characteristics of an initiative under assessment and its sponsoring organisation ('one size does not fit all') in terms of, for example, type and complexity thereof (e.g. technology development, scientific research or legislative proposals) or the type and number of individuals concerned (affected) (e.g. nuclear safety is not to be considered in the same manner as personal data protection). The method and the template for impact assessment might be modular, or 'consisting of separate parts that, when combined, form a complete whole',[47] allowing the addition and/or swapping of one module for another, as impact assessment is responsive to geographical and cultural differences, as well as to variations between legal systems (jurisdictional differences). In addition, as impacts can be appraised in many ways, assessors might resort to other evaluation techniques deemed more appropriate, entirely or in part, possibly in an integrated manner.
14. *Inclusiveness*. Impact assessment is inclusive. This ensures as many stakeholders (including experts and laypersons), relevant societal concerns and relevant development phases as possible, commensurate with the societal concerns at stake, and the type and area of practice of impact assessment, are included in the assessment process.
15. *Receptiveness*. Impact assessment is receptive. The framework, method, template and process evolve as a result of learning from previous experience in parallel evaluation techniques (for example, TA, EIA, risk management, etc.), knowledge from related disciplines (for example, law), and changes within society.
16. *Supportive environment*. Impact assessment requires a supportive environment in order to bear fruit. It needs, *inter alia*, continuous high-level support from policy-makers, and a spirit of cooperation among external and internal stakeholders. Regulators offer guidance and practical assistance in the assessment process, in the form of adequate training, guidelines, explanations and advice, among other things.

2.4 A generic method for impact assessment

The generic method lays the foundations for specific methods for impact assessment of multiple types and in multiple areas of practice. The generic method consists of ten steps (six consecutive steps, three steps executed throughout the entire process, and one step conducted afterwards), grouped into four phases. Some of these steps follow a logical sequence, namely the outcome of one step informs a subsequent one, while others are a function of the principles and conditions embodied in the framework.

These steps, building on a comparative analysis and critical appraisal of multiple methods for conducting the assessment process, are as follows:[48]

Phase I: Preparation of the assessment process
1) *Screening (threshold analysis)*. This step determines whether the process of impact assessment is warranted or necessary for a planned initiative or a set of similar initiatives in a given context. The screening is based on an initial yet sufficiently detailed description of the said initiative, both contextual and technical. The determination is made in accordance with threshold criteria, both internal (i.e. the organisation's own policies) and external (i.e. those set out in legal or other regulatory requirements), or *ad hoc* criteria, such as public pressure. If an assessment process is neither warranted nor necessary, the entire process is then concluded with a reasoned statement of no significant impact.
2) *Scoping*. This step, on the basis of the initial description, is taken to determine the extent of the assessment process and hence identifies:
    a) societal concerns, and their scope, that may be touched on by a planned initiative, such as privacy, personal data protection, (applied) ethics, or the natural and human (biophysical) environment, and the corresponding legal or other regulatory requirements; these concerns will constitute a benchmark of a given assessment process;
    b) categories of stakeholders who might affect, be affected by, be concerned with or be interested in the envisaged initiative(s), or who possess knowledge thereof (experts), as well as the level of their involvement; stakeholders might suggest further stakeholders to be included;
    c) techniques and methods for the appraisal of impacts and for stakeholder involvement, including public participation in decision-making, which will be used throughout a given assessment process;
    d) other evaluation techniques beyond the process of impact assessment that might be necessary or warranted in order to ensure the completeness of the information used in the decision-making process (for example, TA or EIA); and
    e) anything else, as practicable.

    It may be the case that not all of these elements and people are identifiable at the beginning of the assessment process, and hence their identification might need to be revised periodically.
3) *Planning and preparation*. This step defines the terms of reference for the execution of the assessment process. Not all of its elements, however, are of equal importance and applicability. These terms include, among others:
    a) the objectives;
    b) the criteria for the acceptability of negative impacts;
    c) the necessary resources (namely: time, money, workforce, knowledge, know-how, premises and infrastructure);
    d) the procedures and time-frames for the assessment process;
    e) the team of assessors (in-house or outsourced), their roles and responsibilities, and assurance of their professional independence;

f) a detailed list of the stakeholders to be involved (including, for example, their contact details) and a consultation plan, if necessary;
g) the criteria triggering a revision of the assessment process; and
h) the continuity of the assessment process in the event of, for example, changes in the actors involved in the assessment process, disruption, natural disasters or utility failures.

Phase II: Assessment

4) *Systematic description.* This step, on the basis of the initial description (see Step 1), provides a sufficiently detailed, two-part account of the planned initiative. First, there is a *contextual description*, which typically consists of, but is not limited to, a description of:
    a) the planned initiative(s) and of the sponsoring organisation;
    b) the context of deployment of the initiative;
    c) the need for the initiative;
    d) possible interference(s) with societal concern(s); and
    e) the expected benefits and drawbacks.

    Second, a *technical description*. In the case of EIA, this gives an account of, for example, the affected components of the biophysical environment, and, in the case of DPIA, it describes, for example, the categories of personal data and their flows within a processing operation. This description may be subjected to alterations and amendments as the assessment process progresses.

5) *Appraisal of impacts.* In this step, the impacts of the envisaged initiative are evaluated in accordance with the pre-selected techniques (cf. Step 2). These impacts pertain to the societal concern(s) that might be touched upon by the planned initiative, and to the stakeholders who are largely external to the sponsoring organisation. Typically, this appraisal consists of – at least – a detailed identification, analysis and evaluation of the impacts.

    The appraisal techniques range from risk analysis (qualitative or quantitative risk management, or a combination of the two), scenario analysis (planning) and technology foresight, through a legal and regulatory compliance check, legal interpretation techniques, and a proportionality and necessity assessment, to a cost-benefit analysis (CBA) and a strengths, weaknesses, opportunities and threats (SWOT) analysis.

6) *Recommendations.* In this step, concrete, detailed measures (controls, safeguards, solutions, etc.), their addressees, their priorities and the time-frames for addressing them are proposed to minimise the negative impacts of the planned initiative and, if possible, to maximise the positive ones. The assessors justify the distinction made between 'negative' and 'positive' impacts, since this distinction is contextual and subjective. The assessors may take stock of the measures already implemented. On this basis, after the conclusion of the assessment process, the leadership of the sponsoring organisation takes a decision on whether or not to deploy the initiative. An initiative is normally cancelled altogether if the negative impacts are unacceptable (see Step 3b); to carry out such an initiative would be exceptional and would require sufficient justification.

Phase III: Revisiting

7) *Revisiting*. In this step, a decision is made on whether or not to carry out the process again, entirely or in part. This step may occur every time the envisaged initiative is modified (before or after its deployment) or every time the context in which it is going to be deployed, or has already been deployed, changes. This step also ensures the continuity of the assessment process, such as in the case of a transfer of the initiative to another sponsoring organisation.

Ongoing phase

8) *Stakeholder involvement, including public participation, in decision-making*. This is an ongoing, cross-cutting step that runs throughout the entire assessment process, in which stakeholders, including the public and/or their representatives, take part in the assessment process.

Understood broadly, a stakeholder is someone who holds an interest in something, regardless of whether or not they are aware of this and of whether the interest is articulated directly or not. In the context of impact assessment, a stakeholder is an actor that is or might be affecting, affected, concerned by or be interested in the outcome of a planned initiative. A stakeholder may also be an expert who possesses specific knowledge and know-how about the initiative. The concept of stakeholder is therefore open-ended and can include the public (laypeople, etc.), decision-makers, experts, and more. Stakeholders can be individuals or collective entities, regardless of whether they are formally (legally) recognised or not. They may be societal groups, communities, nations, the public at large, civil society organisations, etc. There are multiple (groups of) stakeholders, and hence they can be grouped into internal (e.g. employees or work committees) and external (e.g. customers or non-governmental organisations) ones, and primary (i.e. those with a direct stake in the initiative, for example, investors) and secondary (i.e. those with an indirect interest yet influential, for example, the state) ones, or they can be classified by their attributes, including, but not limited to, power, legitimacy and urgency.

Stakeholder involvement constitutes an integral component of the assessment process, and is normally omitted only in exceptional situations. For example, stakeholder involvement may be judged unnecessary because of similarities with an earlier, similar initiative, because no promising new insights or thoughts are to be gained, or because it would require an effort that would be disproportionate to the results. A decision not to involve stakeholders, or to deviate from the results of such an involvement, must be reasoned and documented. Whenever stakeholder involvement is mandatory, legal remedies are available for the entitled stakeholders, provided that their involvement is absent or insufficient, commensurate with the level of involvement pursued in a given assessment process. In any case, stakeholder involvement does not give rise to any negative consequences for its participants (for example, exploitation). Personal data of identified stakeholders are appropriately protected.

The level of stakeholder involvement can range from: (a) merely being informed or taught about a planned initiative (low level); to (b) dialogue and consultation, in which the stakeholders' views are sought and taken into consideration (middle level); or even to (c) co-decision by the stakeholders and a sponsoring organisation about the deployment of the initiative in question and, subsequently, partnership with the stakeholders in its implementation (high level).[49]

From a practical viewpoint, typically stakeholders are first identified, then informed and consulted and, eventually, their views are considered (in case of consultation) or they are asked for an agreement (in case of co-decision). Information given and sought is robust, accurate, inclusive and meaningful. Information is given to stakeholders in plain language, and hence may require the preparation of specific documentation, for example technical briefings and/or translations. Stakeholders are involved with due respect for confidentiality, including state secrets, trade secrets, personal data or otherwise privileged information. Having gathered the viewpoints of the stakeholders, the assessor considers and takes a position on their views, i.e. on whether they accept them or not; especially in the case of the latter, the assessors are to provide exhaustive justification. (Stakeholders are not assessors; the former provide input, which the latter subsequently take into account or reject.)

There are a plethora of techniques for engaging stakeholder involvement, ranging from information notices to interviews, questionnaires and surveys, to focus groups, roundtables, workshops and citizens' panels, and including structured techniques, such as a 'world café' or use of the 'Delphi method'.[50] An appropriate technique, or a combination of techniques, is selected depending on the level of stakeholder involvement desired, the planned initiative, the context of the deployment of the initiative, and the resources at the disposal of the sponsoring organisation.

Stakeholder involvement can bring several benefits to the assessment process (for example, enhancement of its quality, credibility and legitimacy) and to the outcome (for example, the decision-making process being better-informed), to be contrasted with its drawbacks, which include, *inter alia*, the question of representativeness (over- or under-representation), fairness (for example, manipulation, 'astroturfing'),[51] reluctance, communication barriers, conflict between public and private interests, and the resource-intensive nature of the entire stakeholder involvement process.

9) *Documentation*. This is an ongoing, cross-cutting step, and runs throughout the entire process. Records are kept, in writing or in another permanent form, of all activities undertaken during the assessment process. This step includes the preparation of a final report stemming from the assessment process (or a statement of no significant impact, where applicable). The full spectrum of documentation from a given assessment process, preferably in an electronic format, may be made publicly available, centrally registered, and/or presented for inspection upon request (with due respect for legitimate confidentiality concerns).

10) *Quality control*. In this ongoing, cross-cutting step that runs throughout the entire assessment process, the adherence to a standard of performance is checked (procedural, substantive, or both), either internally (for example, through progress monitoring or a review by the sponsoring organisation) or externally (for example, by an independent regulatory authority through an audit, or by a court of law), or both. The quality control, regardless whether structured or *ad hoc*, can equally well occur during or after the assessment process, or both.

The above-mentioned method for assessing the impacts of an initiative on a societal concern, or concerns, is of a generic nature and needs to be tailored to the specificities and needs of a given area of practice, of the stakeholders (including the public) involved, and of the context of use. Consistent with its purpose, the present textbook offers, in Chapter 8 and Annex 1, a tailor-made method and template, respectively, for integrated impact assessment of border control technologies.

Endnotes

1. The research leading to this Chapter has received funding from the European Union under multiple programmes and schemes (European Commission Directorate-General for Justice and Consumers' action grants, the 7th Framework Programme for Research and Technological Development (FP7), and the Horizon 2020 Framework Programme for Research and Innovation (H2020)), and from l'Institut d'Encouragement de la Recherche scientifique et de l'Innonvation de Bruxelles (Innoviris). The contents are the sole responsibility of the authors, and can in no way be taken to reflect the views of any of the funding agencies.
2. References to legal provisions without any further specification pertain to the General Data Protection Regulation (GDPR, Regulation (EU) 2016/679 of the European Parliament and of the Council of 27 April 2016 on the protection of natural persons with regard to the processing of personal data and on the free movement of such data, and repealing Directive 95/46/EC [General Data Protection Regulation], OJ L 119, 4.5.2016, p. 1–88). The Chapter reflects the law and practice as they stood on 31 March 2021; all hyperlinks are valid as of that day.
3. This Chapter builds on, and sometimes incorporates, the updated and revised text of two earlier works we co-authored: Dariusz Kloza et al., "Data Protection Impact Assessments in the European Union: Complementing the New Legal Framework towards a More Robust Protection of Individuals", d.pia.lab Policy Brief (Brussels: VUB, 2017), 1–4, https://doi.org/10.31228/osf.io/b68em; Kloza et al., "Towards a Method for Data Protection Impact Assessment: Making Sense of GDPR Requirements", 1–8. See also: Dariusz Kloza et al., "Data Protection Impact Assessment in the European Union: Developing a Template for a Report from the Assessment Process," d.pia.lab Policy Brief (Brussels: VUB, 2020), https://doi.org/10.31228/osf.io/7qrfp. We furthermore thank – in alphabetical order – István Böröcz, Alessandra Calvi, Raphaël Gellert, Nikolaos Ioannidis, Ioulia Konstantinou, Eugenio Mantovani, Paul Quinn and Sara Roda for their contributions to the development of the d.pia.lab's architecture of impact assessment.
4. Kloza et al., "Towards a Method for Data Protection Impact Assessment: Making Sense of GDPR Requirements."

5. In its guidelines on risk management, the International Organization for Standardization (ISO) distinguishes between the principles, the framework and the process of risk management. See: ISO, *Risk management – Guidelines*, ISO 31000:2018, Geneva, https://www.iso.org/obp/ui#iso:std:iso:31000:ed-2:v1:en.
6. Oxford Dictionary of English.
7. Oxford Dictionary of English.
8. Kloza et al., "Data Protection Impact Assessment in the European Union: Developing a Template for a Report from the Assessment Process."
9. See, for example, International Association of Privacy Professionals [IAPP] (2020) *2020 Privacy Tech Vendor Report*, Portsmouth, NH, https://iapp.org/resources/article/privacy-tech-vendor-report.
10. See, for example, David Garland, "The Rise of Risk," in *Risk and Morality*, ed. Aaron Doyle and Diana Ericson (Toronto: University of Toronto Press, 2003), 48–83, https://doi.org/10.3138/9781442679382-005.
11. See, for example, Emilio Quincy Daddario, "Technology Assessment. Statement of Emilio Q. Daddario, Chairman, Subcommittee on Science, Research, and Development of the Committee on Science and Astronautics, U.S. House of Representatives" (Washington: United States Government Publishing Office, 1967); Joseph F. Coates, "Some Methods and Techniques for Comprehensive Impact Assessment," *Technological Forecasting and Social Change* 6 (1974): 341–57, https://doi.org/10.1016/0040-1625(74)90035-3; Rinie van Est and Frans W. A. Brom, "Technology Assessment, Analytic and Democratic Practice," *Encyclopedia of Applied Ethics* 4 (2012): 306–20, https://doi.org/10.1016/B978-0-12-373932-2.00010-7; Armin Grunwald, *Technology Assessment in Practice and Theory* (Abingdon: Routledge, 2018), https://doi.org/10.4324/9780429442643.
12. Bram F. Noble, *Introduction to Environmental Impact Assessment. A Guide to Principles and Practice* (Toronto: Oxford University Press, Canada, 2015).
13. See, for example, David Banta, Finn Børlum Kristensen, and Egon Jonsson, "A History of Health Technology Assessment at the European Level," *International Journal of Technology Assessment in Health Care* 25, no. 1 (2009): 68–73, https://doi.org/10.1017/S0266462309090448.
14. See, for example, Claire A. Dunlop and Claudio M. Radaelli, *Handbook of Regulatory Impact Assessment* (Cheltenham: Edward Elgar, 2016).
15. See, for example, Elin Palm and Sven Ove Hansson, "The Case for Ethical Technology Assessment (ETA)," *Technological Forecasting and Social Change* 73, no. 5 (2006): 543–58, https://doi.org/10.1016/j.techfore.2005.06.002.
16. See, for example, David Wright and Charles D. Raab, "Constructing a Surveillance Impact Assessment," *Computer Law and Security Review* 28, no. 6 (2012): 613–26, https://doi.org/10.1016/j.clsr.2012.09.003.
17. See, for example, David Wright and Paul De Hert, eds., *Privacy Impact Assessment* (Dordrecht: Springer, 2012), https://doi.org/10.1007/978-94-007-2543-0; Paul De Hert, Dariusz Kloza, and David Wright, "Recommendations for a Privacy Impact Assessment Framework for the European Union" (Brussels – London, 2012), https://researchportal.vub.be/files/14231615/PIAF_D3_final.pdf. See also Roger Clarke's work on PIA, http://www.rogerclarke.com/DV/#PIA.
18. See, for example, Henk Becker and Frank Vanclay, *The International Handbook of Social Impact Assessment* (Edward Elgar, 2003), https://doi.org/10.4337/9781843768616; Ana Maria Esteves, Daniel Franks, and Frank Vanclay, "Social Impact Assessment: The State of the Art," *Impact Assessment and Project Appraisal* 30, no. 1 (2012): 34–42, https://doi.org/10.1080/14615517.2012.660356.
19. See, for example, Nora Götzmann, *Handbook on Human Rights Impact Assessment* (Edward Elgar, 2019), https://doi.org/10.4337/9781788970006.

20. Roger Clarke, "Privacy Impact Assessment: Its Origins and Development," *Computer Law & Security Review* 25, no. 2 (2009): 123–35, https://doi.org/10.1016/j.clsr.2009.02.002.
21. Rob Kitchin, *The Data Revolution: Big Data, Open Data, Data Infrastructures and Their Consequences*, 2014, https://doi.org/10.4135/9781473909472. See also M Castells, *The Rise of the Network Society: The Information Age: Economy, Society, and Culture* (Malden, MA: Wiley, 2010).
22. See, for example, David Lyon, *Surveillance Studies: An Overview* (Cambridge: Polity Press, 2007).
23. On the experience from carrying out PIA or DPIA processes, see, for example: Jennifer Stoddart, "Auditing Privacy Impact Assessments: The Canadian Experience," in *Privacy Impact Assessment*, ed. David Wright and Paul De Hert (Dordrecht: Springer, 2012), 419–36; Kush Wadhwa and Rowena Rodrigues, "Evaluating Privacy Impact Assessments," *Innovation: The European Journal of Social Science Research* 26, no. 1–2 (2013): 161–80, https://doi.org/10.1080/13511610.2013.761748; Jeroen Van Puijenbroek and Jaap Henk Hoepman, "Privacy Impact Assessment in Practice: The Results of a Descriptive Field Study in the Netherlands," in *CEUR Workshop Proceedings* 1873, 2017: 1–8; Laurens Sion et al., "DPMF: A Modeling Framework for Data Protection by Design," *Enterprise Modelling and Information Systems Architectures (EMISAJ)* 15, no. 10 (2020): 1–53, https://doi.org/10.18417/emisa.15.10.
24. Clarke, "Privacy Impact Assessment: Its Origins and Development."
25. European Commission, *Recommendation on the implementation of privacy and data protection principles in applications supported by radio-frequency identification*, Brussels, 12 May 2009, C(2009) 3200 final.
26. European Commission, *Recommendation on the Data Protection Impact Assessment Template for Smart Grid and Smart Metering Systems*, 2014/724/EU, OJ L 300, 18.10.2014, pp. 63–68.
27. European Commission, *Better Regulation Guidelines*, Brussels, 7 July 2017, SWD (2017) 350.
28. Regulation (EU) 2016/679 of the European Parliament and of the Council of 27 April 2016 on the protection of natural persons with regard to the processing of personal data and on the free movement of such data, and repealing Directive 95/46/EC (General Data Protection Regulation), OJ L 119, 4.5.2016, p. 1–88.
29. Directive (EU) 2016/680 of the European Parliament and of the Council of 27 April 2016 on the protection of natural persons with regard to the processing of personal data by competent authorities for the purposes of the prevention, investigation, detection or prosecution of criminal offences or the execution of criminal penalties, and on the free movement of such data, and repealing Council Framework Decision 2008/977/JHA, OJ L 119, 4.5.2016, p. 89–131.
30. Regulation (EU) 2018/1725 of the European Parliament and of the Council of 23 October 2018 on the protection of natural persons with regard to the processing of personal data by the Union institutions, bodies, offices and agencies and on the free movement of such data, and repealing Regulation (EC) No 45/2001 and Decision No 1247/2002/EC, OJ L 295, 21.11.2018, p. 39–98.
31. Decision of the EEA Joint Committee No 154/2018 of 6 July 2018 amending Annex XI (Electronic communication, audiovisual services and information society) and Protocol 37 (containing the list provided for in Article 101) to the EEA Agreement [2018/1022], OJ L 183, 19.07.2018, pp. 23-26.
32. Proposal for a Regulation of the European Parliament and of the Council concerning the respect for private life and the protection of personal data in electronic communications and repealing Directive 2002/58/EC (Regulation on Privacy and Electronic Communications), 2017/0003(COD). See also https://oeil.secure.europarl.europa.eu/oeil/popups/ficheprocedure.do?reference=2017/0003(COD)&l=en.
33. Protocol amending the Convention for the Protection of Individuals with regard to Automatic Processing of Personal Data, Strasbourg, 10 October 2018, CETS No. 223.

34. Graham Greenleaf, "'Modernising' Data Protection Convention 108: A Safe Basis for a Global Privacy Treaty?," *Computer Law & Security Review* 29, no. 4 (2013): 430–36, https://doi.org/10.1016/j.clsr.2013.05.015; Sophie Kwasny, "Convention 108, a Trans-Atlantic DNA?," in *Trans-Atlantic Data Privacy Relations as a Challenge for Democracy*, ed. Dan Jerker B Svantesson and Dariusz Kloza (Cambridge: Intersentia, 2017), 533–41.
35. Articles 54-55, *Zakon o o zaštiti podataka o ličnosti*, Sl. glasnik RS, br. 87/2018, 13.11.2018.
36. Article 22, *Loi fédérale sur la protection des données* (LPD), 25 septembre 2020, FF 2020 7397.
37. Article 17, *ICRC Rules on Personal Data Protection*, 12 June 2020, https://www.icrc.org/en/publication/4261-icrc-rules-on-personal-data-protection.
38. Ann Cavoukian, *Privacy by Design in Law, Policy and Practice. A White Paper for Regulators, Decision-Makers and Policy-Makers* (Toronto: Information and Privacy Commissioner, Ontario, 2011).
39. Raphaël Gellert and Dariusz Kloza, "Can Privacy Impact Assessment Mitigate Civil Liability? A Precautionary Approach," in *Transformation Juristischer Sprachen, from Tagungsband Des 15. Internationalen Rechtsinformatik Symposions IRIS 2012*, ed. Erich Schweighofer, Franz Kummer, and Walter Hötzendorfer (Wien: Osterreichische Computer Gesellschaft, 2012), 497–505.
40. Dariusz Kloza, "Privacy Impact Assessments as a Means to Achieve the Objectives of Procedural Justice," in *Transparenz. Tagungsband Des 17. Internationaln Rechtsinformatik Symposions IRIS 2014*, ed. Erich Schweighofer, Franz Kummer, and Walter Hötzendorfer (Vienna: Osterreichische Computer Gesellschaft, 2014), 449–58.
41. David Parker, "(Regulatory) Impact Assessment and Better Regulation," in *Privacy Impact Assessment*, ed. David Wright and Paul De Hert (Dordrecht: Springer, 2012), 77–96, https://doi.org/10.1007/978-94-007-2543-0_3.
42. Kloza et al., "Data Protection Impact Assessments in the European Union: Complementing the New Legal Framework towards a More Robust Protection of Individuals."
43. Frank Vanclay, "The Triple Bottom Line and Impact Assessment. How Do TBL, EIA, SIA, SEA and EMS Relate to Each Other?," *Journal of Environmental Assessment Policy and Management* 6, no. 3 (2004): 265–88, https://doi.org/10.1142/S1464333204001729.
44. Ryo Tajima and Thomas B. Fischer, "Should Different Impact Assessment Instruments Be Integrated? Evidence from English Spatial Planning," *Environmental Impact Assessment Review* 41 (2013): 29–37, https://doi.org/10.1016/j.eiar.2013.02.001.
45. Tajima and Fischer.
46. Based on, in particular: Roger Clarke, "An Evaluation of Privacy Impact Assessment Guidance Documents," *International Data Privacy Law* 1, no. 2 (2011): 111–20, https://doi.org/10.1093/idpl/ipr002; David Wright and Paul De Hert, "Findings and Recommendations," in *Privacy Impact Assessment*, ed. David Wright and Paul De Hert (Dordrecht: Springer, 2012), 445–81, https://doi.org/10.1007/978-94-007-2543-0_22; Dariusz Kloza, Niels van Dijk, and Paul De Hert, "Assessing the European Approach to Privacy and Data Protection in Smart Grids. Lessons for Emerging Technologies," in *Smart Grid Security*, ed. Florian Skopik and Paul Smith (Waltham, MA: Elsevier, 2015), 11–47, https://doi.org/10.1016/B978-0-12-802122-4.00002-X; De Hert, Kloza, and Wright, "Recommendations for a Privacy Impact Assessment Framework for the European Union."
47. Cambridge Dictionary of English.
48. Based on, in particular: Kloza et al., "Towards a Method for Data Protection Impact Assessment: Making Sense of GDPR Requirements"; Kloza et al., "Data Protection Impact Assessment in the European Union: Developing a Template for a Report from the Assessment Process."
49. Sherry R. Arnstein, "A Ladder Of Citizen Participation," *Journal of the American Institute of Planners* 35, no. 4 (1969): 216–24, https://doi.org/10.1080/01944366908977225.

50. See Annex 2 in this volume.
51. Astroturfing is a 'deceptive practice of presenting an orchestrated marketing or public relations campaign in the guise of unsolicited comments from members of the public' (Oxford Dictionary of English). The term 'astroturfing' – from an 'artificial grass surface used for sports fields' – was coined in order to directly juxtapose 'grass-roots', i.e. 'ordinary people regarded as the main body of an organization's membership' (Oxford Dictionary of English).

3 Privacy

Nikolaos IOANNIDIS
Vrije Universiteit Brussel. E-mail: nikolaos.ioannidis@vub.be.

3.1 Introduction

3.1.1 Definition of privacy

While the adjective 'private' is an easily comprehendible term in everyday language (meaning that something is not intended for the public), its derivative noun 'privacy' is more complex to grasp. Dictionaries define it today, for example, as the "freedom from unauthorised intrusion" or the "state of being let alone and able to keep certain especially personal matters to oneself".[1] Privacy has been analysed from different perspectives such as legal, as a right, ethical, as a virtue or value,[2] economic, as a utility or interest, or political, as a public or private good.[3]

Nowadays, privacy is frequently intertwined with and threatened by novel and emerging technologies. For the purposes of integrated impact assessment for border control technologies, to which the present textbook is devoted, this Chapter mostly focuses on privacy as a legal right. In operationalising the right to privacy, this Chapter follows the structure below. In the next sub-sections, some further introductory notions on privacy (its importance for society, historical development and relevant regulatory instruments and actors involved) are provided, including the importance of privacy within the assessment process. Section 3.1.2 describes the content of the right to privacy, offering legal and theoretical conceptualisations.

3.1.2 Historical development of the right to privacy in Western legal systems

According to a general consensus among scholars, the history of privacy in modern Western legal systems dates back to a law review article published in 1890 by two Boston lawyers, Samuel Warren and Louis Brandeis.[4] Their idea of privacy came as a reflection on the appearance of new technologies (more specifically, instantaneous photography) that newspapers used to cover gossip stories, "overstepping the limits of propriety and decency, causing harm both to the individuals portrayed and to the community, lowering – it was believed – social standards and morality".[5] At that time, the right to privacy was elaborated merely within the paradigm of tort (delict) law, conceptualised as a civil claim for damages, as opposed to a fundamental or constitutional right. Originally explicated as a "right to inviolate personality", the right to privacy meant that each individual had the right to choose to share or not to share with others information about their "private life, habits, acts, and relations".[6] Alternatively, it was conceptualised as "the right of each individual to protect his or her psychological integrity by exercising control over information which both reflected and affected that individual's personality".[7]

Today, as a civil right, privacy is protected in civil law, within a jurisdiction, or, as a fundamental right, in constitutional law, at a national or regional level. As a civil right, it distinguishes the person from the outside world and is essential for one's autonomy and protection of human dignity. As a fundamental right, privacy is known as the right to respect for private and family life, the home, and correspondence (hereinafter 'the right to privacy'). It encompasses the idea of positive freedom, where a person has the freedom to determine, for example, the extent to which they control their own intellectual activity, and negative freedom, as a demand that others refrain from interference.

3.1.3 The importance of the right to privacy in society

In recent years, the right to privacy in society has gained in importance due to the increased digitalisation and ubiquitousness of computers. As a result, in the online environment, privacy is alternatively called 'informational privacy', 'data privacy' (usually in US literature) or 'online privacy'. Participating in the interconnected world means that individuals are not characterised by their own choices alone; in a community, interaction with other individuals and the way in which information is shared with them is what defines a sphere of activity.

In the past, in small-scale communities, citizens were only able to interact with their neighbours and their immediate community, and on occasions when persons with influential status would receive public critique, privacy interferences were occasional and smaller in scale. Nowadays, by contrast, large-scale monitoring of individuals presents different dangers, and impacts them multi-dimensionally. For instance, personal information obtained via contemporary means is recorded and stored, while more and more aspects of everyday life are transformed into data (e.g. payments through cards, sales via e-commerce, activity upon social media, and interactions with the government online). The development of computer technology makes it possible to store data with virtually no limits to the scope of processing or the storage duration. Furthermore, the information collected can be organised and transferred in an instant.

In sum, the online privacy of individuals is continuously threatened in many ways, for instance, when people share personal information with other users and entities, via the internet, smartphones, social networks, drones, biometric identification terminals or the Internet of Things (IoT). In such scenarios, the right to privacy protects individuals against arbitrary and unjustified use of power by reducing what can be known about them by others, such as public authorities or technology companies.

3.1.4 The importance of the right to privacy in the PERSONA benchmark

The inclusion of privacy as an element of the benchmark of an integrated impact assessment process is therefore indispensable in gaining an adequate understanding of the impacts on the right to privacy in the area of border control.

On the one hand, certain practices in the realms of border control affect the right to privacy of certain religious groups. An example is the obligation to temporarily remove clothing while performing security checks or while taking photos destined for official identity documents. This obligation is particularly sensitive and controversial when it comes to removing religious clothing, such as in the case of Sikhism. A practicing Sikh complained of an interference with his right to freedom of religion by airport authorities, who had obliged him to remove his turban as part of a security check imposed on passengers entering the departure lounge. Defending his freedom of religion and his right to privacy, he argued that there had been no need for the security staff to make him remove his turban, especially as he had not refused to go through the walk-through scanner or to be checked with a hand-held detector.[8] In this case, the same Court held that security checks in airports were necessary in the interests of public safety, however it stressed that, due to the occasional character of the incident, states may decide otherwise. In another case, a practicing Sikh claimed that the requirement for him to appear bareheaded in the identity photograph on his driving licence amounted to interference with his private life and with his freedom of religion and conscience.[9] This self-determination as to how an individual publicly appears falls within the scope of protection of the freedom of religion and the right to privacy. However, the driving licence is an official document which, upon request, could be presented to identify the individual. The European Court of Human Rights (ECtHR) stated that such photos were required by authorities in charge of public safety and law and order, particularly in the context of checks in public places. It held that the interference had been justified in principle, and was proportionate to the aim pursued. The same requirements could be extended to the issuance of an identity card or travel documents.

On the other hand, the increasing use of digital technologies in border control exacerbates existing impacts on the right to privacy. An example is facial recognition. Modern airports have progressively chosen to install automated border gates (or 'smart borders') with hundreds of 'touchpoints' that track travellers in their interactions with airlines and border agencies. Most organisations acknowledge that the potential of facial recognition technology is significant, and its upcoming applications could provide benefits to public safety and security. However, if mismanaged, this technology may potentially lead to a perception of widespread surveillance, and could affect individuals differently, depending on their belonging to specific categories or groups, culminating in 'chilling effects' (e.g. causing distress and anxiety to individuals about the use of such technology), and ultimately eroding their right to privacy or other interconnected fundamental rights.

Additionally, facial recognition technology relies on the collection and processing of biometric information that is unique and permanent. The capacity and sophistication of this technology is continuously evolving (e.g. through self-improving algorithms) and can be used in unforeseen ways or linked with other next-generation technological tools in a manner that creates risks of harm to individuals and distortion of public confidence.[10] Frequently, actors involved in the deployment of such technologies use large-scale datasets, which are often collated. Decisions made about individuals using these identifiers, potentially without their knowledge or consent, may lead to serious risks to their rights and freedoms. Discriminatory effects are frequently given rise to; there could be a non-negligible impact in the ability to exercise certain other fundamental rights, such as the freedom of expression and association. Lastly, damage to reputations or social disadvantages are also possible consequences, sometimes without adequate avenues for recourse.

3.1.5 Relevant regulatory instruments and actors involved

3.1.5.1 Protection and promotion of fundamental rights

In liberal democratic societies, basic principles and rules pertaining to the protection of privacy – as well as other important societal concerns – enjoy a special status in legal systems, and hence are situated at the top of the hierarchy of legal norms, as human (fundamental) rights, heavily intertwined with the essential principles of such a system.[11] Human rights are the rights that "every person has by virtue of merely existing and that aim to secure for such a person certain benefits or freedoms that are of fundamental importance to any human being".[12]

The right to privacy is protected and promoted by a network of legal instruments, supplemented by an enforcement machinery consisting of predominantly international and national courts, yet no single one is solely designated to deal with issues of privacy. In general, the protection of privacy by rulemaking follows a tripartite and hierarchical pattern, namely international, regional and national. International legislation tends to be declarative and less enforceable, while regional and national legislation usually produces tangible legal effects and can be adequately enforceable.

3.1.5.2 International level

Several instruments protect the right to privacy at an international level. At the UN level, Article 12 of the Universal Declaration of Human Rights[13] (UDHR, 1948) reads: "no one shall be subjected to arbitrary interference with his privacy, family, home or correspondence, nor to attacks upon his honour and reputation […]". Further, the 1966 UN International Covenants – one on Civil and Political Rights,[14] the other on Economic, Social and Cultural Rights,[15] which together bind more than 170 countries around the world – stipulate the same provision at Article 17, with the key difference being that the Covenant is binding for contracting parties. Lastly, privacy is specifically protected in the Convention on the Rights of the Child[16] under Article 16: "No child shall be subjected to arbitrary or unlawful interference with his or her privacy, family, home or correspondence, nor to unlawful attacks on his or her honour and reputation."

3.1.5.3 Regional level

In Europe, human rights are protected:

A. At the level of the Council of Europe (CoE), where the main instrument is the European Convention on Human Rights (ECHR, 1950) enforced by the European Court on Human Rights in Strasbourg. The Convention broadly defines the right to private and family life of every person living within the Council of Europe's territorial scope of application (Article 8 ECHR), which is further analysed in Section 1.2.1.

B. At the level of the European Union (EU), where the main instrument is the Charter of Fundamental Rights of the European Union (CFR, 2009)[17] enforced by the Court of Justice of the European Union (CJEU). The right guaranteed in Article 7 of the Charter corresponds to that guaranteed by Article 8 of the ECHR. Article 7 of the CFR is more concise, however, and reads: "Everyone has the right to respect for his or her private and family life, home and communications". It is worth noting here that, in order to take account of developments in technology, the word 'correspondence' from the ECHR has been replaced by the broader word 'communications'.[18] To conform with the Council of Europe standards, the Charter implies that the meaning and scope of this right are the same as those of the corresponding Article of the ECHR.[19] Lastly, the extent to which limitation criteria apply to all fundamental rights recognised in the Charter, are laid out in Article 52(1).[20]

Further regional legal instruments for the protection of privacy include 1969 American Convention on Human Rights[21] (enforced by the Inter-American Court on Human Rights in San Jose, Costa Rica) and the 1981 African Charter on Human and Peoples' Rights[22] (enforced by the African Court on Human and Peoples' Rights in Arusha, Tanzania).

3.1.5.4 National level

At the national level, privacy laws are usually enacted and positioned within a state's founding document, the national constitution, where fundamental principles are enshrined. Constitutions enjoy higher protection within a given jurisdiction and are observed by dedicated supreme courts. The way in which the scope of protection and interpretation of a constitutional right is articulated principally depends on the nation's history, culture and values. For instance, the notion of 'secrecy of correspondence', present in almost every constitution, is protected under the Belgian constitution in Article 29.[23]

Besides its constitutional protection in national law, privacy is further enshrined in virtually any civil code, both within the European Union and beyond. A civil code is a legal instrument, applicable in a given jurisdiction, which codifies and regulates the private law (legal relationships among individuals), indicatively, the law of contracts, law of torts, property law, family law and the law of inheritance. Provisions in the civil code usually protect privacy directly, under the protection of one's image, one's name and one's reputation, or indirectly, through the law of torts (e.g. one person's harmful behaviour against another person's honour, reputation, and privacy).

3.2 The contents of (the right to) privacy

3.2.1 Legal conceptualisations

In relation to conducting the process of integrated impact assessment, the protection of the right to privacy is relevant in situations where a private interest, or the 'private life' of an individual, could be compromised. The concept of 'private life' has been interpreted broadly in case law, as covering intimate situations, sensitive or confidential information, information that could prejudice the perception of the public against an individual, and even aspects of one's professional life and public behaviour. The scope of private life in border control is difficult to define; no general pattern can be drawn. The assessment of whether or not there is, or has been, an interference with private life depends on the context and facts of each individual case.[24]

What is protected by the right to respect for private and family life can be principally understood through the ways in which the European Courts (the ECtHR and the CJEU) have interpreted this fundamental right. There is no standard, universal scope of protection; rather, the interpretation is contextual. Both Courts' opinions on the scope of protection converge. The limitations that may legitimately be imposed on the right to privacy by the Charter are comparable to those in the ECHR. The similarities between the two instruments permit for a simultaneous comparison and research of this right.

This legal provision is divided into two paragraphs, providing for the rule and the exception (conditions for interference therewith), stating that: "1. Everyone has the right to respect for his private and family life, his home and his correspondence. 2. There shall be no interference by a public authority with the exercise of this right except such as is in accordance with the law and is necessary in a democratic society in the interests of national security, public safety or the economic wellbeing of the country, for the prevention of disorder or crime, for the protection of health or morals, or for the protection of the rights and freedoms of others."[25]

Article 8 of the ECHR entails both a negative obligation on public authorities to refrain from any actions that may creep upon private life, but, at the same time, a positive obligation to actively secure the respect for privacy. Not being an absolute right, it may be limited, provided that restrictions fulfil the conditions mentioned in the second paragraph. The ECtHR examines two cumulative conditions in its decisions: a) whether there was an interference with the right to respect for private life under Paragraph 1, and b) whether the interference was legitimate according to Paragraph 2. In the assessment of the test of necessity in a democratic society, the Court often needs to balance the applicant's interests protected by Article 8 and a third party's interests protected by other provisions of the Convention. The same Article protects at least one of the four interests identified in it, namely: (i) private life, (ii) family life, (iii) home, and (iv) correspondence. For the purposes of this Chapter, only private life is directly relevant.

'Private life' is a broad concept not susceptible to any exhaustive definition, and may "embrace multiple aspects of the person's physical and social identity".[26] It involves personal information, which individuals can legitimately expect to not be published without their consent. The notion of private life is not limited to an 'inner circle' in which individuals may live their own personal lives as they choose and exclude the outside world: Article 8 of the ECHR protects the right to personal development, whether in terms of personality or of personal autonomy, and encompasses the right of each individual to approach others in order to establish and develop relationships with them and with the outside world.

The same logic extends to professional and business activities.[27] Private life encompasses the right of an individual to form and develop relationships with other human beings, including relationships of a professional or business nature. Therefore, restrictions imposed on access to a profession have been found to affect 'private life'.

As well as the general sphere of private life, the scope of private life also concerns three more specific categories, i.e. a) physical, psychological and moral integrity, b) identity and autonomy and c) privacy in a strict sense.[28] Under the first category fall, for instance, sexual orientation, disability issues, mental diseases and reproductive rights, and any personal information relating to these. Within the boundaries of the second category are, indicatively, the right to gender, ethnic and racial identity, the choice of a desired appearance, the right to a name, marital or parental status, and the right to citizenship and residence. Lastly, aspects of privacy in a strict sense are, among others: the pivotal right to one's image and photographs about oneself, the publishing of photos, images, and articles, the defence against defamation, claims relating to data protection, the right to access one's personal information, police surveillance, stop and search police powers, and information about one's health.

3.2.2 Theoretical conceptualisations

To assess the various impacts of an initiative on the right to privacy, assessors can benefit from theoretical conceptualisations, which could be done in different ways. One could articulate privacy, for example, as descriptive, normative or reductionist, control or use-based, and/or property or privacy-based, resulting in "a right to control access to and uses of places, bodies, and personal information",[29] or "the ability to determine for ourselves when, how, and to what extent information about us is communicated to others".[30] For the purpose of performing the process of integrated impact assessment, this Section adopts the typology of Koops et al., as illustrated in the template (under 'privacy screening'). Organising privacy-related theory via a typology is an explanatory step by which the application of (notions of) privacy in border control may be better understood.

The analysis of the identified types of privacy is structured in a two-dimensional model, consisting of eight basic types of privacy (bodily, intellectual, spatial, decisional, communicational, associational, proprietary and behavioural privacy), with an overlay of a ninth type (informational privacy) that overlaps, but does not coincide with, the eight basic types (Fig. 1). Furthermore, demarcating various aspects of privacy helps explain why privacy cannot merely be reduced to informational privacy, how the concept of privacy relates to the right to privacy, and how the right to privacy varies depending on the context of use.

1. *Bodily (physical) privacy*: Bodily privacy encapsulates the right to protect the physical body of the individual. It connotes a negative freedom for anyone except for the concerned individual: one can exclude the others from unsolicited touching, restraining or restricting one's body (sometimes including mental integrity). It further protects any unreasonable search and seizure, supplemented with additional restrictions for certain parts of the body, in particular the 'private parts'. A relevant illustration of this type of privacy is the compulsory provision of samples of body fluids and body tissue, as well as fingerprints. This type therefore concerns the physical body *per se*, and not clothing, bags, pockets etc., which fall within the scope of another type of privacy.

2. *Spatial privacy*: Spatial privacy is the interest of a person to mark the existence of a reasonably understood private space or territory (individually controlled), by excluding and/or restricting other people's access to it or managing its use. It is comprised of an intimate zone (around the person) and an extended zone, in which the person is residing or inhabiting and is supposed to be acting privately (e.g. the area of the house). In both the intimate and extended zone, the individual sets the conditions for exposure. This type of privacy is triggered by, for example, the performance of unlawful 'searches' that enable law enforcement to observe activities as they are taking place inside the home. A person should be able to (stressing the ability/control to do so) control (increase/decrease) the degree of openness to others by 'tweaking' the modalities of their intimate zone, this referring to a limited information flow within trusted relationships. An interference with spatial privacy in border control is rare, since it is

connected to the private property (home). Nonetheless, interrogation about how one acts at home and preferences in terms of social engagement, intimate partners, family members or close friends could fall within the scope of this type of privacy.

3. *Communicational privacy*: Communicational privacy is the ability of a person to restrict access to communications or to control the use of information communicated to third parties. The meaning of (tele)communications is continuously evolving, and is arguably one of the cornerstones of constitutional privacy protection, linked also to the freedom of expression. Historically, it would be solely associated with written (i.e. postage) letters and telegraphy, but nowadays it is interpreted broadly, in order to accommodate newer forms of communicating at a distance, such as telephone calls, emails, instant messages and voice messages. This list is constantly expanding and evolving. Communicational privacy protects the secrecy of such communications, including their contents, channels and the traffic data. Communications may be mediated or unmediated, resulting in different practices of controlling such messages. Relevant examples of communicational privacy in the area of border control are those of law enforcement guards intercepting personal communications, confiscating and accessing others' electronic devices, 'eavesdropping', or generally checking the content of stored communications without due reason.

4. *Proprietary privacy*: Proprietary privacy is the interest of an individual in their use of property as a means to shield activity, facts, things, or information from public view. At its core, it is closely associated to spatial privacy, being similar in the fact that the user has the right to exclude others from their property. They differ, however, in that proprietary privacy concerns tangible objects, while spatial privacy concerns a 'defined' area. Proprietary privacy is interfered with when, for instance, a person is compelled by a third party to reveal content in their purse, wallet, backpack, pockets, against their will. In other words, people choose to conceal certain objects, facts, situations or even body parts behind their (mobile) property and, thus, choose whether and to which extent they expose to public view what they have concealed. The nature of computer devices (including smartphones, laptops, wearables and IoT objects) is hybrid, and falls first of all within the scope of proprietary privacy, on the basis of being hardware.

5. *Intellectual privacy*: Intellectual privacy is the right of an individual to privacy of thought and mind, and the development of opinions and beliefs. This type of privacy, although separate, could be included in the scope of protection of several associated privacy rights, such as the freedom of thought. The direct influencing of a person's mind is not within the abilities of today's technologies, however indirect methods of inspecting people's minds though electromagnetic signals (or at least identifying patterns by tracing brain activity) is a technique that is widely used. However, in border control scenarios, it is not expected that people's minds be interfered with; the mind is censed to be an inviolable area.

6. *Decisional privacy*: Decisional privacy is the right of a person to defend against (state) intrusions into citizens' rights to hold or make certain choices pertaining to the intimate sphere; these could regard their lives and how they live them, such as choices about same-sex marriage, abortion or assisted suicide. Generally, decisional privacy protects human autonomy and expresses the intellectual privacy, mentioned above, with this being deemed the thought process and decisional privacy being the execution process, i.e. the manifestation of thought. All facts in relation to proactive, sexual and family choices, as well as disclosure of information about these, therefore fall within its scope of protection. In border control, this type of privacy is tangibly interfered with when technologies reveal sensitive information or facts about such situations, e.g. an obligation to reveal a tattoo upon the torso, illustrating upsetting or appalling images.
7. *Associational privacy*: Associational privacy is the right of individuals to choose their interactions and acquaintances, i.e. friendships, communities and groups they belong to (akin to the freedom of assembly). Such choices are protected under the concept of associational privacy, which can materialise in strictly private places, intimate settings or semi-public spaces, depending on the degree of exposure chosen. Associational privacy does not constitute the core of private life, but is an emanation thereof, while in the context of border control, it can be interfered with when multiple individuals are associated, i.e. a group of travellers from a certain country or with certain shared characteristics, friends belonging to the same organisation, religion, community etc.
8. *Behavioural privacy*: Behavioural privacy is the right of individuals to choose their public demeanour, which cannot be hidden from others observing it. Characteristics that fall under this type of privacy are facial characteristics, clothes, smell, gait, gestures, voice, language, mood, etc., that also, to a certain extent, cannot be instantly identified unless particular attention is given to the individual. Borders are representative of places, where natural persons would be compelled to protect their behavioural privacy, especially where they have to briefly undress or uncover areas of their body and thus make gestures that they would otherwise not need to do in public. Behavioural privacy is also related to the level of transparency and exposure chosen, yet some characteristics of the person cannot be hidden from public view (e.g. religious outfit). This type of privacy is interfered with when a technology substantially hinders or excludes a person from choosing how they behave publicly, due to a fear of being criticised about such mannerisms, e.g. how they walk, how they speak, how they move their hands or face, etc.
9. *Informational privacy*: Informational privacy is considered an interest of an individual in preventing information about themselves being collected and in controlling information about themselves that others may have a legitimate access to. It is both a type and meta-type of privacy, in the sense that, firstly, it refers to a distinctive type of privacy and, secondly, it overlaps with all other types. Interference with informational privacy essentially entails that the affected person lacks control over how information

about the eight aforementioned types is managed. Informational privacy is bifurcated into a positive freedom (informational self-determination) and a negative freedom (exclusion of others to information). This type of privacy has served as the foundation for the recent development of the distinct right to personal data protection, to a great extent also overlapping with it. The right to data protection is assessed separately, in the process of a data protection impact assessment (DPIA), and is a vital part of the integrated impact assessment. In border control, virtually all personal data fall, additionally, under the scope of informational privacy.

Figure 1: A typology of privacy

	personal zone "solitude"	intimate zone "intimacy"	semi-private zone "secrecy"	public zone "inconspicuousness"
(emphasis on) freedom from "being let alone"	bodily privacy	spatial privacy	communicational privacy	proprietary privacy
		informational privacy		
(emphasis on) freedom to "self-development"	intellectual privacy	decisional privacy	associational privacy	behavioral privacy

Koops, B. J., Newell, B. C., Timan, T., Škorvánek, I., Chokrevski, T., & Galič, M. (2017). *A typology of privacy*. In University of Pennsylvania Journal of International Law (Vol. 38, Issue 2, pp. 483–575).

Endnotes

1. Merriam-Webster, *Privacy*, https://www.merriam-webster.com/dictionary/privacy#synonyms.
2. Helen Nissenbaum, *Privacy in Context: Technology, Policy, and the Integrity of Social Life* (California: Stanford University Press, 2010).
3. Mireille Hildebrandt, *Law for Computer Scientists and Other Folk* (Oxford: University Press, 2020), https://lawforcomputerscientists.pubpub.org/.
4. Warren, Samuel D., and Louis D. Brandeis. "The Right to Privacy." *Harvard Law Review* 4, no. 5 (1890): 193-220. https://doi.org/10.2307/1321160.
5. Ibid.
6. Glancy, D.J. The Invention of the Right to Privacy, *Arizona Law Review* 21, 4 (1979), http://law.scu.edu/wp-content/uploads/Privacy.pdf.
7. Ibid.
8. ECtHR, *Phull v. France*, Application no. 35753/03.

9. ECtHR, *Mann Singh v. France*, application no. 24479/07.
10. Global Privacy Assembly, *Adopted resolution on facial recognition technology*, 42nd Closed Session, 2020, https://edps.europa.eu/sites/edp/files/publication/final_gpa_resolution_on_facial_recognition_technology_en.pdf.
11. Serge Gutwirth, *Privacy and the Information Age* (Lanham, Md.: Rowman & Littlefield, 2002).
12. Gustavo Arosemena, "Human Rights," in *Introduction to Law* (Cham: Springer, 2017), 303–29, https://doi.org/10.1007/978-3-319-57252-9_13.
13. United Nations, Universal Declaration of Human Rights (UDHR), 10 December 1948.
14. United Nations (UN), International Covenant on Civil and Political Rights, 16 December 1966.
15. United Nations (UN), International Covenant on Economic, Social and Cultural Rights, 16 December 1966.
16. Convention on the Rights of the Child, New York, 20 November 1989.
17. The Treaty of Lisbon amended the Treaty of the European Union (TEU), in which Article 6(1) now reads: "The Union recognizes the rights, freedoms and principles set out in the Charter of Fundamental Rights of the European Union of 7 December 2000, as adapted at Strasbourg, on 12 December 2007, which shall have the same legal value as the Treaties."
18. Article 7 ('Respect for private and family life') of the Charter of Fundamental Rights of the European Union, OJ C 326, 26.10.2012, p. 391-407.
19. Article 52(3) of the Charter reads: "In so far as this Charter contains rights which correspond to rights guaranteed by the Convention for the Protection of Human Rights and Fundamental Freedoms, the meaning and scope of those rights shall be the same as those laid down by the said Convention. This provision shall not prevent Union law providing more extensive protection."
20. Article 52(1) of the Charter reads: "Any limitation on the exercise of the rights and freedoms recognised by this Charter must be provided for by law and respect the essence of those rights and freedoms. Subject to the principle of proportionality, limitations may be made only if they are necessary and genuinely meet objectives of general interest recognised by the Union or the need to protect the rights and freedoms of others."
21. American Convention on Human Rights, San Jose, Costa Rica, 22 November 1969.
22. African Charter on Human and Peoples' Rights, Nairobi, Kenya, 01 June 1981.
23. Article 29 of the Belgian Constitution reads: "Le secret des lettres est inviolable. La loi détermine quels sont les agents responsables de la violation du secret des lettres confiées à la poste", http://www.ejustice.just.fgov.be/cgi_loi/change_lg.pl?language=fr&table_name=loi&la=F&cn=1994021730.
24. European Union Agency For Fundamental Rights, European Court of Human Rights, and European Data Protection Supervisor, *Handbook on European Data Protection Law* (Luxembourg: Publications Office of the European Union, 2018), 6.
25. Article 8 ECHR.
26. ECtHR, *S. and Marper v. the United Kingdom*, No. 30562/04 and 30566/04, 4 December 2008.
27. ECtHR, *Bărbulescu v. Romania*, No. 61496/08, 5 September 2017.
28. European Court of Human Rights, "Guide on Article 8 of the European Convention on Human Rights Right to respect for private and family life, home and correspondence," (2020), https://www.echr.coe.int/documents/guide_art_8_eng.pdf.
29. Adam D. Moore, "Defining Privacy," *Journal of Social Philosophy* 39, no. 3 (2008): 411-428, https://ssrn.com/abstract=1980849.
30. Alan F. Westin, "Privacy and Freedom", *Washington and Lee Law Review* 25, no. 1 (1967): 166-170, https://scholarlycommons.law.wlu.edu/cgi/viewcontent.cgi?Article=3659&context=wlulr.

4 Personal data protection

Nikolaos IOANNIDIS
Vrije Universiteit Brussel. E-mail: nikolaos.ioannidis@vub.be.

4.1 Introduction

4.1.1 Definition and development of the right to personal data protection

The terms 'privacy' and 'data protection' are oftentimes understood as one and the same concept. Indeed, the right to personal data protection has evolved from the right to respect for private life, since the development of computers and the Internet in the second half of the 20th century brought considerable risks and new challenges to the latter. To address the need for specific rules about the collection and use of personal information, a new concept of privacy emerged around the 1970s,[1] known in some jurisdictions as 'informational privacy' (i.e. the privacy of personal information usually related to personal data stored in computer systems) or as the 'right to informational self-determination' (i.e. an individual's right to control the disclosure, retention, and dissemination of their personal information[2]). Throughout the years, these concepts evolved and eventually led to the development of special legal regimes that provide for what is known today as 'personal data protection'.

Despite their common origin and overlapping content, privacy and data protection are distinct fundamental rights.[3] While the right to privacy aims to create a personal sphere in which individuals are able to develop their personalities freely, the right to personal data protection is understood as a precondition to the exercising of other rights. In other words, whereas the right to privacy consists of a general prohibition of interference as a 'passive right', the right to personal data protection is considered to be an 'active right', which motivates a system of checks and balances to protect natural persons' personal data.

For the purposes of integrated impact assessment for border control technologies, to which the present textbook is devoted, this Chapter will focus on the right to data protection, and in particular on how it is protected by the General Data Protection Regulation (GDPR).[4] In operationalising the right to data protection, this Chapter follows the structure below. In the following sub-sections, some further introductory notions pertaining to data protection (its importance for society, relevant regulatory instruments and connections with other fundamental rights) are provided. Next, the Chapter delves into specific concepts of data protection law, following the terminology of the GDPR, to guide the assessors throughout the assessment process. Following this, Section 4.1.2 overviews key concepts and actors, Section 4.1.3 looks at principles of EU data protection law, Section 4.1.4 describes legal requirements, and Section 4.1.5 summarises data subject rights.

4.1.2 The importance of data protection in society

Although the right to data protection originates from the need to control the processing of personal information by public authorities, the banking sector, or health insurance companies, nowadays, the same data are processed by big private corporations, including technological companies. The use of artificial intelligence (AI) and profiling algorithms has allowed the processing of large amounts of personal and non-personal data[5] that people commonly share on digital platforms, such as social media sites, e-commerce sites, or health apps. These data have been characterised as "the new oil", as they are exploitable resources for which companies are able to develop strategies to generate revenue and profits.[6] For instance, browsers and websites collect the personal data of users and perform data-driven price differentiation, i.e. the same product or service is offered at different prices depending on the socio-economic status of a person. Another example is the use of recommendation systems upon social media and e-commerce platforms, in which personal data are processed to decide on what to recommend to the end user.

In this context, data protection rules are crucial to ensuring the security of individuals' data and regulating the collection, usage, transfer and disclosure of personal data. Such rules would permit individuals to maintain some control over their personal information and how this is shared with others, as well as make them aware that certain public authorities and private entities collect their data.

4.1.3 The role of data protection in the benchmark

The need for data protection rules is particularly pressing in the context of border control, where so-called 'smart borders', which store personal data, e.g. names and surnames, date, time and place of entry or exit of third-country nationals, travel documents or biometric data, have become widespread. One recurring argument for introducing smart borders is the need for law enforcement authorities to benefit from the best possible tools in order to quickly identify the perpetrators of terrorist acts and other serious crimes.[7] Furthermore, the adoption of pan-European databases would enable the provision of authorised users with fast, seamless, systematic and controlled access to relevant information systems pertaining to individuals who cross borders.

In the light of these developments, focusing on the right to personal data protection as one of the elements of the benchmark of this integrated impact assessment is helpful in controlling for the possible abuse of power by border control authorities and, more generally, in assessing the risks of certain processing operations to the rights and freedoms of natural persons.[8]

The goal of this Chapter is to guide the assessors in assessing whether a given initiative complies with the requirements of necessity and proportionality, accountability, and data protection principles such as purpose limitation and quality of data.[9] A robust assessment is critical when developing new instruments that rely on the use of information technology; the approach provided in this textbook aims to embed personal data protection rules in the technological basis of a proposed instrument.

4.1.4 List of relevant regulatory instruments and systems

To guide the assessors, this Section provides a brief overview of data protection regulatory instruments and systems. As with the right to privacy, the right to personal data protection is not universally protected by a single piece of legislation, but by a multitude of provisions depending on the jurisdiction. This Section follows a tripartite and hierarchical categorisation, through i) international, ii) regional, and iii) national laws.

International law

United Nations: The UN has not explicitly recognised the right to personal data protection as such, in contrast to the right to privacy.[10] Only recently, in 2013 and after the Edward Snowden revelations,[11] the UN adopted the resolution "The Right to Privacy in the Digital Age", while the General Assembly affirmed that the rights held by people offline must also be protected online. Consequently, it called upon all contracting parties to respect and protect the right to privacy in digital communication.[12] This is the closest semblance to modern data protection laws issued by the UN to date.

Council of Europe: Along with the ECHR,[13] the Council of Europe adopted, in 1981, the "Convention for the protection of individuals with regard to automatic processing of personal data" (Convention 108). This Convention is the first and, to this day, only international legally binding instrument dealing with data protection.[14] The Convention underwent a modernisation process, completed with the adoption of an amending Protocol (Convention 108+).[15] Furthermore, the Council of Europe actively issues recommendations with regard to internet actors' accountability.[16]

European Union law

Primary law: The Treaty on the Functioning of the European Union (TFEU) and the Charter of Fundamental Rights of the European Union ('Charter' or CFR) deal with the right to personal data protection. Article 16 of the TFEU, under the part of the treaty dedicated to the general principles of law, creates a new legal basis, granting the EU the competence to legislate on data protection matters. Article 8 of the Charter enshrines the right to the protection of personal data as a fundamental right.

Secondary law: The body of law founded upon the principles and objectives of the treaties is known as secondary law; this includes, among other things, regulations and directives. From 1995 until May 2018, the principal European Union (EU) legal instrument on data protection was Directive 95/46/EC, also known as the Data Protection Directive.[17] The Directive was adopted on the model of Convention 108, and acted as an instrument for achieving the objectives set by the internal market agenda.

The Directive was replaced by the GDPR,[18] which consolidates principles and rules on data protection, has an extraterritorial effect (i.e. it applies also outside the EU), and enhances the principle of accountability, thus being viewed as an exemplary document for other jurisdictions around the world.

In parallel, three more instruments currently complement the GDPR in data protection matters. First, Directive 2016/680 or the "law enforcement Directive" applies to the protection of natural persons with regard to the processing of personal data by competent authorities for the purposes of the prevention, investigation, detection or prosecution of criminal offences or the execution of criminal penalties, and on the free movement of such data. Second, Directive 2002/58/EC,[19] also called the "ePrivacy Directive", applies to personal data and the protection of privacy in electronic communications, with regards to security, data breaches and confidentiality of communications (including metadata). Third, Regulation 2018/1725[20] lays down the data protection obligations of the EU institutions and bodies during the processing of personal data by them, and development of new policies (European Institutions Data Protection Regulation (EUDPR)). The principles and key rules of this Regulation do not substantially differ, on the contrary, they are based on the provisions of the GDPR, with the exception of certain provisions inextricably tied to the nature and specificities of the function of EU institutions.

National laws

The first national data protection legislation was a novelty in one (West) German State (Hesse) in 1970. Since then, an increasing number of countries worldwide have progressively enacted (reformed) data protection legislation, including the Member States of the EU. As an illustration, the decade 2010-2019 saw 62 new countries enacting data protection laws, more than in any previous decade. In total, as of today, an impressive number of 142 countries have legislated for data protection.[21] The adoption of firm data protection legislation in parts of the world with significant economic activity is highly important for, among other things, data transfers of personal data, ensuring a consistently high level of protection.

4.1.5 Connection with other fundamental rights

Data protection law does not have the single purpose of protecting only one fundamental right, but rather acts as an umbrella mechanism for multiple fundamental rights whenever affected by the processing of personal data. The interrelationship between the right to personal data protection and other fundamental rights is twofold: (a) since data protection is not an absolute right, it must be considered in relation to its function in society and be balanced against other fundamental rights, in accordance with the principle of proportionality, and (b) the EU data protection framework underlines the respect for all fundamental rights; the freedoms and principles recognised in the Charter and as enshrined in the Treaties of the EU. Furthermore, it is assumed that certain types of processing may create significant risks to other fundamental rights and freedoms, therefore explicitly extending the material scope of its protection outside the domain of personal data alone, and towards other fundamental rights and freedoms, when personal data are involved.

Typically, such rights could be: (a) the right to non-discrimination, (b) the freedom of thought, conscience, and religion, (c) the freedom of expression and information, (d) the right to an effective remedy and to a fair trial and (e) the respect for private and family life, home, and communications (right to privacy). Furthermore, it is observed that case law of the Court of Justice of the EU (CJEU) and the European Court of Human Rights (ECtHR) often involves two or more affected rights. For instance, it is highly probable that a specific type of personal data processing operation does not present risks for a single person but may produce significant societal and legal effects or exacerbate systemic group discrimination. In the realm of border control, the use of automated technologies in identifying migration flows and managing resources is increasingly reinforcing structures of discrimination already inherent in migration decision-making.[22]

4.2 Key concepts and actors

4.2.1 Personal data and data subject

The concepts of personal data and data subject are inextricably linked. 'Personal data' is defined as "information relating to an identified or identifiable natural person".[23] The definition of personal data is extremely broad and may also comprise 'special categories of data'[24] (also called 'sensitive data'), which, by their very nature, may pose greater risks to the data subjects when processed. Due to their character, processing of these data requires higher attention to be afforded by the data controller and other involved parties. These categories of data include personal data 'revealing racial or ethnic origin, political opinions, religious or philosophical beliefs, or trade union membership, genetic data, biometric data for the purpose of uniquely identifying a natural person, data concerning health or data concerning a natural person's sex life or sexual orientation'.[25]

If the processing of data does not concern an identified or identifiable person (a human being), then data protection law does not apply.[26] For example, if the process of anonymisation has been conducted, meaning that all identifying elements are eliminated from a set of personal data, and the data subject is no longer identifiable, then data protection law does not apply. In order to determine whether a natural person is identifiable, one must take into account all reasonable means (including available technology) that are likely to be used to directly or indirectly identify the individual. Establishing a link with a natural person can be achieved by reference to an 'identifier' such as a name, an identification number, locational data, an online identifier or to one or more properties specific to the physical, physiological, genetic, mental, economic, cultural or social identity of that person.[27]

4.2.2 Data controller

In the context of personal data processing, the key decision-making figure is the data controller. In the private sector sphere, this is usually a natural or legal person, while in the public sector, this is an authority (e.g. a ministry, a governmental agency, etc.). The data controller is the one who determines the means and purposes of processing the personal data of natural persons.[28] This mostly answers the question of 'why' and 'how' the personal data should be processed.[29] To determine whether or not an entity acts as a data controller, the assessors look at the decision to collect or process the personal data, the purpose or outcome of the processing, which personal data is collected and from which individuals, whether there will be a contract for this, which decisions or inferences are drawn during or after processing, etc.

4.2.3 Data processor

A 'data processor' means a natural or legal person, public authority, agency or other body that processes personal data on behalf of the data controller.[30] As a general rule, the data processor processes personal data by only following specific instructions regarding the processing. For instance, data processors do not decide to collect personal data from individuals on their own initiative, do not decide what personal data should be collected from individuals, do not decide the lawful basis for the use of that data, do not decide what purpose or purposes the data will be used for, and do not decide whether to disclose the data, or to whom.[31]

4.2.4 Data protection authorities

EU data protection law is applied and enforced in each national jurisdiction independently. This is ensured by the function of independent supervisory authorities (SAs), also called data protection authorities (DPAs). Specifically, each Member State shall provide for the institution and function of one or more independent public authorities to be responsible for monitoring the proper application and enforcement of data protection laws in their jurisdiction.[32]

Supervisory authorities are tasked with the following activities:[33]
- they promote data protection at the national level, advising data subjects, data controllers and the government;
- they hear complaints and assist data subjects with alleged violations of data protection rights;
- they supervise controllers and processors, and they conduct investigations on the application of the Regulation;
- they monitor relevant (technological) developments, insofar as they impact the protection of personal data, such as the development of information and communication technologies;
- they possess investigative, corrective, authorisation and advisory powers, for example, they may carry out investigations in the form of data protection audits;
- they notify the controller or the processor of an alleged infringement of the Regulation, or obtain, from the controller and the processor access to all personal data and premises (such as data processing equipment and means);
- they can issue warnings to a controller whose intended processing operations are likely to infringe provisions of the Regulation;
- they can impose a temporary or definitive limitation including a ban on processing and,
- they are the ones to impose the administrative fines, where necessary.[34]

4.3 Principles of EU data protection law

4.3.1 Lawfulness, fairness, transparency

Three fundamental principles in data protection law jointly act as the starting point for the more detailed provisions on processing. Largely, these concern the data controller. The most important are i) lawfulness, ii) fairness and iii) transparency. Their general articulation as principles is further specified according to the circumstances in which they are applied. In other words, their application in the area of border control entails different risks compared to personal data processing for marketing purposes.

In order to process personal data, the data controller must have a lawful basis to do so. This basis functions as an enabler for processing personal data within the scope of the purposes identified. Lawful processing requires the consent of the data subject or one of the five other legitimate grounds provided in the data protection legislation. It also implies that the data controller has reviewed the purposes of the processing activities, and has selected the most appropriate lawful basis (or bases) for each activity.

Personal data must be processed fairly. This means that processing must be done in ways that people would reasonably expect, and not in ways that have unjustified adverse effects on them, or in ways that could mislead them. This does not mean, however, that every processing that would negatively affect an individual should be considered 'unfair'.

The principle of transparency requires that any information addressed to the public or to the data subject be concise, easily accessible and easy to understand, and that clear and plain language and, additionally, where appropriate, visualisation be used.[35] Among other things, the following information is provided beforehand: the identity and the contact details of the controller, the purposes of the processing for which the personal data are intended, and also the legal basis for the processing, the legitimate interests pursued, the legitimate interests, the period for which the personal data will be stored, etc.[36] Transparency in processing facilitates the exercising of the data subject's rights.

4.3.2 Purpose limitation

The principle of purpose limitation means that personal data must be collected for specified, explicit and legitimate purposes and not further processed in a manner that is incompatible with those purposes. In other words, any processing of personal data must be performed for a specific well-defined purpose, and if this happens for additional purposes, these must be specified and compatible with the original one.[37] Its objective is primarily legal certainty, along with predictability and user control.[38] Neither processing personal data for undefined or unlimited purposes is lawful, nor is processing based on the assumption that it may be useful at some point in the future.

It is the data controller who defines the purposes of processing. In assessing the compatibility of the initial specific purpose with any additional ones, the controller shall take the following into consideration: any link between those purposes and the purposes of the intended further processing; the context in which the personal data have been collected; the reasonable expectations of data subjects; the nature of the personal data; the consequences of the processing for data subjects; the existence of appropriate safeguards.[39]

4.3.3 Data minimisation

Data minimisation means that personal data shall be adequate, relevant and limited to what is *necessary* in relation to the purposes for which they are processed. All these three words, '*adequate, relevant and limited*' are subject to the discretionary power of by the data controller. The criteria for the assessment of necessity of processing are not straightforward, and neither is the extent to which the purpose of the processing can be reasonably fulfilled by other means. What is deemed 'appropriate' in the case of extensive processing systems is not listed, in order to avoid prescriptiveness and to allow greater conformity with technological advancements. The data controller shall proceed to an assessment of the measures adopted, so as to ensure that data processing does not entail a disproportionate interference in the fundamental rights and freedoms at stake. This also includes periodic review of the stored data, and deletion of those that are not necessary.

4.3.4 Data accuracy

A data controller must ascertain that data are accurate and kept up-to-date by guaranteeing that data that are inaccurate are erased or rectified without delay.[40] At the same time, some categories of personal data shall remain non-updated (e.g. a medical record that should be compared to and complemented by future examinations). The data subject shall have the right to restriction of processing by the controller when the accuracy of the personal data is contested.[41]

4.3.5 Storage limitation

The data controller shall ensure that personal data are deleted or anonymised as soon as they are no longer needed for the purposes for which they were collected. Personal data shall be kept in a form that permits identification of data subjects for no longer than what is necessary for the purposes for which the personal data are processed. Storage limitation functions in conjunction with purpose limitation, since these both allow for the same exception of further processing solely for archiving purposes in the public interest, scientific or historical research purposes, or statistical purposes.[42] Data subjects must be appropriately informed about the standard retention periods through the privacy policy.[43] This principle enables compliance with individuals' requests for erasure under 'the right to be forgotten'.

4.4 Legal requirements

4.4.1 Lawfulness of processing

Pursuant to the principle of lawfulness, personal data may be lawfully processed if they meet one of the following criteria (lawful grounds):[44]

a) *Consent*: the data subject has given consent to the processing of their personal data for one or more specific purposes. Consent is considered freely given if the data subject has genuine or free choice or is able to refuse or withdraw consent without detriment.[45] It shall be as easy to withdraw as to give consent, at any time. Consent may not always be a lawful ground: for instance, employees are not in a position to freely give, refuse or revoke consent, given their dependency within the employer/employee relationship. Consent must also be informed (data subjects must have received sufficient information), specific (for concrete processing purposes) and unambiguous (without reasonable doubts).

b) *Contract*: processing is necessary for the performance of a contract to which the data subject is party, or in order to take steps at the request of the data subject prior to entering into a contract. This lawful ground applies where either of two conditions are met: the processing in question is objectively necessary for the performance of a contract with a data subject, or the processing is objectively necessary in order to take pre-contractual steps at the request of a data subject.[46]

c) *Legal obligation*: processing is necessary for compliance with a legal obligation to which the controller is subject. For instance, employers must process data about their employees for social security and taxation reasons, and businesses must process data about their customers for taxation purposes.[47]

d) *Vital interests*: processing is necessary in order to protect the vital interests of the data subject or of another natural person. An illustration would be when monitoring epidemics and their development, or where there is a humanitarian emergency.[48]

e) *Public interest*: processing is necessary for the performance of a task carried out in the public interest or in the exercise of official authority vested in the controller. This is most relevant to public authorities, and the underlying task, function or power must have a clear basis in law. Furthermore, there should be no less intrusive way by which an authority is able to reasonably perform its tasks or exercise its powers.

f) *Legitimate interest*: processing is necessary for the purposes of the legitimate interests pursued by the controller or by a third party, except where such interests are overridden by the interests or fundamental rights and freedoms of the data subject that require protection of personal data, in particular where the data subject is a child. In this respect, the legitimate interests of the controller are first identified, and then a balancing exercise must be conducted between those interests and the interests or fundamental rights and freedoms of the data subject. A classic example of legitimate interest is direct marketing.

4.4.2 Accountability and compliance

The principle of accountability[49] stipulates that the data controller shall be responsible for, and be able to demonstrate compliance with, all the data protection principles mentioned above. This means that they shall actively and continuously implement measures to promote and safeguard data protection in their processing activities. Demonstrating compliance with the Regulation is an obligation towards data subjects, but also towards the data protection authorities. Three prominent newly introduced tools for accountability include the data protection officer, the data protection impact assessment, and the data protection by design & by default.

Security of processing
The principle of data security is probably the most complicated and disputed one. It is connected to a data protection principle, that of integrity and confidentiality. It requires that the security, integrity and confidentiality of personal data is guaranteed, so as to prevent adverse effects for the data subject. Measures adopted could be either of a technical or an organisational nature. The appropriateness of security measures must be determined on a case-by-case basis and be reviewed regularly.

Criteria for such choice are the state of the art, the costs of implementation and the nature, scope, context and purposes of processing, as well as the risk of varying likelihood and severity for the rights and freedoms of natural persons.

Measures that are deemed technically appropriate, among others, are: the pseudonymisation and encryption, the confidentiality, integrity, availability and resilience of processing systems and services, restoration of the availability and access to personal data in a timely manner in the event of a physical or technical incident, and a process for regularly testing, assessing and evaluating the effectiveness of technical and organisational measures for ensuring the security of the processing.[50]

Measures that correspond to good organisational rules could be: regular provision of information to all employees about data security rules and their obligations under data protection law, especially regarding their confidentiality obligations, clear distribution of responsibilities and a transparent outline of competences in matters of data processing, and ensuring that authorisations to access personal data have been assigned by the competent person and require proper documentation.[51]

Data protection officer
The role of the data protection officer (DPO) has been formulated in such a way so as to be the key role in the accountability mechanism. DPOs are responsible for the due completion, and liable for reporting the success of a compliance project, yet without being accountable themselves. It is the data controller who is accountable for the compliance of the processing operations with the law. DPOs are obligatorily appointed where processing is conducted by a public authority, where processing results in systematic monitoring, or

where the processing concerns special categories of data or personal data relating to criminal convictions or offences.[52]

DPOs are independent: they do not receive instructions from the management, they facilitate compliance by implementing the rules and communicating with the supervisory authorities, while they are involved, properly and in a timely manner, in all issues which relate to the protection of personal data within the organisation.[53] Duties of DPOs include, for example, advising on the undertaking of data protection impact assessments, training personnel, and creating and maintaining records of processing activities within an organisation.

Data protection impact assessment

The requirement to conduct data protection impact assessments (DPIAs) in several innovative laws around the world is not coincidental. The recently reformed personal data protection law in the EU introduced a requirement for data controllers to assess the impacts of data processing operations that are "likely to result in a high risk to the rights and freedoms of natural persons" with regard to the protection of personal data.[54] The level of risk varies depending on the nature and scope of processing. Large-scale operations and those involving the processing of sensitive data present much higher risks for data subjects compared to smaller-scale data controllers who processes their employees' personal phone numbers.

The Regulation foresees a list of processing operations that are considered high-risk and for which a prior impact assessment is necessary: where there is systematic and extensive evaluation of personal aspects (profiling), where special categories of data or personal data relating to criminal convictions or offences are processed, and where processing involves the large-scale, systematic monitoring of publicly accessible areas.[55] The content of the impact assessment shall include, among other things, an assessment of the necessity and proportionality of the processing operations and the possible risks to the rights of individuals, as well as mitigation measures for the risks identified. To demonstrate compliance, data controllers must maintain a record of the processing activities carried out under their responsibility.[56]

Data protection by design and by default

Data protection by design and by default refers to the effective implementation of data protection principles and appropriate technical and organisational measures to safeguard data subjects' rights and freedoms. The concept is an evolution of what was previously known as privacy by design, and is currently a legal requirement. It is inspired by the fair information practices, as articulated by the Information and Privacy Commissioner of Canada.[57]

Data protection 'by design' applies to the development of new services, systems, processes or products that involve personal data processing. It involves implementation of appropriate technical and organisational measures designed to implement the data protection principles, and the integration of safeguards into the processing necessary to fulfil the legal requirements and protect data subjects' rights. This way, privacy and data protection are guaranteed at the design phase of any system, service, product or process, and then throughout the lifecycle.

Data protection 'by default' requires that the data controller ensures processing of the data that is necessary to achieve a specific purpose. It links to the fundamental data protection principles of data minimisation and purpose limitation. A misunderstanding could be that it requires the adoption of a 'default to off' solution, but this is not true: This principle translates as the need to specify the personal data before the processing starts, to appropriately inform individuals, and to only process the data that are needed for the purpose.[58]

Data breaches
One additional accountability mechanism is that relating to data breaches. A personal data breach refers to a security breach leading to the accidental or unlawful destruction, loss, alteration or unauthorised disclosure or access to processed personal data.[59] Data breaches can be highly detrimental to the data protection rights of individuals who, as a result of the breach, lose control over their personal data. They are subsequently exposed to risks, such as identity theft or fraud, financial loss or material damages, loss of confidentiality of personal data protected by professional secrecy, and damage to their reputation.[60]

When a personal data breach is detected, and if it is likely to result in a high risk to the rights and freedoms of natural persons, the controller shall communicate the personal data breach to the data subject without undue delay. The notification must include a description of the nature of the data breach, of data subjects affected, and a description of the possible consequences. If the data breach is likely to result in high risks for the data subjects, then the data controller must inform the data subjects in clear and plain language. At the same time, the controller is responsible for informing the supervisory authorities.

4.4.3 Data transfers

The level of protection of personal data is deemed to accompany them in function of the country that the personal data are. Data protection law regulates transfers of personal data which are undergoing processing or are intended for processing after transfer to a third country or to an international organisation.[61] In other words, if and whenever personal data are transferred outside the EU, then they are subject to specific rules in processing. With regard to the principle of free movement of personal data in the EU, this shall be neither restricted nor prohibited for reasons connected with the protection of natural persons with regard to the processing of personal data.[62]

Depending on the recipient of personal data, there are different tools to frame the data transfers. The strongest, but also the least common, is the adequacy decision.[63] A third country may be declared as offering an adequate level of protection, under a European

Commission decision, meaning that data can be transferred to another company in that third country without the data exporter being required to provide further safeguards or conditions.[64] If an adequacy decision has not been signed, then data controllers can transfer personal data based on binding corporate rules,[65] which are legally binding to every member of the group. Alternatively, they can use standard contractual clauses approved by the European Commission; lastly, it is possible to adhere to a code of conduct or certification mechanism.

Data transfers are subject to the discretion of the data controller ("…has provided appropriate safeguards, and on condition that enforceable data subject rights and effective legal remedies for data subjects are available"). This means that the burden of proving that, by transferring personal data to third countries, the level of protection there fulfils the minimum requirements in the EU – first and foremost, that data subject rights are not prejudiced and that appropriate remedies are in place – lies upon the data controller. In such cases, a data transfer impact assessment, a risk assessment of the factors related to the transferral of data to third countries, may be needed to complement the DPIA or as a standalone document. In this, the necessity, proportionality, and technical and organisational measures are evaluated, as well as the level of protection of fundamental rights.

4.5 Data subject rights

4.5.1 Right to be informed

The transparency principle requires that any personal data processing should generally be transparent to individuals. To this end, the data controller is obligated to provide information to the data subjects. This holds whether personal data are collected from the data subject directly or have not been obtained from the data subject, but instead from third parties. Such an obligation does not depend on a request from the data subject.[66] Rather, the controller must proactively comply with the obligation, regardless of whether the data subject shows an interest in the information or not.

A broad comprehensive obligation is established when communicating this information to data subjects.[67] As described in the transparency principle, data controllers must provide, at the time the data are obtained or prior to the processing, in concise, transparent, intelligible, easily accessible, clear, plain and easily understandable language, all the necessary information, usually in the form of a privacy notice or a website privacy policy. This information is provided free of charge. Frequently, information on data processing is structured in such a way so as to respond to the following questions: *Who are we? What data do we collect from you? Why are we collecting your data? How do we process your data? What are your rights?*

4.5.2 Right of access by the data subject

The right to access one's own data (right of access) is a pivotal right[68] and is also set out as one of the elements of the fundamental right to the protection of personal data in the Charter of Fundamental Rights, i.e. in primary law.[69] The right of access gives individuals the right to obtain a copy of their personal data, as well as other supplementary information. It helps data subjects to understand how and why the data controller is using their data, and check whether this is being done lawfully. The data controller must provide, upon request by the data subject, at least information on the following: purposes of processing, categories of personal data processed, recipients of the data, storage periods, existence of data subject rights, and the logic involved in automated processing of data, in the case of automated decisions.[70]

4.5.3 Right to rectification

EU law provides for a right to rectification of personal data.[71] The data subject shall have the right to obtain from the controller without undue delay the rectification of inaccurate personal data concerning them. This right includes completing data which were previously incomplete, or inaccurate personal data, which must be rectified without undue or excessive delay.

4.5.4 Right to erasure ('right to be forgotten')

Data subjects have the right to have their own personal data erased, pursuant to the principle of data minimisation.[72] This is applicable, for instance where the personal data are no longer necessary in relation to the purposes for which they were collected or otherwise processed, the data subject withdraws consent, or the data has been unlawfully processed.[73] Nevertheless, this right is not absolute: it needs to be balanced against other bases, such as the freedom of expression, the public interest, scientific or historical research purposes or statistical purposes.

4.5.5 Right to restriction of processing

Data subjects are entitled to obtain from the controller restriction of processing of their personal data where the accuracy of the personal data processed by the data controller is disputed or is unknown, the processing itself is unlawful, the processing of personal data is not necessary for the purposes intended, or the data subject has objected to the processing.[74] This right enables the data subject to limit the way that a data controller uses their personal data, often as an alternative to deleting them.

4.5.6 Right to data portability

Applying the right to data portability essentially means that data subjects are entitled to have their personal data transmitted directly from one controller to another if this is technically feasible. This involves receiving the personal data in a structured, commonly used and machine-readable format and then transmitting those data to another controller without hindrance. The right to data portability is permitted when the lawful basis is either consent or contract, and the processing is carried out by automated means.[75]

4.5.7 Right to object

Data subjects have the right to object to the processing of their personal data in certain circumstances, such as where a task is carried out in the public interest, or in the exercising of official authority or legitimate interests. The right to object is raised to an absolute right in the case of direct marketing.[76] The right to object serves in striking the correct balance between the data subject's data protection rights and the legitimate rights of the data controller. Furthermore, it constitutes a powerful weapon against profiling.

4.5.8 Right not to be subject to automated decision-making, including profiling

In principle, data subjects must not be subject to automated decisions that give rise to legal or similarly significant effects.[77] This right is passive, in the sense that it equates to a general prohibition and does not require the data subject to proactively seek an objection to such a decision.[78]

This provision could concern, for instance, an automatic refusal of an online credit application or e-recruiting practices. Automated decision-making based on profiling may take the form of analysing or predicting aspects concerning the data subject's performance at work, economic situation, health, personal preferences or interests, reliability or behaviour, location or movements, etc. If such processing is conducted, it must be accompanied by adequate safeguards for the data subject, such as the right to obtain human intervention on the part of the controller, to express their point of view, and to contest the decision.[79]

4.5.9 Data subject rights in border control

The national DPAs supervise the application of the data protection rules in their respective countries, while the EDPS monitors the application of the data protection rules for the central system managed by eu-LISA.[80] In accordance with data protection principles, all individuals whose data is processed in the Schengen Information System II are accorded specific rights. These rights are: a) the right of access to data relating to them stored in SIS II; b) the right to correction of inaccurate data or deletion when data have been unlawfully stored; c) the right to bring proceedings before the courts or competent authorities to correct or delete data, or to obtain compensation.

Lastly, data subject rights do not always prevail, they are not absolute; restrictions may be imposed, particularly when other interests are at stake. Such restrictions shall respect the essence of the right to data protection (its core) and shall be necessary and proportionate measures in a democratic society. Common grounds for imposing restrictions on data subject rights are national and public security, prevention, investigation, detection or prosecution of criminal offences, defence, protection of judicial independence, and protection of the data subject or the rights and freedoms of others.

Endnotes

1. The first data protection legislation in the world was passed in 1970, in the (West) German state of Hesse.
2. Alan F. Westin, "Privacy and Freedom", *Washington and Lee Law Review* 25, no. 1 (1967): 166-170, https://scholarlycommons.law.wlu.edu/cgi/viewcontent.cgi?Article=3659&context=wlulr.
3. European Union Agency For Fundamental Rights, European Court of Human Rights, and European Data Protection Supervisor, *Handbook on European Data Protection Law* (Luxembourg: Publications Office of the European Union, 2018), https://doi.org/10.2811/58814.
4. Regulation (EU) 2016/679 of the European Parliament and of the Council of 27 April 2016 on the protection of natural persons with regard to the processing of personal data and on the free movement of such data, and repealing Directive 95/46/EC. OJ L 119, 4.5.2016, p. 1–88.
5. Maja Brkan, "Do algorithms rule the world? Algorithmic decision-making and data protection in the framework of the GDPR and beyond", *International Journal of Law and Information Technology* 27, no. 2 (2019): 91–121, https://doi.org/10.1093/ijlit/eay017.
6. Jathan Sadowski, "When Data Is Capital: Datafication, Accumulation, and Extraction," *Big Data and Society* 6, no. 1 (2019): 1–12, https://doi.org/10.1177/2053951718820549.
7. European Data Protection Supervisor (EDPS) *Opinion 4/2018 on the Proposals for two Regulations establishing a framework for interoperability between EU large-scale information systems* (2018), https://edps.europa.eu/sites/edp/files/publication/2018-04-16_interoperability_opinion_en.pdf.
8. *European Commission Communication from the Commission to the European Parliament and the Council, Stronger and Smarter Information Systems for Borders and Security* (2016), https://eur-lex.europa.eu/legal-content/EN/TXT/HTML/?uri=CELEX:52016DC0205&from=EN.
9. Ibid.
10. The main instruments of the United Nations (UN), stipulating provisions about privacy, are the non-binding Universal Declaration of Human Rights (UDHR) and the International Covenant on Civil and Political Rights (ICCPR).

11. These revelations have increased public concern about information security and privacy resulting from disclosures detailing the extent of the National Security Agency's (NSA) surveillance activities.
12. United Nations (UN), The Right to Privacy in the Digital Age, http://undocs.org/A/RES/68/167.
13. The right to personal data protection is not enshrined in the European Convention on Human Rights (ECHR) *per se*. Rather, it is inferred from the scope of Article 8, which guarantees the right to respect for private and family life, home and correspondence.
14. Ibid.
15. Protocol amending the Convention for the Protection of Individuals with regard to Automatic Processing of Personal Data (CETS No. 223).
16. The precautionary measure of human rights impact assessment is stipulated in 'Recommendation CM/Rec (2020)1 of the Committee of Ministers to member States on the human rights impacts of algorithmic systems.'
17. Directive 95/46/EC of the European Parliament and of the Council of 24 October 1995 on the protection of individuals with regard to the processing of personal data and on the free movement of such data, OJ L 281, 23.11.1995, p. 31–50.
18. Regulation (EU) 2016/679 of the European Parliament and of the Council of 27 April 2016 on the protection of natural persons with regard to the processing of personal data and on the free movement of such data, and repealing Directive 95/46/EC.
19. Directive 2002/58/EC of the European Parliament and of the Council of 12 July 2002 concerning the processing of personal data and the protection of privacy in the electronic communications sector (Directive on privacy and electronic communications).
20. Regulation (EU) 2018/1725 of the European Parliament and of the Council of 23 October 2018 on the protection of natural persons with regard to the processing of personal data by the Union institutions, bodies, offices and agencies and on the free movement of such data, and repealing Regulation (EC) No 45/2001 and Decision No 1247/2002/EC.
21. Graham Greenleaf, "2020 Ends a Decade of 62 New Data Privacy Laws," *Privacy Laws & Business International Report* 163 (2020): 24-26, https://papers.ssrn.com/sol3/papers.cfm?abstract_id=3572611.
22. Petra Molnar, *Technological Testing Grounds, Migration Management Experiments and Reflections from the Ground Up* (2020), https://edri.org/wp-content/uploads/2020/11/Technological-Testing-Grounds.pdf.
23. GDPR, Art. 4 (1).
24. GDPR, Art. 9.
25. GDPR, Art. 9 (1).
26. Article 29 Working Party, "Opinion 4/2007 on the concept of personal data", WP 136, 20 June 2007, p. 22.
27. GDPR, Art. 4 (1).
28. GDPR, Art. 4 (7).
29. Information Commissioner's Office (ICO), Controllers and processors, https://ico.org.uk/for-organisations/guide-to-data-protection/guide-to-the-general-data-protection-regulation-gdpr/key-definitions/controllers-and-processors/.
30. GDPR, Art. 4 (8).
31. Information Commissioner's Office (ICO), Controllers and processors, https://ico.org.uk/for-organisations/guide-to-data-protection/guide-to-the-general-data-protection-regulation-gdpr/key-definitions/controllers-and-processors/.
32. GDPR, Art. 51.
33. GDPR, Art. 57-58.
34. GDPR, Art 83.

35. GDPR, Art. 12 (1).
36. GDPR, Art. 12 (2) and Recital 58.
37. GDPR, Art. 5 (1) (b).
38. Ibid.
39. GDPR, Recital 50.
40. GDPR, Art. 5 (1) (d).
41. GDPR, Art. 18 (1) (a).
42. GDPR, Art. 5 (1) (e).
43. Information Commissioner's Office (ICO), Controllers and processors, https://ico.org.uk/for-organisations/guide-to-data-protection/guide-to-the-general-data-protection-regulation-gdpr/key-definitions/controllers-and-processors/.
44. GDPR, Art. 6 (1).
45. GDPR, Recital 42.
46. European Data Protection Board, Guidelines 2/2019 on the processing of personal data under Article 6(1)(b) GDPR in the context of the provision of online services to data subjects, adopted on 9 April 2019, https://edpb.europa.eu/sites/edpb/files/consultation/edpb_draft_guidelines-art_6-1-b-final_public_consultation_version_en.pdf.
47. Ibid.
48. Ibid.
49. GDPR, Art. 5 (2).
50. GDPR, Art. 32 (1).
51. Ibid.
52. GDPR, Art. 37 (1).
53. GDPR, Art. 37 (3) and (4).
54. Dariusz Kloza et al., "Data Protection Impact Assessments in the European Union: Complementing the New Legal Framework towards a More Robust Protection of Individuals."
55. GDPR, Art. 35 (1).
56. GDPR, Art. 30.
57. Ann Cavoukian, "Privacy by Design, the 7 foundational principles implementation and mapping of fair information practices", https://www.ipc.on.ca/wp-content/uploads/resources/pbd-implement-7found-principles.pdf.
58. Information Commissioner's Office, "Data protection by design and default", https://ico.org.uk/for-organisations/guide-to-data-protection/guide-to-the-general-data-protection-regulation-gdpr/accountability-and-governance/data-protection-by-design-and-default/#dpd3.
59. GDPR, Art. 4 (12).
60. GDPR, Recital 75.
61. GDPR, Art. 44.
62. GDPR, Art. 1 (3).
63. GDPR, Art. 45.
64. The European Commission has so far only recognised Andorra, Argentina, Canada (commercial organisations), the Faroe Islands, Guernsey, Israel, the Isle of Man, Japan, Jersey, New Zealand, Switzerland and Uruguay as providing adequate protection.
65. Information Commissioner's Office, Binding Corporate rules, https://ico.org.uk/for-organisations/binding-corporate-rules/#:~:text=Binding%20Corporate%20Rules%20(BCRs)%20are,Directive%2095%2F46%2FEC.
66. European Union Agency for Fundamental Rights, Council of Europe-European Court of Human Rights, European Data Protection Supervisor, "Handbook on European Data Protection Law", 207.
67. GDPR, Art. 12-14.
68. GDPR, Art. 15.

69. Charter of Fundamental Rights, Art. 8 (2).
70. GDPR, Art. 15.
71. GDPR, Art. 16.
72. European Union Agency for Fundamental Rights – Council of Europe-European Court of Human Rights – European Data Protection Supervisor.
73. GDPR, Art. 17.
74. GDPR, Art. 18.
75. GDPR, Art. 20.
76. GDPR, Art. 21.
77. GDPR, Art. 22.
78. Article 29 Working Party, "Guidelines on Automated Individual Decision-Making and profiling for the purposes of Regulation 2016/679", WP 251, 3 October 2017, p. 15.
79. General Data Protection Regulation, Art. 22 (3).
80. European Agency for the operational management of large-scale IT systems in the area of freedom, security and justice (eu-LISA).

5 Ethics and border control technologies

Simone Casiraghi,* J. Peter Burgess** and Kristoffer Lidén***
* Vrije Universiteit Brussel. E-mail: simone.casiraghi@vub.be.
** École Normale Supérieure, Paris & Vrije Universiteit Brussel.
   E-mail: james.peter.burgess@ens.fr.
*** Peace Research Institute Oslo. E-mail: kristoffer@prio.org.

5.1 Introduction

5.1.1 Definition of ethics

The two terms 'ethics' and 'morals' are sometimes used interchangeably in everyday language, but they are not synonymous. The concepts, originating from the Greek *ethos* and the Latin *mores*, respectively, both mean something like habit or custom. While the term 'morals' refers to *de facto* habits, customs and traditions, 'ethics' refers to a systematic reflection, a philosophical critique, and an evaluation thereof. Ethics is understood for the purpose of this Chapter, in the context of border control, as a synonym for moral philosophy, which is a branch of philosophy that deals, roughly, with a rational and practical reflection on what conduct is good or bad and right or wrong.

If ethics is defined as a systematic reflection on moral issues raised by emerging technologies, the purpose of this Chapter is to provide a toolkit to guide such systematic ethical reflection in the context of border control. In particular, the Chapter provides assessors with a list of recurring arguments (and recurring fallacies against which to evaluate them) that will allow them to assess the ethics component of the benchmark in the integrated impact assessment process. Thus, the structure of the Chapter is as follows: In the next sub-sections, some further introductory notions on ethics (its importance for society, historical development and literature overview) will be provided, including its importance in the assessment process and the actors involved in it. Section 5.1.2 will provide assessors with the key concepts to conduct the ethics steps of the impact assessment process according to the Template included in Annex 1. The approaches that are often used at the level of applied ethics are explored, with specific examples from the context of border control. Moreover, a list of argumentative fallacies will be provided as tools through which to assess or complement these approaches.

5.1.2 The importance of ethics for society

Performing an ethics assessment involves, put simply, systematic moral reflections about how a given initiative can be 'good' and 'bad', right and wrong, or beneficial and harmful. Recent technological developments have affected every dimension of people's lives; social contacts, jobs, how they eat, travel, play, and so on. European values and moral norms have been affected in this process as well: concepts like autonomy, freedom and responsibility have been challenged and modified by the new affordances of technologies and socio-technical infrastructures.[1] For example, identity is shaped by algorithmic profiling (with systems 'predicting' people's online behaviour and purchases) and biometrics (with people's bodily parts becoming the most important identifier by which access to certain services is enabled).

More concretely, research and innovation (R&I) efforts at the European Commission (EC) in the security domain are said to contribute to tackling 'societal challenges' such as fighting crime, human trafficking and terrorism, or strengthening security through border management.[2] At the same time, the same technological developments resulting from R&I can lead to undesirable impacts on individuals and groups, distributing burdens and benefits unequally.[3] New socio-technical arrangements create genuinely new challenges, some argue, or exacerbate existing societal problems, such as systemic forms of racism and discrimination,[4] thus requiring reflection in order to identify harmful effects and take action against them.

5.1.3 The role of ethics in the benchmark

Ethics, when framed within such a definition, can be of help in an integrated impact assessment process, not as an alternative to a legal assessment based on fundamental rights, but rather as an argumentative support. The scope of this Chapter is therefore the integration of ethics of technology into the impact assessment process, with the intention of introducing a 'how to' method to assessing the uses and implementations of new and emerging border technologies. The ethical component of the impact assessment method is meant to support and/or expand upon the data protection component, which constitutes the 'backbone' of such a method.[5] This especially means that, besides the necessity and proportionality assessment and risk assessment that are mandated by law as part of a Data Protection Impact Assessment (DPIA),[6] the integrated impact assessment method adds an 'ethics assessment' to the appraisal techniques, in order to further expand on the assessment of the risks to rights and freedoms of natural persons. Such an expansion gives assessors a broader political and societal view on the impacts of border control technologies in addition to individual data protection issues[7] by also looking at arguments relating to the values these technologies aim to uphold, their (supposed) neutrality, or the unequal distribution of burdens and benefits among groups of people.

However, assessors need to pay attention to the use of the term 'ethics' when it comes to assessing the impacts of emerging technologies. On the one hand, ethics is currently an inflated term or buzzword, used with different meanings depending on the interests at stake for specific groups. Reference to ethics can be made by academics, humanitarian or non-governmental organisations, civil society representatives, technology companies (e.g. the ethical principles of Google or Microsoft) or political institutions (such as the European Commission), with each pursuing possibly different – and even competing – goals. On the other hand, both academics and civil society organisations[8] have warned about the excessive use of 'AI (Artificial Intelligence) ethics' which could become an obstacle to traditional regulation, and a way of self-legitimising industry practices.[9] Given the proliferation of ethics principles, guidelines and methods in recent years,[10] assessors may be provided with tools that can guide them throughout the assessment process and, more generally, can consider the current debates, without the risk of considering ethics an empty signifier. Before turning specifically to the approach of the integrated impact assessment method, however, it is useful to quickly look at the historical development of applied ethics and ethics assessment tools.

5.1.4 Historical development of applied ethics

The historical roots of the word 'ethics', as part of a philosophical enterprise, can be traced back to Ancient Greece, to the work of Plato and Aristotle in the 5th and 4th centuries BCE, among others. In the West, ethics remained for centuries predominantly a matter limited to philosophical discussion.[11]

Until recently, then, ethics primarily had an academic and theoretical role. In the second half of the 20th century, however, ethics, first and foremost in the form of bioethics, began to acquire a political and institutionalised role.[12] The main explanation that is often given for this political turn is the increased risks associated with research on human subjects through biotechnical medicine. However, this explanation is overly simplistic.[13] An additional explanation is that the rise of institutionalised ethics reflected the need to establish a more open dialogue between science and society.[14] Since the 1970s, the EU has sought to strike a balance between facilitating and promoting science on the one hand and respect for the pluralism of European values on the other, as a response to value conflicts in areas including medicine and food and agriculture.[15]

Following bioethics, computer ethics, environmental ethics, and, more recently, robo-ethics, big data ethics and AI ethics proliferated as forms of 'applied ethics', i.e. forms meant to address specific challenges in different domains by applying rigorous philosophical reasoning in an attempt to solve moral dilemmas or guide decision-making. Applied ethics involves an inter-disciplinary discussion, often outside academia, and related to policy making and decision-making processes in private (e.g. companies) or public institutions (e.g. research committees or advisory bodies).

Among the methods for performing applied ethics, ethical technology assessment and ethical impact assessment have emerged as new anticipatory methods (i.e. techniques of anticipatory governance to tackle impact of technologies *before* they materialise), as well as approaches such as Responsible Research and Innovation (RRI),[16] to combine the more strategic and technical dimension of R&I with the more normative one of responsibility.[17] Such anticipatory and responsible approaches have opened up the topic of 'ethics' to a multi-disciplinary arena of actors, instead of keeping it confined to the realms of philosophers or academics.

5.1.5 The profile for assessing ethics

Today, the landscape of applied ethics is multifaceted. Compliance with ethics requirements, depending on the initiative, may be assessed by a variety of bodies such as:
- Research Ethics Committees (RECs), at public (e.g. universities) or private (e.g. companies) organisations, which calculate the risks and benefits of a given initiative and ensure participants give informed consent,[18]
- National ethics committees or councils,[19] at EU or Member State level, or
- Groups of ethics experts recruited in an *ad hoc* manner.[20]

An integrated impact assessment process, however, requires a team of assessors that works together across several domains. Looking at the composition of ethics committees and ethics advisory boards, members may be drawn from medicine, business, engineering, computer science, or elsewhere, depending on the field to which ethics is applied. It is therefore a challenge to identify the profile required to perform the ethics steps of the integrated impact assessment process.

There are no clear-cut solutions to this challenge. Moreover, giving a definitive answer to these questions would risk making 'ethics' a type of expertise inaccessible to some profiles. Instead, engaging in ethical discussions is, and should be, open to different profiles, provided that assessors are open to critical thinking (including in their own daily activities) and willing to familiarise themselves with the key concepts provided in Section 5.2. In any case, assessors with a background in humanities, and more particularly in philosophy (specialised in philosophy of technology, applied ethics, RRI), social sciences (specialised in surveillance studies, critical security studies or science and technology studies) or law and technology (including criminology), might need less effort to acquaint themselves with the approach described here.

If in the team of assessors there are no persons able to carry out this part of the assessment process, or it is not possible to hire extra personnel to carry out the assessment, this could mean two main things. First, it would provide an opportunity for personnel of the institution in charge of the assessment to be encouraged to acquire new expertise through, for example, training. Alternatively, it may offer a chance to open up the assessment process to stakeholder involvement, for example through the team of assessors organising events or sessions with external experts or members of the public who can provide relevant input or support.

5.1.6 Literature overview

Despite recent tendencies of coupling and blurring ethical and legal considerations of technologies in areas such as security research,[21] ethics and law are better understood as distinct, with each having its own questions and approaches.[22] This separation is reflected in the benchmark of the integrated impact assessment process. The interdisciplinarity of ethics, however, coupled with the fact that there is no specific 'ethics of border control technologies', (as there are, for example, bioethics, business ethics and computer ethics as established forms of applied ethics),[23] might confuse assessors when it comes to choosing instruments (texts, methods, techniques) to support the assessment process. However, there are at least two groups of sources that could provide support to assessors. These are:

A. Generic anticipatory or assessment methods that can be applied to the case of ethics of border control. A plethora of methods by which to undertake ethics in R&I exist, but the main groups can be classified in:[24]
   - *Ex-ante* methods, i.e. aiming at addressing ethical issues at an early stage of the R&I process, such as Ethical Technology Assessment,[25] Pragmatist New and Emerging Science and Technology (NEST) ethics,[26] or scenario approaches;[27]
   - Intra methods, taking place at the design or testing phase, like Value-Sensitive Design,[28] ethical impact assessment, or mediation theory;[29] or
   - *Ex-post* methods, i.e. those performed on concrete applications of already-finished R&I processes, like checklist approaches or principle-based ethics.[30]

B. Texts by scholars and activists[31] who address issues of surveillance and management of 'smart border' solutions,[32] which can help assessors to identify recurring arguments in the assessment process. In particular, the following are to be considered recurring challenges:[33]
   - Reduction of dynamic and biographical identity of travellers to static biological samples;[34]
   - Creation of 'technologies of power', which enable institutions to control citizens and exploit their bodies; a dark side to the promise of more efficient and objective identification practices;[35]
   - Excessive economic costs of border control technologies in comparison to the advantages they bring, such as high maintenance costs, technical seatbacks, or difficulty in adjusting to regulations;[36]

- Increased chances of vulnerabilities such as hacking, identity theft and manipulation of data;[37]
- Risks of discrimination and replication of racial prejudices, especially concerning the treatment of citizens from third countries, who often need to undergo extra checks and, depending on their ethnicity or social background, might be more readily associated with terrorism or smuggling.[38]

5.2 Ethical arguments and fallacies

5.2.1 Ethics and technology arguments

This Section presents a list of ethical arguments that assessors need to identify, analyse and assess.[39] The list includes the most recurrent arguments (and related counter-arguments) that are prevalent in the literature and in public debates on border control technologies. Engaging with ethical arguments is not a standalone exercise, but an argumentative support to the legal and social acceptance aspects of the integrated impact assessment process.

Universality of principles and/or values: A technology is developed on the basis of values or principles that are assumed to be universal. The idea is that there is a set of 'core' of principles that are applicable, or values that are shared, across cultures.[40] In turn, from these values, one can 'deduct', *a priori*, a core number of universal principles (4 in the case of bioethics) that are applicable in any practice. The same arguments are replicated today in the fields of Artificial Intelligence (AI)[41] and biometrics,[42] both of which that have been utilised in border control. Opponents of this argument stress that people might disagree on what values or principles count. In this case, values or principles might apply only to a specific situation (or culture, or even technological context), but not to another. A bigger problem is that principles and values might be dictated or decided upon by those who are already in power, and later 'exported' to other (more specifically, more vulnerable or less powerful) people, under the alleged assumption of universality.

Technological determinism: A technology will *inevitably* bring about some positive or negative effects. This argument can take optimist or pessimist forms. Technology optimists argue in favour of technological developments as a panacea for long-lasting social problems. Almost any form of technological progress will bring about some social progress, including in the context of border control. Biometrics and smart borders, for instance, are often seen as a 'silver bullet' for identification: they are portrayed as more reliable, accurate and efficient than traditional means of identifying people. They can 'solve' problems of airport security (by identifying potential threats) or migration flows (by speeding-up border checks). Technology pessimists instead insist on the negative effects of technologisation, often with nostalgic tones. Technology is a form of alienation, and a deterministic force than cannot be stopped. It makes humans interchangeable forces, and takes away their individualism. One form of alienation in border control stems from the massive use of biometric systems. A rich and dynamic identity of a person, which includes their personal story, interests or personality, is flattened over their static bodily identity, represented by a digital token (e.g. a fingerprint, facial image or retinal scan).[43]

Neutrality of technology: *Per se*, technology is neutral, that is, it is neither beneficial nor harmful: it depends on the use that is made of it to achieve a certain goal. An example is Live Facial Recognition (LFR)[44] deployed by some national law enforcement authorities, such as the London Metropolitan Police (UK), the police in Hamburg and Berlin (Germany) and in Nice (France).[45] Some would claim LFR is neutral: it can be used responsibly to make public spaces safer, by preventing and investigating criminal offences, but it can also be misused, e.g. when its use is not strictly necessary or it has detrimental effects on a person that is wrongly identified as a criminal.[46] However, many oppose this neutrality thesis as too simplistic. Technological artefacts cannot be considered in isolation, but always as parts of social worlds. In other words, there are no such things as technological artefacts in and of themselves, but they always mediate and are mediated by society.[47] For example, programmers already project (willingly or not) certain possible uses, values or biases upon a technology, for example, amplifying racial hierarchies.[48] Consequently, technologies could have unforeseen effects or uses that were not considered at the design phase, or that are not strictly related to the original goal. For instance, higher rates of misidentification by LFR algorithms could lead to disproportionate interference with certain ethnic groups, e.g. through unnecessary police stops and requests to show proof of identity.[49]

Arguments from precedence: New technologies are not really 'new', but rather they re-propose the same benefits and challenges of older ones. In the case of border control technologies, in a positive sense, an analogy is often made between biometric and non-biometric passports or identity documents. Identity documents have existed for a long time, and people have become accustomed to them; biometric documents do not pose additional problems (they are still vulnerable to, for example, theft and falsification); therefore, one should not worry about identity documents that include biometric features.[50] Opponents of the argument of precedent claim that the changes of emerging technologies are so disruptive, rapid and large-scale that the analogy with precedent technologies no longer holds.[51] Since biometric systems might collect a huge amount of data, combine different types of biometric samples (e.g. fingerprint, retina, gait, voice, etc.) and store them in possibly interoperable databases, the purpose(s) of which might not be clearly defined in advance, they are worthy of greater attention.

Change of ethical values: Technologies change our values, leading to moral progress or moral decline.[52] Some argue that technologies help people to progress ethically, e.g. to take better decisions in ethical dilemmas, act according to higher ethical standards, or better discern values and principles at stake. This happens both at an individual and a societal level. For example, in the context of border control, biometric identification techniques could be seen as enhancing the impartiality of border checks. The process of recognition is carried out by automated systems, thus boosting the fairness of the outcomes. The idea is that, while people can have biases, automated machines do not, and are consequently more equitable. Newer verification systems based on a combination of biometric traits are also seen to outperform the current limitations of other automated biometrics, such as fingerprinting, in terms of neutrality and reliability. Opponents of the argument of ethical progress stress instead how, despite cases of progress in recent years, ethical decline has also taken place. Considering something to be 'progress' is highly dependent upon a specific point of view: what counts as progress for one person might not for another. Technological developments often increase inequalities between areas of the world and groups within society, enhancing the welfare of the Western countries at the expense of the Global South, or making big companies richer at the expense of unaware customers.[53] Moreover, machines and algorithms are designed by humans, and as such they can embody prejudices and biases subconsciously introduced by their programmers.[54]

Slippery slope: Using a metaphor, once one makes the first steps on the slope, it becomes impossible to stop until bad consequences happen. In relation to technology, the idea is that some relatively innocuous or small-scale technological developments could bring about, if developed on a large scale, a cascade of uncontrollable and unpredicted negative effects.[55] Alternatively, technology supporters might claim that if a new technology is not implemented now, people will suffer all types of terrible consequences. Opponents of this argument say that people are able to escalate easy generalisations from one specific case to multiple ones; that there is no convincing evidence that simply allowing some exceptions to moral rules will bring about a collapse of the whole system of rules; finally, that the possibility of exceptions does not necessarily mean that these exceptions will also occur on a larger scale.

'Function creep': In short, function creep means the use of a specific initiative (e.g. a border control technology) for a purpose for which it was not originally intended.[56] With reference to biometric technologies, storing biometric data in a central database might permit that such data are (re-)used for purposes not initially foreseen, like profiling or criminal investigations. An example is when Europol and law enforcement agencies were granted access to the information stored in the Visa Information System (VIS) for detection and investigation of terrorist offences.[57] This is not in line with the original purpose of the system,[58] which was established in 2004[59] to improve the management of a common EU visa policy and to enhance the security of visas. However, in 2008, when the Regulation for the VIS was adopted,[60] access was granted under certain circumstances, a purpose that was not foreseen when the system was established in 2004.[61]

5.2.2 Normative ethics

A specific subset of ethical arguments is related to normative ethical positions. Roughly, the crux of this issue is which specific ethical rules should govern conduct. This Section follows a tripartition between deontological, consequentialist and distributive justice arguments.[62]

Deontological arguments define rules on the basis of fundamental moral principles. An action is considered to be 'morally right' if it conforms to certain principles, rights, duties, prohibitions, or responsibilities, and/or if the actor has certain intentions, regardless of the consequences of such action. Roughly speaking, the definition of duty precedes that of what counts as 'good'.[63] Deontological arguments can be also weaker (admitting exceptions or performing balancing between principles or duties) or stronger (requiring moral integrity and no exception, with certain actions being categorically prohibited). The main examples of deontological arguments in the technological domain are drawn from principle-based ethics, human rights and codes of professional conduct.

- In principle-based ethics, principles are abstract action guides (*do x*), but sometimes they can also categorically prohibit a certain action (*don't do y*). As a concrete example, the High-Level Expert Group on AI defines their principles as 'ethical imperatives' that AI practitioners should *always* strive to adhere to.[64]
- In human rights ethics, human rights are moral entitlements that any person has and that have to be considered before the consequences. Sometimes, fundamental rights enshrined in legal texts[65] are also taken as foundations of ethical principles in the public discourse, such as in the EU's debates on privacy and new technologies.[66]
- In codes of professional conduct, sets of rules or principles exist that should guide the conduct of practitioners when exercising their profession. Codes of conduct can be written by companies, but also by professional associations. One of the earliest expressions of professional ethics is the Hippocratic Oath, which has been used in the medical profession for centuries. Examples of codes of conduct can also be found in border control.[67]

The main shortcomings of deontological rules are that they are often difficult to live up to, they require a strong commitment, and they admit few-to-no exceptions. Also, there is often a gap between abstract principles and more concrete situations, which makes it difficult to apply the principles. To overcome the rigidity of deontology and its vagueness in guiding action, consequentialist arguments are often offered as alternatives.

Consequentialist arguments (among which: utilitarian) state that actions are right or wrong only on the basis of their outcomes (i.e. consequences). In other words, among the possible actions available, one chooses the option that maximises the expected outcomes (or degree of utility).[68] Thus, contrary to deontology, there are no *a priori* wrong acts (e.g. murder) and an act is right whenever it is the one that produces the best possible consequences relative to any other. Consequentialist arguments can take many forms, depending on how the consequences or degree of utility are quantified: for example, in terms of pleasure, satisfaction of preferences or economic factor.[69] Consequentialist arguments fit well with risk-based approaches and cost-benefit analyses precisely because they offer more quantitative, calculable ways to solve moral dilemmas.

To recognise a consequentialist argument, a rule-of-thumb could be to look at whether a trade-off is proposed. A classic trade-off in border control discourses is that of security versus privacy: surveillance technologies require the giving away of some privacy (e.g. by allowing the processing of one's sensitive data and sharing them with third parties) in exchange for extra security (e.g. less risk of identity theft, less risk of dangerous people entering a plane).

Trade-off discourses can be criticised for being overly simplistic: problems that are presented as mathematical, quantifiable and objective are in fact value-laden. The risk of these discourses is that political conflicts and power asymmetries are reframed as mere technical ones.[70] For example, it could be shown how, in a specific case (say, the introduction of a system of new-generation cameras at an airport), privacy and security *should not* be understood as an abstract trade-off, that can simply be solved by using metrics that assign a numeric value to privacy and another to security. The language of trade-off[71] is often enforced in contexts (cultures, organisations) that systematically favour security (e.g. to defend travellers from terrorist attacks), while both privacy and security could be enforced without losses for either of the two.[72] Another criticism is that consequences are often uncertain and not easy to predict, especially when it comes to emerging technologies. A classic example is environmental consequences of technologies, for instance how the use of cars has increased pollution in cities. Finally, consequentialism fails to take seriously the distinction between persons,[73] since what counts is the aggregate results of consequences, also at the cost of serious damages for small groups of people, like minorities. This is a problem in border control, where technologies are often beneficial for large groups of people (*bona-fide* travellers) but can be unavailable or detrimental for smaller groups (third country nationals, high-risk categories, or refugees).

Distributive justice arguments[74] state that an action is deemed morally problematic whenever some benefit to which a person is entitled is denied (without any compelling reason) or whenever there is an unequal distribution of benefits and burdens.

Justice arguments can take a more positive or negative stance. In a positive sense, it can be admitted that, at first, the distribution of a new technology is not proportionate. It is inevitable that a small amount of people could initially benefit from it, but eventually everyone will profit from it. A small group 'paves the way' for the more large-scale use of technology. In a negative sense, the same biometric features and identification technologies that are used can be indeed quite convenient and efficient for some, but they are also used to restrict the movement of others by those who are in power.[75] This could lead, on the one hand to the reinforcement of privileges of some groups (like EU and US citizens) and, on the other, to the increased discrimination against other groups (like asylum seekers). An example of this is the old Fast Low Risk Universal Crossing (FLUX Alliance) traveller program for US and Dutch frequent intercontinental travellers, which is based on biometric identifiers including fingerprints and retinal imaging.[76] So-called 'low risk passengers', i.e. with no criminal records, customs or immigration conviction, can apply for the program. If the interview and security threat assessment is successful, they can have, at the cost of paying an additional fee, the advantage of skipping queues and border checks.

5.2.3 Types of ethical fallacies

As shown in the previous Sections, ethical arguments can always be criticised. One way of showing that an argument is not convincing is to demonstrate a deficit in the structure of the argument (also known as a logical fallacy). A fallacious argument is a reasoning that seems convincing at first, but is based on weak assumptions, and/or the conclusions do not follow from the premises. The list of fallacies provided here is tailored down to ethical arguments relevant for the context of border control, which are therefore referred to as 'ethical' fallacies. The list could give assessors some critical tools to challenge what is usually taken for granted or under-emphasised in public discourse.

The list below is not exhaustive, but was selected on the basis of application to the arguments outlined in Section 5.2.[77] Taking inspiration from this list, assessors could expand the list of fallacies for their assessments.

Begging the question, or *petitio principii*: These are arguments that include in their premises the argument they aim to demonstrate. Such an argument is technically valid, but useless in demonstrating its conclusions. A classic example could be this: 'The technology is ethical because it is compliant with ethical principles'. In this example, the conclusion (i.e. the fact that a technology is ethical) does not add anything new to the premises (the fact that the technology complies with ethical principles).

Ad hominem: An argument is refuted on the basis of the person (or company or institution) that is proposing the argument. This argument is fallacious because it should focus on the merit of the argument (validity of premises, line of reasoning, clarity of exposition) and not on some (possibly irrelevant) qualities of the proposer. An example could be that 'The ethics principles endorsed by Person X are unreliable because Person X is known for not respecting such principles in their private life'. The argument can be fallacious, *if* it is not based on content or process to draw the principles endorsed by Person X, but *only* on the bad name that Person X bears in public discourse.

Appeal to a (moral) authority, or ipse dixit: This is an argument where the opinion of an authority is used as irrefutable evidence to support the argument. For example, it can be said that 'A technology is ethical because X said that' or that 'A technology is ethical because it is compliant with the principle issued by X'. Reference to 'moral' authorities is not warranted here, since it is not clear who has established that an author or ethical advisory body is an authority, why they cannot be wrong, or whether the people who decided on the principle were democratically elected or chosen to do so. The argument is fallacious because the soundness of the opinions of the authority are taken for granted and not questioned.

Confusion of ethics and law: In these arguments, the boundary between the law and ethics is blurred. This can happen in both directions. 'If a technology is legal, then it is ethical' is fallacious, because the legal compliance of a technology does not automatically make it morally acceptable. But also, the converse is problematic 'if a technology is ethical, then it must be legal'. This is questionable when it is consistently argued that 'the law lags behind' and cannot maintain the pace of technological development; therefore, ethics is needed to go 'beyond the law'.⁷⁸ If ethics is not properly defined, and ethics principles are arbitrarily constructed, they may be in contrast with the law (e.g. with fundamental rights).

Naturalistic fallacy: These arguments are characterised by the unwarranted deduction of prescriptions (*X should* …) from descriptions (*X is* …). Simply put, if something took place a number of times, it *must* be true: 'If a country is implementing measures to deploy interoperable large-scale databases, then people should accept them'. This is fallacious because a normative conclusion (people *should* …) is derived from descriptive premises (a country *is* implementing …). To be sound, the argument needs to have both conclusions and premises either in the descriptive or prescriptive form.

Ambiguity: A key word can assume multiple meanings. Usually, the correct meaning is deduced from the context, but when this is not the case, an argument can take different meanings, thus becoming weaker. An example is the use of the word 'ethics' as a subject of a sentence ('ethics can help to', 'ethics can contribute to', 'ethics can clarify', etc.). For example: 'Ethics will help the border guards to identify the risk of the biometric technology'. In this case, ethics can mean, for example, a specific training, a textbook, a set of arguments, or a group of ethics experts. But the problem is that it is unclear what type of ethics people are talking about, what type of ethics experts are involved, or who selected these. If this is not specified, the argument loses its force and can be misused.

Privacy fallacy: 'If you haven't done anything wrong, you have nothing to hide'. This argument is fallacious on many levels. First, not *only* do people that did something wrong need to be protected by privacy. Being exposed can carry risks, regardless of the fact that one has something to hide. For example, people might be discriminated against by banks, insurers or employers if their health records are made public. Second, one might not have done anything wrong, but still, due to a failure of the system, be found guilty or wrongly stigmatised as a criminal, only because they belong to a certain ethnic group.

Appeal to emotion: These are arguments that appeal to the subject's emotion in order to encourage them to accept arguments whose premises are weak or dubious. One example could be appeal to fear of anxiety of 'external threats', like the need to develop invasive technologies against the menace of terrorism, in spite of the majority of terrorist attacks in Europe resulting from actions of internal 'residual terrorists' (e.g. far-right groups or separatists) and not of international groups.⁷⁹

Technocratic fallacy: These arguments take the form of 'It is an engineering issue how X is dangerous; therefore, engineers should decide whether X is acceptable'.⁸⁰ 'Dangerous' could also be changed to 'secure', 'privacy-friendly', and so on. The argument is fallacious because engineers (or other experts) may be competent in deciding how X is dangerous, but not the extent to which it is morally acceptable.

False analogy: These are arguments that use analogical reasoning; since something is morally accepted/acceptable in a certain case, then is *must* be accepted in a similar case, too. For instance, 'Since biometric technologies have been accepted in criminal investigations for their accuracy, then they must be used in everyday life too'. Arguments like this could be fallacious because the properties used to make the analogy are not relevant to drawing the conclusions. The reasons that make biometrics acceptable in criminal investigations are not the same as those that (would) make them acceptable in public life.

Endnotes

1. European Data Protection Supervisor Ethics Advisory Group, "Towards a Digital Ethics," 2018.
2. See Annex I Part III of Regulation (EU) No 1291/2013 of the European Parliament and of the Council of 11 December 2013 establishing Horizon 2020 – the Framework Programme for Research and Innovation (2014-2020) and repealing Decision No 1982/2006/EC, OJ L 347, 20.12.2013, p. 104–173.
3. Zach Campbell, Caitlin L Chandler, and Chris Jones, "Sci-Fi Surveillance: Europe's Secretive Push into Biometric Technology," *The Guardian*, 2020.
4. Ruha Benjamin, *Race After Technology: Abolitionist Tools for the New Jim Code* (Cambridge, UK: Polity Press, 2019); Petra Molnar, EDRi, and the Refugee Law Lab, "Technological Testing Grounds. Migration Management Experiments and Reflections from the Ground Up," 2020.
5. Dariusz Kloza et al., "Data Protection Impact Assessment in the European Union: Developing a Template for a Report from the Assessment Process," d.pia.lab Policy Brief (Brussels: VUB, 2020), https://doi.org/10.31228/osf.io/7qrfp.
6. See Chapter 4 in this Volume.
7. Nina Boy, Elida Jacobsen, and Kristoffer Lidén, "Societal Ethics and Biometric Technology," PRIO (2018), https://www.prio.org/utility/DownloadFile.ashx?id=1708&type=publicationfile.
8. See: https://edri.org/our-work/attention-eu-regulators-we-need-more-than-ai-ethics-to-keep-us-safe/.
9. Paul Nemitz, "Constitutional Democracy and Technology in the Age of Artificial Intelligence," *Philosophical Transactions of the Royal Society A: Mathematical, Physical and Engineering Sciences* 376, no. 2133 (2018): 1–25, https://doi.org/10.1098/rsta.2018.0089; Ben Wagner, "Ethics as an Escape from Regulation: From Ethics-Washing to Ethics-Shopping?," in *Being Profiled. Cogitas Ergo Sum*, ed. Mireille Hildebrandt (Amsterdam: Amsterdam University Press, 2018), 84–89; Karen Yeung, Andrew Howes, and Ganna Pogrebna, "Why Industry Self-Regulation Will Not Deliver 'Ethical AI': A Call for Legally Mandated Techniques of 'Human Rights by Design,'" in *The Oxford Handbook of Ethics of AI*, ed. Markus D. Dubber, Frank Pasquale, and Sunit Das (Oxford, UK: Oxford University Press, 2020).
10. Niels van Dijk and Simone Casiraghi, "The 'Ethification' of Privacy and Data Protection in the European Union. The Case of Artificial Intelligence," *Brussels Privacy Hub Working Paper*, 6, 2020.
11. It is impossible to give a comprehensive account of the history of ethics intended as moral philosophy in the present Chapter. For an overview, see Alasdair MacIntyre, *A Short History of Ethics. A History of Moral Philosophy from the Homeric Age to the Twentieth Century* (Notre Dame, Indiana: University of Notre Dame Press, 1998).
12. Alan Petersen, *The Politics of Bioethics* (London: Routledge, 2011); Ulrike Felt et al., *Taking European Knowledge Society Seriously*, Office for Official Publications of the European Communities (Luxembourg, 2007).
13. Felt et al.

14. Nancy S. Jecker, Albert R. Jonsen, and Robert A. Pearlman, *Bioethics. An Introduction to the History, Methods and Practice* (Sudbury, MA: Jones and Bartlett Publishers, 1997).
15. Examples are the 'mad cow' crisis or the transatlantic trade wars over hormone-treated beef in the 1990s. Sheila Jasanoff, *Designs on Nature. Science and Democracy in Europe and the United States* (Princeton, New Jersey: Princeton University Press, 2007).
16. RRI became increasingly important in the years around 2010, especially in the EU's Framework Programme Horizon 2020. Rene Von Schomberg, "A Vision of Responsible Research and Innovation," in *Responsible Innovation. Managing the Responsible Emergenve of Science and Innovation in Society* (Wiley, 2013), 51–74.
17. Robert Gianni, John Pearson, and Bernard Reber, eds., *Responsible Research and Innovation. From Concepts to Practices*, *Responsible Research and Innovation* (London & New York: Routledge, 2018), https://doi.org/10.4324/9781315457291.
18. Allison Ross and Nafsika Athanassoulis, "The Role of Research Ethics Committees in Making Decisions about Risk," *HEC Forum : An Interdisciplinary Journal on Hospitals' Ethical and Legal Issues* 26, no. 3 (2014): 203–24, https://doi.org/10.1007/s10730-014-9244-6.
19. The most well-established are often specialised in health and life sciences, such as *Der Duetsche Ethikrat* in Germany (see https://www.ethikrat.org/en/the-german-ethics-council/) or the *Comité, Consultatif National d'Éthique* in France (see https://www.ccne-ethique.fr/en).
20. For example, the ethics review process of an EU-funded research proposal. For a description of the process in the security domain, see Matthias Leese, Kristoffer Lidén, and Blagovesta Nikolova, "Putting Critique to Work. Ethics in EU Security Research," *Security Dialogue* 50, no. 1 (2018): 59–76.
21. Examples are also Ethical, Social and Legal Implications (ELSI) of emerging technologies in the United States (Michael S Yesley, "What's ELSI Got to Do with It? Bioethics and the Human Genome Project," *New Genetics and Society* 27, no. 1 (2008): 1–6, https://doi.org/10.1080/14636770701843527), mostly related to genomics and nanotechnology, and Responsible Research and Innovation (RRI) in the EU (Gianni, Pearson, and Reber, *Responsible Research and Innovation. From Concepts to Practices*).
22. Gloria González Fuster and Serge Gutwirth, "Ethics, Law and Privacy. Disentangling Law from Ethics in Privacy Discourse", *Proceedings of the 2014 IEEE International Symposium on Ethics in Science, Technology and Engineering* (2014).
23. With relative curricula, courses, dedicated conference and journals, and so on.
24. Wessel Reijers et al., "Methods for Practising Ethics in Research and Innovation: A Literature Review, Critical Analysis and Recommendations," *Science and Engineering Ethics* 24, no. 5 (2018): 1437–81, https://doi.org/10.1007/s11948-017-9961-8.
25. Elin Palm and Sven Ove Hansson, "The Case for Ethical Technology Assessment (ETA)," *Technological Forecasting and Social Change* 73, no. 5 (2006): 543–58, https://doi.org/10.1016/j.techfore.2005.06.002; Asle H. Kiran, Nelly Oudshoorn, and Peter Paul Verbeek, "Beyond Checklists: Toward an Ethical-Constructive Technology Assessment," *Journal of Responsible Innovation* 2, no. 1 (2015): 5–19, https://doi.org/10.1080/23299460.2014.992769.
26. Tsjalling Swierstra and Arie Rip, "Nano-Ethics as NEST-Ethics: Patterns of Moral Argumentation about New and Emerging Science and Technology," *NanoEthics* 1, no. 1 (2007): 3–20, https://doi.org/10.1007/s11569-007-0005-8.
27. Gill Ringland, "The Role of Scenarios in Strategic Foresight," *Technological Forecasting and Social Change* 77, no. 9 (2010): 1493–98, https://doi.org/10.1016/j.techfore.2010.06.010.
28. Batya Friedman, Peter Kahn, and Alan Borning, *Value Sensitive Design: Theory and Methods* (University of Washington Technical, 2002), https://faculty.washington.edu/pkahn/articles/vsd-theory-methods-tr.pdf.

29. Ibo van de Poel et al., *Ethics, Technology and Engineering: An Introduction* (Wiley Blackwell, 2011). Peter-Paul Verbeek, *What Things Do. Philosophical Reflections on Technology, Agency and Design* (Pennsylvania State University Press, 2005).
30. High-Level Expert Group on Artificial Intelligence, "The Assessment List for Trustworthy Artificial Intelligence," 2020.
31. These authors do not necessarily call themselves 'ethics experts' or 'ethicists', but their inputs are relevant for the benchmark in this Chapter.
32. The EU's 'smart borders' are automated systems to speed up and facilitate the border check procedure of the majority of travellers, and specifically (but not exclusively) to hinder and stop those migrants that pose a threat to the security of the Union through their status of irregular migrants, criminals or terrorists. See: European Commission, "Stronger and Smarter Information Systems for Borders and Security", COM/2016/0205 final.
33. These challenges are further expanded in the Section 5.2.
34. Katja Franko Aas, "'The Body Does Not Lie': Identity, Risk and Trust in Technoculture," *Crime, Media, Culture* 2, no. 2 (2006): 143–58, https://doi.org/10.1177/1741659006065401; Katja Franko Aas, "'Crimmigrant' Bodies and Bona Fide Travelers: Surveillance, Citizenship and Global Governance," *Theoretical Criminology* 15, no. 3 (2011): 331–46, https://doi.org/10.1177/1362480610396643; Btihaj Ajana, "Recombinant Identities: Biometrics and Narrative Bioethics," *Journal of Bioethical Inquiry* 7, no. 2 (2010): 237–58, https://doi.org/10.1007/s11673-010-9228-4; David Lyon, *Surveillance as Social Sorting: Privacy, Risk and Automated Discrimination, Surveillance as Social Sorting: Privacy, Risk and Automated Discrimination* (London & New York: Routledge, 2005), https://doi.org/10.4324/9780203994887.
35. Chris Jones, "Automated Suspicion: The EU's New Travel Surveillance Initiatives," 2020; Chris Jones, Jane Kilpatrick, and Mariana Gkliati, "Deportation Union: Rights, Accountability, and the EU's Push to Increased Forced Removals," 2020.
36. Julien Jeandesboz, "Smartening Border Security in the European Union: An Associational Inquiry," *Security Dialogue* 47, no. 4 (2016): 292–309, https://doi.org/10.1177/0967010616650226.
37. Pinja Lehtonen and Pami Aalto, "Smart and Secure Borders through Automated Border Control Systems in the EU? The Views of Political Stakeholders in the Member States," *European Security* 26, no. 2 (2017): 207–25, https://doi.org/10.1080/09662839.2016.1276057.
38. Matthias Leese, "The New Profiling: Algorithms, Black Boxes, and the Failure of Anti-Discriminatory Safeguards in the European Union," *Security Dialogue* 45, no. 5 (2014): 494–511, https://doi.org/10.1177/0967010614544204.
39. The way in which these recurring arguments are presented is inspired by NEST ethics as presented in Tsjalling Swierstra, "Introduction to the Ethics of New and Emerging Science and Technology," in *Handbook of Digital Games and Entertainment Technologies*, 2015, https://doi.org/10.1007/978-981-4560-52-8_33-1; Swierstra and Rip, "Nano-Ethics as NEST-Ethics: Patterns of Moral Argumentation about New and Emerging Science and Technology."
40. Tom L. Beauchamp, "Common Morality, Human Rights, and Multiculturalism in Japanese and American Bioethics," *Journal of Practical Ethics* 3, no. 2 (2015): 18–35.
41. High-Level Expert Group on Artificial Intelligence, "Ethics Guidelines for Trustworthy AI," 2019.
42. For example, the ethics principles published by the Biometrics Institute, a multi-stakeholder international community, at: https://www.biometricsinstitute.org/ethical-principles-for-biometrics/.
43. Ajana, "Recombinant Identities: Biometrics and Narrative Bioethics."
44. See Chapter 6 in this Volume.
45. European Union Agency for Fundamental Rights, "Facial Recognition Technology: Fundamental Rights Considerations in the Context of Law Enforcement," 2019.

46. Pete Fussey and Daragh Murray, 'Independet Report on the London Metropolitan Police Service's Trial of Live Facial Recognition Technology' 128, 43, http://repository.essex.ac.uk/24946/.
47. Verbeek, *What Things Do. Philosophical Reflections on Technology, Agency and Design*.
48. Benjamin, *Race After Technology: Abolitionist Tools for the New Jim Code*.
49. Silkie Carlo, Jennifer Krueckeberg, and Griff Ferris, "Face Off: The Lawless Growth of Facial Recognition in UK Policing," *Big Brother Watch* (2018): 56.
50. For a critique of this argument, see Simone Casiraghi, 'Should (Your) Identity Documents Use Biometrics?' (2018), https://www.eticasconsulting.com/wp-content/uploads/2018/04/Origins_-FINAL.pdf.
51. Julian Savulescu, Ruud ter Meulen, and Guy Kahane, eds., *Enhancing Human Capacities* (Oxford, UK: Wiley-Blackwell, 2011).
52. Hanno Sauer, "Butchering Benevolence Moral Progress beyond the Expanding Circle," *Ethical Theory and Moral Practice*, 2019, https://doi.org/10.1007/s10677-019-09983-9.
53. Christian Fuchs, "The Political Economy of Privacy on Facebook," *Television and New Media* 13, no. 2 (2012): 139–59, https://doi.org/10.1177/1527476411415699.
54. Kevin Macnish, "Unblinking Eyes: The Ethics of Automating Surveillance," *Ethics and Information Technology* 14, no. 2 (2012): 151–67, https://doi.org/10.1007/s10676-012-9291-0.
55. Wibren van der Burg, "The Slippery Slope Argument," *Ethics* 102, no. 1 (1991): 42–65.
56. Bert-Jaap Koops, "The Concept of Function Creep," *Law, Innovation and Technology*, 1 (2021): 29–56, https://doi.org/10.1080/17579961.2021.1898299.
57. The fact that the expansion of scope was regulated does not hinder the fact that it is still an expansion of scope that was not foreseen in advance.
58. See also the principle of purpose limitation in data protection explained in Chapter 4 in this Volume.
59. Council Decision of 8 June 2004 establishing the Visa Information System (VIS), OJ L 213, 15.6.2004, p. 5–7.
60. Regulation (EC) No 767/2008 of the European Parliament and of the Council of 9 July 2008 concerning the Visa Information System (VIS) and the exchange of data between Member States on short-stay visas (VIS Regulation), OJ L 218, 13.8.2008, p. 60–81.
61. Els J. Kindt, *Privacy and Data Protection Issues of Biometric Applications. A Comparative Legal Analysis*, Privacy and Data Protection Issues of Biometric Applications (Dodrecht, Heidelberg, London, New York: Springer Netherlands, 2013), https://doi.org/10.1007/978-94-007-7522-0.
62. Scholars usually refer also to virtue ethics (VE). For clarity reasons, VE approaches were not included because they are not widespread 1) in the debates on border control, and 2) in the assessment methods overviewed in Section 5.1.6. For more information on virtue ethics and technology, see Shannon Vallor, *Technology and the Virtues. A Philosophical Guide to a Future Worth Wanting* (New York: Oxford University Press, 2016).
63. Immanuel Kant, *Groundwork in the Metaphysics of Morals* (Cambridge: Cambridge University Press, 2012).
64. High-Level Expert Group on Artificial Intelligence, "Ethics Guidelines for Trustworthy AI."
65. See Chapters 3 and 4, in this Volume.
66. High-Level Expert Group on Artificial Intelligence.
67. For example, European Border and Coast Guard Agency (Frontex), *Code of Conduct Applicable to All Persons Participating in Frontex Operational Activities* (Luxembourg: Publications Office of the European Union, 2020). Council of Europe, The European Code of Police Ethics (Council of Europe Publishing 2001), https://polis.osce.org/european-code-police-ethics.
68. John Stuart Mill, *Utilitarianism* (Cambridge, MA: Cambridge University Press, 2014). Original work published in 1861.

69. Amartya Sen and Bernard Williams, eds., *Utilitarianism and Beyond* (Cambridge: Cambridge University Press, 1982).
70. Andrea Saltelli, "Ethics of Quantification or Quantification of Ethics?," *Futures* 116, no. October 2019 (2020): 102509, https://doi.org/10.1016/j.futures.2019.102509; Felt et al., *Taking European Knowledge Society Seriously*.
71. Trade-offs are also legally criticised from a proportionality perspective, in which fair mediation of values must be struck, as opposed to the application of the crude mechanics of scale (i.e. if one value goes up the other goes down). Jeremy Waldron, "Security and Liberty: The Image of Balance," *Journal of Political Philosophy* 11, no. 2 (2003): 191–210. See also Chapter 4 in this Volume.
72. Marc van Lieshout et al., "Reconciling Privacy and Security," *Innovation the European Journal of Social Science Research* 26, no. 1–2 (2013): 119–32, https://doi.org/10.1080/13511610.2013.723378.
73. John Rawls, *A Theory of Justice* (Cambridge, MA: Belknap Press of Harvard University Press, 1971).
74. They can also be seen as a subset of consequentialism or deontology.
75. Louise Amoore, "Biometric Borders: Governing Mobilities in the War on Terror," *Political Geography* 25, no. 3 (2006): 336–51, https://doi.org/10.1016/j.polgeo.2006.02.001; Irma van der Ploeg, "Biometrics and Privacy A Note on the Politics of Theorizing Technology," *Information, Communication & Society* 6, no. 1 (2003): 85–104, https://doi.org/10.1080/1369118032000068741; Aas, "'Crimmigrant' Bodies and Bona Fide Travelers: Surveillance, Citizenship and Global Governance"; Aas, "'The Body Does Not Lie': Identity, Risk and Trust in Technoculture."
76. Aas, "'Crimmigrant' Bodies and Bona Fide Travelers: Surveillance, Citizenship and Global Governance."
77. van de Poel et al., "Ethics, Technology and Engineering: An Introduction."
78. van Dijk and Casiraghi, "The 'Ethification' of Privacy and Data Protection in the European Union. The Case of Artificial Intelligence."
79. Mark Maguire and Pete Fussey, "Sensing Evil: Counterterrorism, Techno-Science, and the Cultural Reproduction of Security," *Focaal-Journal of Global and Historical Anthropology* 2016, no. 75 (2016): 31–44.
80. Sven Ove Hansson, "Fallacies of Risk," *Journal of Risk Research* 7, no. 3 (2004): 353–60, https://doi.org/10.1080/1366987042000176262.

6 Social acceptance and border control technologies

Simone CASIRAGHI,* J. Peter BURGESS** and Kristoffer LIDÉN***
* Vrije Universiteit Brussel. E-mail: simone.casiraghi@vub.be.
** École Normale Supérieure, Paris & Vrije Universiteit Brussel.
E-mail: james.peter.burgess@ens.fr.
*** Peace Research Institute Oslo. E-mail: kristoffer@prio.org.

6.1 Introduction

6.1.1 Definition of the social acceptance

Social acceptance of technology is a concept that indicates the degree to which 'a new technology is accepted – or merely tolerated – by a community'.[1] Acceptance, in turn, refers to the act of receiving something that is offered, of giving an affirmative reply to it, and accommodating to it with approval.[2] In this sense, social acceptance differs from ethics and stakeholder involvement. To distinguish one from the other, ethics refers to a systematic reflection, a philosophical critique, and an evaluation of customs, habits and traditions in a given context.[3] Therefore, while ethics is a normative concept, and as such requires mostly a desk-based research (although supplemented by stakeholder involvement), social acceptance, in turn, is a mainly empirical concept, and as such needs to be assessed on the basis of verifiable information or experience.[4]

Yet, the two concepts – social acceptance and ethics – are interrelated and complementary. What is portrayed as acceptable influences how people actually accept a technology. If, for example, the media say biometrics are acceptable despite the infringements of privacy and other fundamental rights, this narrative can have an influence upon how users actually come to accept them. *Vice versa*, the way some people react to a technology may change what they consider to be ethically acceptable: the fact that some activists protest against invasive surveillance methods, e.g. by covering their face in public spaces with a mask, can have an effect upon users that had not previously perceived a problem as having existed with such methods. On the one hand, a social acceptance assessment can help the assessors refine the list of arguments for the ethics assessment in Chapter 5. On the other, the recurring arguments included in the ethics assessment can act as an inspiration in the development of acceptance assessment techniques (e.g. formulating questions for questionnaires).

Social acceptance and stakeholder involvement are also distinct concepts. The basic idea of the two concepts is to allow for wider representation. In the context of impact assessment, this translates into allowing multiple stakeholders[5] to participate in the assessment process, opening up the process beyond the team of assessors. Also, the list of techniques is, in principle, the same, and their choice depends on the timespan and resources available, and the goal of the assessment. The execution of the techniques and their scope, however, differs. Stakeholder involvement is a broader concept: the idea is to involve any stakeholder in order to allow them to have a say on (ideally) every specific phase of the process in a continuous, ongoing manner (e.g. types of risks, how to assess risks, result of the threshold analysis, recommendations, etc.). In the social acceptance assessment, the idea is to assess how a more limited group of pre-defined stakeholders accommodates or gives a positive reply to a given initiative at a specific point during the assessment process, i.e. Step 5 of the integrated impact assessment process (Appraisal of impacts).

Given these preliminary distinctions, the structure of the Chapter will be as follows: In the next sub-sections, some further introductory notions on social acceptance (its importance for society, historical development and literature review) and about the social acceptance component of the benchmark will be outlined, including its importance in the assessment process and the actors involved in it. Section 6.2 will provide the assessors with the key concepts critical in conducting the social acceptance steps of the impact assessment process according to the Template included in Annex 1. To do this, the perspectives, techniques and types of stakeholders, as well as common misconceptions about what social acceptance is about, are explored.

6.1.2 The importance of social acceptance for society

The introduction of new technologies to society can give rise to widespread adoption, but also to episodes of discomfort, denial or even social resistance. Classic examples of the latter include the construction of nuclear plants or chemical factories that led to local protests.[6] In such cases, local communities might protest against top-down decisions that put their environment, health or local activities in danger. But similar episodes have happened with the introduction of surveillance and biometric technologies. For example, the EU-funded project iBorderCtrl (2016-2019), in which a 'smart' Automated Deception Detection System (ADDS) was being developed, was harshly criticised, by the press and some civil society organisations for, among other aspects,[7] its scientific developments and possible discriminatory outcomes.[8] From this it can be seen that sometimes technologies as such are not accepted by the public, even before the products are put on the market (e.g. during the research phase). In other cases, users do not adopt, or even actively 'resist', new technologies until after they are introduced to the market, or they simply express their fears about potential misuse.[9]

An example is the use of Live Facial Recognition (LFR) by the police in public spaces in the UK. A survey by the Ada Lovelace Institute,[10] which was intended to assess the 'public attitudes' to LFR, showed some positive acceptance of the public towards its use. 70% of the respondents supported the use of LFR by police in criminal investigation, and 50% supported its use in airports in place of passport control.[11] A similar survey of the London Policing Ethics Panel[12] showed how 57% of the respondents thought the use of LFR by the police was acceptable and 75% that it would make it easier for the police to catch criminals.[13]

The same research, however, also evidenced some tensions regarding the public attitude towards LFR in the UK. For instance, the report by the Ada Lovelace Institute shows how, of those interviewed, 36% 'did not know anything about' LFR and 48% 'knew little about it'.[14] On the use of LFR, 61% were uncomfortable with its use on public transport,[15] and the percentages of people wanting it to be deployed for purposes like tracking shopping behaviour, monitoring children at school or people at work were extremely low (below 10%).[16] Similarly, the survey of the London Policing Ethics Panel showed how, overall, 43% of the people surveyed did not think that police use of LFR was acceptable, and 50% responded that it would not make them feel safer.[17] Moreover, 41% reported that they saw it as being invasive of people's privacy[18] and 81% responded that they believed the ways in which police collect personal data should be strictly controlled.[19]

Debates like the one on LFR have shown that taking into account a nuanced perspective of public perceptions of emerging technologies is relevant, even if the results on performance, reliability and cost efficiency are encouraging. Like in the UK, introducing surveillance technologies without a proper public consultation might raise public outrage and political criticism.[20] Failing to take these considerations into account early on may give rise to negative impacts not only on policymakers and industries developing technologies (in regard to which strategies or products cannot be thoroughly implemented or delayed, or which image might suffer reputational damages), but also on the public, who may not be aware of how they work and their risks, may not trust the private sector, or may not unconditionally support their deployment.

6.1.3 The role of social acceptance in the benchmark

While there are already well-established forms of data protection impact assessment, privacy impact assessment and, to a lesser extent, ethics impact assessment,[21] which together constitute the other components of the benchmark of the integrated impact assessment method, there is no such a thing as 'social acceptance impact assessment'. Incorporating social acceptance into an integrated assessment method for border control technologies has to date not been attempted.

The reasons for social acceptance being part of the integrated impact assessment method are complementary. First, the method broadens its scope beyond traditional methods of assessing legal and ethical aspects of emerging technologies (traditionally more expert-based) and opens up the debate to 'lay experts'[22] of the technology, especially travellers themselves.

Second, the concept of social acceptance can be, and has often been, interpreted in too narrow and instrumental a way, often as a way to self-legitimate a pre-defined technological program.[23] Even when performed robustly, assessing only *de facto* acceptance of a given initiative (with a dedicated method) is insufficient. The mere fact that (some) travellers accept border technologies is not enough to deem them ethically desirable or legally compliant. Therefore, social acceptance is only one part of the quadripartite benchmark in the integrated impact assessment process.

6.1.4 Historical development of social acceptance

Social acceptance did not play an important role in the history of impact assessment,[24] but the concept of social acceptance developed in several disciplines, most notably psychology, and has recently been studied extensively in relation to technologies. There are at least two main strands to consider:

A. Information Technology (IT) acceptance research: This strand has roots in psychology, sociology and Information Systems (IS) literature. The research carried out in this area stems from the idea that, while the presence of IT has increased dramatically in organisations since the 1980s, IT first needs to be accepted and used by employees to be beneficial for the same organisations. Explaining the mechanisms behind acceptance and usage of single technologies resulted in the creation of several theoretical models, which are nowadays used and refined in multiple domains like, among others, health IS, bioinformatics and social networking[25] to predict the technological behaviour of certain users in a given context.[26]

B. Social acceptance of energy projects and other large-scale infrastructures: This strand stems from practical policy and risk management literature, and takes into account the acceptance of both policies and politically contentious technologies. Rather than focusing on organisations and their employees, the emphasis is on the impact of disruptive or risky technologies on local communities. In this sense, the concept has been widely used in a variety of fields since the 1980s (e.g. nuclear waste management or carbon capture and storage), but more recently it has become a crucial point of discussion in social sciences debates around renewable and wind energy.[27]

6.1.5 The profile needed for assessing social acceptance

Since social acceptance is not regulated by law, there are no formal bodies or institutions in charge of supervising or assessing social acceptance, which is predominantly an enterprise carried out by individual researchers or groups.

Even by restricting the analysis to the two strands outlined in Section 6.1.4, researchers on social acceptance will still be drawn from multiple domains. At the same time, there is no specific profession or role that manifests an expertise in social acceptance of border control technologies. This might create confusion when composing the team of assessors.

Differently from ethics, some 'hard skills' are needed to perform a social acceptance assessment, although the extent to which this is the case depends on the techniques that are selected, as some techniques may require greater levels of specialisation than others. Given the sources referred to in this Chapter, assessors with a background in psychology, social sciences and information studies would possess a robust set of quantitative and qualitative methodological skills for performing the assessment. Alternatively, or as a complement, having a background in the humanities is also useful, and more particularly in philosophy or law and technology (including criminology). These latter profiles, however, may need some more time to become acquainted with certain traditional stakeholder involvement techniques.[28]

As for the case of ethics, the team of assessors may have no persons able to carry out this part of the assessment process, or it may lack the possibility to hire extra personnel to execute it. This could mean two main things. First, it could be a good opportunity to encourage some members of the institution in charge of the assessment to acquire new expertise through, for example, training. Alternatively, it is a chance to open up the assessment process to stakeholder involvement, i.e. the team of assessors may organise events or sessions with external experts or members of the public who can provide relevant input or support in the social acceptance assessment.

6.1.6 Literature overview

Unlike personal data protection, privacy and ethics, social acceptance of technologies is neither a well-established (academic) field within a clear-cut academic discipline, nor does it have a tradition of dedicated methods and techniques in the context of impact assessment. Yet, established scientific methods for the assessment of social perceptions are of direct relevance. To give a short overview, the two strands identified in Section 6.1.4 can be related to the context of border control:

Information Technology (IT) acceptance research: The most commonly used models that promote this approach are the Technology Acceptance Model (TAM)[29] and the Unified Theory of Acceptance and Use of Technology (UTAUT).[30] The latter is inspired by the former, and many other models have been proposed in between. TAM and UTAUT were first developed to assess acceptance in IS, subsequently spreading to other field like health IS, bioinformatics and social networking.[31] The main feature of TAM and UTAUT is that of predicting the intentions of a user in their use of a technology and explaining the subsequent usage behaviour. The basic methodological idea is that there are several constructs that determine usage and acceptance, such as perceived usefulness or ease of use, and that these can be studied empirically. Despite their success, such models have been simultaneously criticised for being both overly complicated and overly simplistic. They are deemed overly complicated because they take into account too many independent variables (or constructs) at once, without clearly defining the relationships between them, while they are deemed overly simplistic because they overlook the fact that group, social and cultural aspects also play a role in technology acceptance.[32]

Social acceptance of energy projects and other large-scale infrastructures: In the literature on social acceptance of technologies in the energy field, in particularly wind energy,[33] it has been pointed out how social acceptance can be studied from the angles of three intertwined perspectives that touch upon different groups of stakeholders:[34]

1. A socio-political perspective related to policy and institutional frameworks and wider public opinions. This is social acceptance at the most general level, like that described in the surveys on LFR in Section 6.1.2.
2. A community perspective related to residents and local authorities living in the sites of energy projects. This is about acceptance by local stakeholders related to the initiative, such as residents and local authorities.
3. A market perspective related to the process of market adoption and innovation. This is not only about consumers (the more consumers accept, the more they are willing to switch to a new technology and buy), but also about investors and companies who develop technologies.

Drawing an analogy from the case of border control technologies, in the early 2000s, authorities and policymakers found little reason to consult the public,[35] as there was nothing to debate and no opt-out from this large-scale experiment in the use of biometrics to manage mobility risks.[36] When the European Commission (EC), and especially the Directorate-General for Migration and Home Affairs (DG HOME),[37] started focusing on the societal dimension of security technologies, the industry's perspective played a major role: 'the problems associated to the societal acceptance of security technologies results in a number of negative consequences. For industry it means the risk of investing in technologies which are then not accepted by the public, leading to wasted investment. For the demand side it means being forced to purchase a less controversial product which however does not entirely fulfil the security requirements'.[38] More recently, the EU and DG Home have been promoting different initiatives to include various stakeholders, and not only practitioners and industry.[39]

When the focus on the market perspective prevails over the community perspective, the role of the wider public or specific communities could be reduced to that of being informed or 'convinced' that these border solutions are the best possible alternatives available. This is the case when passengers, for instance, are merely considered from the perspective of customer satisfaction when asked about emerging security technologies.[40]

To show the assessors that social acceptance plays an important role from all the three perspectives listed above, the next Section zooms in on some key concepts that will facilitate assessors' undertaking of the social acceptance assessment.

6.2 Social acceptance concepts and misconceptions

6.2.1 What social acceptance is about

This Section presents a list of social acceptance concepts that the assessors need to consider in the assessment process. The list is based on the current discussions in the academic domains identified in Section 6.1.

6.2.1.1 Engagement vs deficit model

In technology discourses, when social acceptance is considered merely as an obstacle to overcome and as a necessary condition to support innovation, it is often assumed that opposition to technologies is due to an ignorance about or lack of information as to the benefits of the specific technology.[41] In studies of public understanding of science, this is referred to as the 'deficit model'.[42] The deficit model assumes that an individual does not accept a type of (border control) technology because they lack an awareness of the advantages that such technology offers, like security, efficiency or convenience. The public therefore needs to be 'educated' by experts to become aware of the technologies in question and to be steered to trust them. The idea is that *only if* the public is correctly informed, *then* it could understand the reasons behind the massive deployment of new border technologies. Relying on a deficit model could transform the acceptance assessment process into a mere self-legitimating exercise, in which acceptance is assumed beforehand, and not subjected to public scrutiny. Opposed to the deficit model, according to the 'engagement model', individuals are not only 'instructed' but involved in a dialogue with scientists and policy makers.[43] The idea is to move the engagement 'upstream',[44] take the lay knowledge of the citizens seriously, and possibly achieve a two-way dialogue between the latter and scientists.

The engagement model, however, has also its limits. Even when individuals are engaged, it is unclear whether they passively react to a pre-established political and technological agenda, or if instead they challenge the agenda itself.[45] Engagement will always be somehow partial, as it is not possible to take all views into account from the start. Rather, engagement is a matter of trial and error. The goal is to conceive engagement as a way 'to make visible the invisible, to expose to public scrutiny the values, visions and assumptions that are usually hidden', which, in practice, involves asking questions like: 'Why this technology? Why not another? Who needs it? Who is controlling it? Who benefits from it? Can they be trusted? What will it mean for me and my family?'.[46]

The fact that a technology is feasible does not necessarily mean that it is accepted or acceptable. Thus, questioning the very desirability of the technology's goals and values, as well as the interests it will serve, is essential. Asking about acceptance is not merely collecting preferences about one or another feature or about perception of risks, but it is about recognising the normative and political choices by which the debate is framed.[47]

6.2.1.2 Three types of perspectives

It was noted above (Section 6.1.6) how at least three perspectives from which to study social acceptance have been identified; i.e. socio-political, community and market.[48] For a comprehensive assessment, the assessors must consider all three perspectives, and – at the very least – not focus *exclusively* on the market or socio-political perspective. In the context of border control, these three levels mean the following:

1. The socio-political acceptance is about the generic, aggregated acceptance of a border technology. It is about the attitude of the generic traveller who crosses a border crossing point. The assessors have already been warned about the possible pitfalls of an over-reliance on this level of analysis: there is no 'generic' traveller *per se*, but different travellers with competing interests and values. However, an analysis at this level could be a starting point from which to provide some preliminary input for the assessment, allowing the assessors to focus on more specific issues or groups.

2. The community acceptance is the one that probably goes most unnoticed in border control technologies. *Per se*, community acceptance refers to the acceptance of local stakeholders. In the context of border control, this concept could be extended not only to the specific sites where a technology is being tested or deployed (e.g. a specific land, air or sea border of a specific country), but also to the specific (vulnerable) groups *on which* this technology is tested. Since vulnerable communities, such as non-citizens, might not have access to resources and human rights protections, it is more difficult for them to have a choice or a say in (not) accepting border control technologies. In turn, it is 'easier' for local authorities to exploit the situation and test technologies on them. Some authors have argued how the deployment of automated decision systems for migration and asylum purposes can be seen as a 'human laboratory' of high-risk experiments in automated decision-making.[49] Similar patterns have taken place in the EU, for instance in refugee camps at the EU's external borders, like in Greece or Italy,[50] or elsewhere, such as in Canada.[51]

3. The market acceptance is about the market adoption of a particular technology. It has more to do with how end-users (e.g. border police) are able to 'switch' from more traditional to more innovative technological solutions and accept this change as beneficial for their operations. As for any EU-funded Horizon 2020 research projects, the market acceptance is related to the exploitation of projects' results, and could include

the assessment of possible skills shortages (e.g. among border guards), inadequate finances (e.g. to buy the technologies or build the required infrastructure), traditional value chains that are less keen to innovate, incompatibility between parts of the technological system (e.g. for lack of standards), or mismatch between market needs and the solution.[52]

6.2.1.3 Stakeholders

Especially when the focus of social acceptance is on the socio-political and community perspectives, involving travellers is necessary to move to an upstream engagement model and avoid a deficit model of participation in which decisions are taken by experts and more powerful stakeholders (such as companies or governments). In fact, there are many different travellers to consider, each with local, regional and national conflicting interests and values.[53] Among them, acceptance may vary greatly depending on the group considered, especially when it comes to border control technologies. An initial rule-of-thumb to guide the assessor would be to look at the traveller categories in the Schengen Borders Code,[54] which can be divided in two macro-categories:[55]

– European Union (EU)/European Economic Area (EEA)/Helvetic Confederation (CH) citizens
– Non-EU/EEA/CH citizens, including the sub-categories:
  - Refugees,
  - Travellers on a Schengen Visa,
  - Travellers with ETIAS travel authorisation,
  - Family members of EU citizens, and
  - Third country nationals enjoying the right of free movement under EU law.

At the community level, not only EU citizens but also non-EU and even non-citizens or refugees are considered when it comes to social acceptance, because the latter categories are particularly affected and are more vulnerable to the risks posed by border technologies. When it is not possible to engage with these categories, a valid alternative is to engage with their representatives or with civil society organisations that can give voice to their concerns (such as the NGOs that are part of the European Digital Rights (EDRi) network), or with institutions tasked with investigating issues relating to fundamental rights (such as the European Union Agency for Fundamental Rights (FRA)).

There are also other stakeholders to consider at the community and socio-political level when it comes to acceptance, however, especially border guards and customs officers who need to operate the technologies. Asking border guards and customs officers about the acceptance of technologies (e.g. whether they fear automated technologies would take their job away or whether they think such technologies would reduce their overall workload) is important, but should not substitute or be confused with the acceptance assessment of travellers.

On the market level, at the very least, industrial stakeholders, scientific experts and policy makers need to be taken into consideration. Industrial stakeholders could include technology or security service developers and providers. Scientific experts include people from academia and research institutes with a wide range of expertise, from hard sciences and applied sciences, such as engineering and computer science, to humanities, such as law, political science or philosophy. Finally, policy makers also include legislators and representatives from EU bodies and agencies related to border control, such as the European Border and Coast Guard Agency (Frontex), the European Union Agency for the Operational Management of Large-Scale IT Systems in the Area of Freedom, Security and Justice (eu-LISA) or the EC's DG HOME.

6.2.1.4 Techniques and disciplines for assessing social acceptance[56]

In Section 6.1.2, surveys and questionnaires were given as examples of techniques for assessing acceptance and public attitudes toward a particular border control technology (LFR), but these techniques do not fit the different groups and perspectives detailed above in the same ways. In parallel, the same techniques can fit different levels of analysis, e.g. a questionnaire to assess market acceptance or socio-political acceptance.

Surveys fit the socio-political level.[57] For instance, polls and questionnaires are very generic and give a useful and wide, but possibly superficial, input. Interviews, online platforms and study groups are also advisable, because they can provide more nuanced results, but can also take more time to undertake, require greater expertise to be correctly executed, and only allow the collection of a smaller sample (in the same amount of time, just a few people can be interviewed while hundreds are able to complete a questionnaire). When different groups of travellers are considered at the same time, they have the possibility to confront one another through methods like consultive groups, roundtables or workshops. To make the input of travellers more robust, participants could be asked to fill in questionnaires immediately after a facility tour or technology demonstration of the initiative under assessment (e.g. a video, a graphical representation, or simulation of a technology).[58]

For the community level, it is advisable to resort to interviews, focus groups, hotlines and consultive groups. These techniques allow the assessors to hear the personal stories of vulnerable people, and how each of them experiences their own individual challenges. This would involve the sharing of sensitive details, so it is advisable that formats where opinions can be given in an anonymised way, and without being revealed to a bigger group, be promoted. A questionnaire or survey would give overly generic results at this level, although it can be valuable to ensure anonymity if enough space is given to elaborate on specific questions (e.g. a preference for open-ended questions over close-ended ones, where the respondent can elaborate on their answer instead of picking from pre-selected options).

On the market level, the assessors need to bring together stakeholders with different background and interests, and make them confront one another. Therefore, a plethora of other methods are advisable, including the Delphi process, workshops, roundtables, scenario planning and/or advisory groups.⁵⁹ Furthermore, surveys and focus groups for market research, or market validation questionnaires, provide a valid alternative if limited time and resources are available for the assessment process.

6.2.2 What social acceptance is *not* about

The concept of social acceptance is often accompanied by a number of key assumptions in the public debate that serve to limit its scope. Including social acceptance in an integrated assessment process allows the assessors to look critically at these assumptions, in order to help the assessors perform a robust social acceptance assessment. Some of these assumptions are listed below.⁶⁰

'The majority of people support the technology': It is often emphasised in public surveys how support for border technologies or trust for authorities is high. The assumption of strong support and trust is then taken as a starting point for the discussion on the large-scale implementation of these technologies. Regardless of the fact of whether this has an empirical basis or not, a critical appraisal of these polls and surveys is sometimes lacking. Aspects to consider are, for instance:

– Who commissioned the poll, since a poll's goal and ultimate aim can be very different if it is commissioned by a company, a research consortium, a governmental organisation or an NGO. A company producing technologies might place more emphasis on the positive results of a survey for its economic advantage, while an NGO fighting for the respect of human rights might be more interested in stressing the negative results on vulnerable populations.
– How and by whom the questions are analysed, since depending on the message that one wants to convey with the results, certain relevant information might be underrated (for example the fact that awareness of how the technology works is very low), or certain not-so-relevant information overly emphasised. Findings can be presented as 'objective facts' that can be quantitatively measured, not worth discussing, although there are a variety of subjective factors at play that cannot simply be reduced to numeric values.⁶¹ Since the methods employed and the design of the study are decided beforehand, a bias to these can be introduced by the results that one wants to demonstrate.
– The point in time when the surveys were conducted, since the timeframe of the research can influence the results of a survey. If people are asked about the acceptance of a nuclear plant immediately before and immediately after a nuclear incident, like that at Chernobyl, the results obtained from the pool would show a huge contrast.
– The selection of the samples, to make sure that participants are selected in a representative way. If travellers were asked about a new technology introduced at an airport, the results would vary significantly if the interviewees were mostly white, European middle-aged men, with few women, elderly, people of colour or with disabilities being asked their opinions, to if the composition of the pool of those questioned were the other way round.

'Social acceptance should be achieved for a greater goal': In political debates about technologies, there is often an assumption that social acceptance is an obstacle to overcome for the sake of another goal, be it innovation, industrial growth or public security. Accordingly, media and policy discourses 'impose' how technologies should be accepted at any cost for such greater goals.

One example is the 'biometrics imaginary' that was first recently created in the US, and subsequently in the EU.[62] Especially in the wake of 9/11, a great number of initiatives were undertaken to increase security in the US and worldwide. Among these, interoperability efforts were taken as crucial to connect different databases and therefore fight terrorism (e.g. by sharing watchlists). Interoperability has been used in the collective imaginary as a crucial component of security, while cultural and legal barriers to its implementation needed to be overcome. In the EU, enhancement of border control and interoperability has been portrayed as a means by which to promote European integration, against potential threats coming from external borders. Another example, outside the EU, is the case of the establishment of an Israeli national biometric database, as a result of the controversial Israeli Biometric Project (IBP).[63] The scope of the project was officially countering the forgery of ID cards and passports. Behind the official motivation, however, the idea was to create a national centralised biometric database to enhance surveillance. Despite the strong social resistance to the project, it was shown how a part of the Israeli press consistently constructed a legitimising discourse of threat to national security, portraying Israel as a vulnerable victim and 'others' (e.g. Iranians) as dangerous enemies.[64] Motives to support the IBP included cultural motives central to Jewish-Israeli history. This allowed to create a convergence between two aspects of identity: a national, cultural Israeli identity and an administrative procedure of biometric identification.

'Opponents are ignorant': This argument assumes too hastily that any form of opposition equals ignorance or lack of expertise, and that the knowledge of experts is by definition more valuable than lay knowledge. It undermines legitimate forms of opposition that can stem from different reasonings than those of the purported advantages of the technology, for example a fear for the infringement of human rights (such as privacy) or other culture-specific motivations. In fact, an increased level of knowledge or education could lead to a lower level of acceptance for certain technologies. Getting to know how one's data are managed, how they are made interoperable and searchable, and how they could be misused or misinterpreted, might increase the opposition to privacy-intrusive technologies among the broader public. If people are unaware or ignorant, by contrast, they might more passively accept such a technology and believe the advantages that are advertised to them. Some objectors to these technologies appear highly informed, for example certain NGOs in Europe, like the EDRi network, which includes, among others, Statewatch, an NGO that has published extensively on security and border control.[65] Another famous case is that of the philosopher Giorgio Agamben, who, in 2004, having to travel to the US for a guest lecture on a visa, decided to cancel the journey because he refused to have his fingerprint taken upon arrival.[66] Although some people do not accept border technologies, their position does not necessarily result from ignorance, and needs to be taken seriously in both public debate and policy choices.

'Opponents are threats': Opposition to border technologies is also equated with threat, and, in turn, acceptance is an 'antidote' to such threats. Some groups of the public are excluded from engagement not because of their lack of knowledge, but because of the perceived risks they can cause, for example, in relation to public security (terrorists, political protesters, or activists), public health or irregular migration. In the case of border control, the threats are represented by so-called 'high-risk' travellers, who also evoke fear amongst the population. High-risk travellers, the argument goes, do not accept these technologies since they aim to evade these stricter controls, while 'low-risk' passengers, the category within which the vast majority of travellers and EU citizens fall, will accept them for the sake of public security, health and convenience. This argument assumes that there is a clear-cut distinction between low-risk and high-risk, which is in turn equated with a collective identity of 'us' (i.e. low-risk) vs. 'them' (i.e. high-risk).[67] While *we* tend to accept the technologies, *they* do not. However, the ways in which a person may end up being categorized as low or high risk are determined by opaque criteria that might reflect discriminatory biases of the designers and border guards, such as racial biases.[68] The problem is that not all those who are labelled 'high-risk' are serious threats or potential terrorists, and therefore their reasons for not accepting technologies are grounded in bases other than evading stricter controls and pursuing their criminal intents.

'Acceptance is a matter of single technologies and individual users': In many studies on social acceptance of technology in the fields of psychology and IS studies, an implicit assumption exists that social acceptance is mostly (1) an issue of individual users, and (2) a matter of single technologies.[69] These criticisms are also relevant to the case of border control technologies. Most individuals make judgements about technologies depending on perceived usefulness, motivations or expectations, but these are all conditional on social circumstances and cultural identities.[70] For instance, in the case of the lie detector developed by the project iBorderCtrl, people from Western countries, who may be familiarised with lie detectors (e.g. from movies or books), could have, at first sight, few problems with them. However, the same might not apply to people whose way of communicating is different, for example when it is considered inappropriate to have eye contact with persons of the opposite sex.[71] Secondly, it is misleading to consider technological artefacts in isolation, regardless of the socio-technical systems in which they are introduced and, in particular, regardless of the *political* and power relations that are at play.[72] Acceptance in border control is never mere acceptance of an artefact that can make travellers and border guards' lives more (or less) easy, but acceptance of a political architecture, as well: these technologies *have to be* used to strengthen the external borders of the EU and to better control migration flows.

Endnotes

1. Behnam Taebi, "Bridging the Gap between Social Acceptance and Ethical Acceptability," *Risk Analysis* 37, no. 10 (2017): 1817–27, https://doi.org/10.1111/risa.12734.
2. Susana Batel, Patrick Devine-Wright, and Torvald Tangeland, "Social Acceptance of Low Carbon Energy and Associated Infrastructures: A Critical Discussion," *Energy Policy* 58 (2013): 1–5, https://doi.org/10.1016/j.enpol.2013.03.018.
3. See Chapter 5 in this Volume.
4. Social acceptance also goes by the name of 'public acceptance' or 'societal acceptance'. The term 'social acceptance' was chosen for this Volume, due to the fact that it is in line with the EC's terminology and the literature overviewed.
5. See Chapter 2 in this Volume.
6. Ibo van de Poel, "A Coherentist View on the Relation Between Social Acceptance and Moral Acceptability of Technology," in *Philosophy of Technology After the Empirical Turn*, ed. Maarten Frassen, Pieter E. Vermaas, Peter Kroes, Anthoine W. M. Meijers (Springer, 2016) 178, https://doi.org/10.1007/978-3-319-33717-3_11.
7. The project was also targeted as an example of (mis)information and (mis)communication, since some of the crucial deliverables of the project (e.g. those on ethics) were not made available to the public.
8. See, for instance, Daniel Boffey, "EU Border 'lie Detector' System Criticised as Pseudoscience," *The Guardian*, November 2018, https://www.theguardian.com/world/2018/nov/02/eu-border-lie-detection-system-criticised-as-pseudoscience and Eleftherios Chelioudakis, "Greece: Clarifications Sought on Human Rights Impacts of IBorderCtrl," 2018, https://edri.org/our-work/greece-clarifications-sought-on-human-rights-impacts-of-iborderctrl/.
9. van de Poel, "A Coherentist View on the Relation Between Social Acceptance and Moral Acceptability of Technology."
10. "Beyond Face Value: Public Attitudes to Facial Recognition Technology," 2019. The Ada Lovelace Institute is an independent research institute and deliberative body whose mission is to ensure data and Artificial Intelligence work for people and society. It was established by the Nuffield Foundation, in collaboration with the Alan Turing Institute, the Royal Society and the British Academy in the UK. See https://www.adalovelaceinstitute.org/.
11. Ada Lovelace Institute.
12. The London Policing Ethics Panel is an independent panel established by the Mayor of London to give ethical advice on policing issues that may impact public acceptance. See http://www.policingethicspanel.london/.
13. London Policing Ethics Panel, "Final Report on Live Facial Recognition," 2019.
14. Ada Lovelace Institute, "Beyond Face Value: Public Attitudes to Facial Recognition Technology", 5.
15. Ada Lovelace Institute, 9.
16. Ada Lovelace Institute, 13.
17. London Policing Ethics Panel, "Final Report on Live Facial Recognition", 20.
18. London Policing Ethics Panel, 21.
19. London Policing Ethics Panel, 27.
20. Silkie Carlo, Jennifer Krueckeberg, and Griff Ferris, "Face Off: The Lawless Growth of Facial Recognition in UK Policing," *Big Brother Watch* (2018): 56.
21. See Annex 3 in this Volume.
22. Simone van der Burg, "A Lay Ethics Quest for Technological Futures: About Tradition, Narrative and Decision-Making," *NanoEthics* 10, no. 3 (2016): 233–44, https://doi.org/10.1007/s11569-016-0273-2.

23. Mhairi Aitken, "Why We Still Don't Understand the Social Aspects of Wind Power: A Critique of Key Assumptions within the Literature," *Energy Policy* 38, no. 4 (2010): 1834–41, https://doi.org/10.1016/j.enpol.2009.11.060.
24. See Chapter 2 in this Volume.
25. Neil Charness and Walter R Boot, "Technology, Gaming, and Social Networking," in *Handbook of the Psychology of Aging*, ed. K Warner Schaie and Sherry Willis (San Diego: Academic Press, 2016), 389–407, https://doi.org/10.1016/B978-0-12-411469-2.00020-0.
26. Viswanath Venkatesh et al., "User Acceptance of Information Technology: Toward a Unified View," *MIS Quarterly* 27, no. 3 (2003): 425–78.
27. Yann Fournis and Marie José Fortin, "From Social 'Acceptance' to Social 'Acceptability' of Wind Energy Projects: Towards a Territorial Perspective," *Journal of Environmental Planning and Management* 60, no. 1 (2017): 1–21, https://doi.org/10.1080/09640568.2015.1133406.
28. See Annex 2 in this Volume.
29. Fred D Davis, "Perceived Usefulness, Perceived Ease of Use, and User Acceptance of Information Technology," *MIS Quarterly* 13, no. 3 (1989): 319–40, https://doi.org/10.2307/249008.
30. Venkatesh et al., "User Acceptance of Information Technology: Toward a Unified View."
31. Charness and Boot, "Technology, Gaming, and Social Networking."
32. Richard P. Bagozzi, "The Legacy of the Technology Acceptance Model and a Proposal for a Paradigm Shift," *Journal of the Association for Information Systems* 8, no. 4 (2007): 244–54, https://doi.org/10.17705/1jais.00122.
33. Ellis Geraint and Gianluca Ferrero, "The Social Acceptance of Wind Energy. Where We Stand and the Path Ahead," 2016, https://doi.org/10.2789/696070.
34. Rolf Wüstenhagen, Maarten Wolsink, and Mary Jean Bürer, "Social Acceptance of Renewable Energy Innovation: An Introduction to the Concept," *Energy Policy* 35, no. 5 (2007): 2683–91, https://doi.org/10.1016/j.enpol.2006.12.001.
35. Ben Hayes, "Arming Big Brother The EU's Security Research Programme," 2006; Ben Hayes, "NeoConOpticon. The EU Security-Industrial Complex," 2009.
36. Kristrun Gunnarsdóttir and Kjetil Rommetveit, "The Biometric Imaginary: (Dis)Trust in a Policy Vacuum," *Public Understanding of Science* 26, no. 2 (2017): 195–211, https://doi.org/10.13140/RG.2.1.4207.4325.
37. See, for example, how the promotion of the social acceptance of security technologies is one of the objectives aimed for in order to enhance the competitiveness of European industry: European Commission, Work Programme 2018-2020 'Secure societies – Protecting freedom and security of European citizens', Decision C(2020)1862.
38. European Commission, *Security Industrial Policy. Action Plan for an innovative and competitive Security Industry,* COM(2012) 0417 final, 5.
39. Examples include the 'Europe for Citizens Programme' and its funding streams (Council Regulation (EU) No 390/2014 of 14 April 2014 establishing the 'Europe for Citizens' programme for the period 2014-2020 OJ L 115, 17.4.2014, p. 3–13) and the 'Community of Users on Secure, Safe and Resilient Societies' (Philippe Quevauviller, ed., *A Community of Users on Secure, Safe and Resilient Societies* (1st edn, Publications Office of the European Union 2018)).
40. Leon Hempel et al., "Towards a Social Impact Assessment of Security Technologies: A Bottom-up Approach," *Science and Public Policy* 40, no. 6 (2013): 740–54, https://doi.org/10.1093/scipol/sct086.
41. See Section 6.2.2.
42. Rob Flynn, *Risk and the Public Acceptance of New Technologies*, ed. Rob Flynn and Paul Bellaby, *Risk and the Public Acceptance of New Technologies* (London: Palgrave Macmillan UK, 2007), https://doi.org/10.1057/9780230591288.

43. Alan Irwin and Brian Wynne, "Introduction," in *Misunderstanding Science?*, ed. Alan Irwin and Brian Wynne (Cambridge: Cambridge University Press, 1996), 1–18, https://doi.org/10.1017/CBO9780511563737.001.
44. James Wilsdon and Rebecca Willis, *See-Through Science: Why Public Engagement Needs to Move Upstream* (London: Demos, 2004).
45. Melissa Leach, Ian Scoones, and Brian Wynne, eds., *Science and Citizens. Globalization and the Challenge of Engagement* (London & New York: Zed Books, 2005).
46. Wilsdon and Willis, *See-Through Science: Why Public Engagement Needs to Move Upstream*.
47. Flynn, "Risk and the Public Acceptance of New Technologies".
48. Wüstenhagen, Wolsink, and Bürer, "Social Acceptance of Renewable Energy Innovation: An Introduction to the Concept."
49. Petra Molnar, EDRi, and the Refugee Law Lab, "Technological Testing Grounds. Migration Management Experiments and Reflections from the Ground Up," 2020.
50. Chris Jones, "Automated Suspicion: The EU's New Travel Surveillance Initiatives," 2020; Raphael Tsavkko Garcia, "How the Pandemic Turned Refugees Into 'Guinea Pigs' for Surveillance Tech," *OneZero*, 2021.
51. Petra Molnar and Lex Gill, "Bots at the Gate: A Human Rights Analysis of Automated Decision-Making in Canada's Immigration and Refugee System," *International Human Rights Program & Citizen Lab*, 2018, 88.
52. See the entry 'Dissemination and exploitation of results' of the H2020 Online Manual: https://ec.europa.eu/research/participants/docs/h2020-funding-guide/grants/grant-management/dissemination-of-results_en.htm.
53. Flynn, "Risk and the Public Acceptance of New Technologies".
54. Regulation (EU) 2016/399 of the European Parliament and of the Council of 9 March 2016 on a Union Code on the rules governing the movement of persons across borders (Schengen Borders Code), OJ L 77, 23.3.2016, 1–52.
55. Ibid., 1-52.
56. See also Annex 2 in this Volume.
57. Surveys are conducted by trained interviewers who select a representative sample, ensure the questions are unbiased and formulated clearly, and take into account the statistical significance of the research. See James L. Creighton, *The Public Participation Handbook: Making Better Decisions through Citizen Involvement* (Jossey-Bass, 2005), 128; Louis M. Rea and Richard A. Parker, *Designing and Conducting Survey Research. A Comprehensive Research Guide*, Third (Jossey-Bass, 2005).
58. US Environmental Protection Agency, *RCRA Public Participation Manual*, 1996, 56. See also Annex 2 in this Volume.
59. For an overview of such methods, see Annex 2 in this Volume.
60. Adapted from Aitken, "Why We Still Don't Understand the Social Aspects of Wind Power: A Critique of Key Assumptions within the Literature."
61. Andrea Saltelli, "Ethics of Quantification or Quantification of Ethics?," *Futures* 116 (2020): 102509, https://doi.org/10.1016/j.futures.2019.102509.
62. Kjetil Rommetveit, "Introducing Biometrics in the European Union: Practice and Imagination," *The International Library of Ethics, Law and Technology* 17 (2016): 113–26, https://doi.org/10.1007/978-3-319-32414-2_8.
63. Avi Marciano, "The Discursive Construction of Biometric Surveillance in the Israeli Press: Nationality, Citizenship, and Democracy," *Journalism Studies* 20, no. 7 (2019): 972–90, https://doi.org/10.1080/1461670X.2018.1468723.
64. Marciano.

65. Chris Jones, Jane Kilpatrick, and Mariana Gkliati, "Deportation Union: Rights, Accountability, and the EU's Push to Increased Forced Removals," 2020, https://www.statewatch.org/deportation-union-rights-accountability-and-the-eu-s-push-to-increase-forced-removals Jones, "Automated Suspicion: The EU's New Travel Surveillance Initiatives," https://www.statewatch.org/media/1235/sw-automated-suspicion-full.pdf.
66. Giorgio Agamben, "Bodies Without Words: Against the Biopolitical Tatoo," *German Law Journal* 5, no. 2 (2004): 168–69.
67. Katja Franko Aas, "'Crimmigrant' Bodies and Bona Fide Travelers: Surveillance, Citizenship and Global Governance," *Theoretical Criminology* 15, no. 3 (2011): 331–46, https://doi.org/10.1177/1362480610396643.
68. Ruha Benjamin, *Race After Technology: Abolitionist Tools for the New Jim Code* (Cambridge, UK: Polity Press, 2019).
69. Bagozzi, "The Legacy of the Technology Acceptance Model and a Proposal for a Paradigm Shift."
70. Flynn, "Risk and the Public Acceptance of New Technologies".
71. Petra Molnar, "Emerging Voices: Immigration, Iris-Scanning and IBorderCTRL-The Human Rights Impacts of Technological Experiments in Migration" (OpinioJuris, 2019), http://opiniojuris.org/2019/08/19/emerging-voices-immigration-iris-scanning-and-iborderctrl-the-human-rights-impacts-of-technological-experiments-in-migration/.
72. Molnar and Gill, "Bots at the Gate: A Human Rights Analysis of Automated Decision-Making in Canada's Immigration and Refugee System," https://citizenlab.ca/wp-content/uploads/2018/09/IHRP-Automated-Systems-Report-Web-V2.pdf.

7 Border management law in the European Union

Alessandra CALVI
Vrije Universiteit Brussel. E-mail: alessandra.calvi@vub.be.

7.1 Introduction

7.1.1 The concept of border management

The twofold goal of border management is to facilitate the efficient flow of *bona fide* travellers while preventing the entry of irregular travellers.[1] Traditionally, border management encompasses an ensemble of activities aimed at controlling the flow of goods and individuals across borders, and administering immigration, migrant flows and asylum requests. At the European Union level, instead, the focus of the so called "integrated border management" is rather on persons than on goods. Integrated border management is considered a necessary corollary to the free movement of persons and central to improve migration management (see *infra*). Its aims include efficiently managing the crossing of the external borders and addressing migratory challenges and potential future threats at those borders, while fully respecting fundamental rights.[2] In recent decades, the way in which border management in the European Union (EU) and in other Western democratic countries in general has been practiced has undergone significant changes, becoming increasingly technologised and digitalised. Traditional physical borders have been supplemented by new digital borders in the form of large-scale information systems that target primarily the movements of third-country nationals,[3] weakening the role played by the physical aspect of border management, including the actual crossing of territorial borders.[4] New border control technologies, which have become increasingly reliant on systematic and large-scale processing of personal data, especially biometric data, have been deployed with the objective of enhancing the efficiency of mobility control and increasing security.[5] Checks at territorial borders have become progressively automated and combined with checks before and during travel, as well as after arrival, now commonly in place.

At the same time, geographical frontiers are increasingly surveilled in order to prevent their crossing by irregular migrants.[6] Technological experiments in various domains of border management activities are being increasingly undertaken, with these ranging from predicting population movements in the Mediterranean and Aegean Seas by monitoring social media activities to applying artificial intelligence (AI) for risk-scoring purposes.[7]

These changes also concern the actors involved in actual border management. While border management has been first and foremost entrusted with specially trained state officials (see e.g. Article 16 Schenghen Borders Code), due to the progressive externalisation and privatisation of border control (see *infra*), the role of non-national state actors, such as private companies (e.g. air carriers) and even individuals, as well as of supranational and international actors, such as the EU and its many agencies (e.g. Frontex), and even third countries, has increased.[8] At the same time, the technologisation of border control has amplified the importance of technology providers.[9] The proliferation of technology and data actors has led to an increasingly complex regulatory framework governing border management in the EU, triggering at the same time criticism due to its possible detrimental effects on fundamental rights, particularly data protection and privacy (see *infra*) and, consequently, on democracy and the rule of law. These three elements are inherently and indivisibly linked. While each one seems to operate independently of the others, separating them in practice risks causing the system of values enshrined in Article 2 Treaty on the European Union (TEU) to collapse.[10]

The purpose of this Chapter is to support assessors in mapping the relevant legal and regulatory framework applicable to border control technologies and, therein, to emphasise those legal requirements – grouped into the three categories of data protection, privacy and ethics[11] – that have to be complied with in order to assure, to the highest extent possible, that border control technologies remain aligned with democratic principles, the rule of law and fundamental rights.

Border management law, which encompasses a patchwork of European, national and international legal and otherwise regulatory instruments (see *infra*), represents a *sui generis* component of the benchmark against which border control technologies have to be assessed under the integrated impact assessment process as proposed in this textbook. Within this process, unlike the other elements of the benchmark (namely data protection, privacy, ethics and social acceptance), border management law is not *per se* a societal concern, but rather contains provisions that do protect societal concerns. In other words, from border management law, it is possible to extrapolate legal requirements enshrining data protection, privacy and ethics that, to be lawful, border control technologies must abide by. The adherence to these requirements is expected to enhance the social acceptance of the technology under assessment.

The structure of this Chapter is as follows: Sections 7.1.2 and 7.1.3 will illustrate some of the fundamental rights and other societal concerns that can be affected by border management laws and policies, as well as by border control technologies. Section 7.2 will delve into the historical development of border management law and policies in the EU. Section 7.3 will provide an overview of the legal and regulatory instruments regulating border management law. Section 7.4 will focus on the actors involved in border management, and, finally, Section 7.5 will overview the data protection, privacy and ethics requirements enshrined in multiple components of EU border management law that may be relevant for the integrated impact assessment process.

Border management laws and policies are instilled with certain values of a society, values that vary depending on geopolitical and historical circumstances.[12] In other words, border management activities, policy goals and necessities are fluid and subject to change over time. They may promote the respect of fundamental rights, democracy and the rule of law, or conversely advance xenophobic and racially discriminatory ideologies.[13] Given that border management is so heavily politicised, it is natural to assume that the utilisation of border control technologies is not neutral either.[14]

7.1.2 How border management laws and policies affect fundamental rights: the case of EU large-scale databases and their interoperability

Several fundamental rights and other societal concerns can be affected by border management laws and policies, as well as by border control technologies. This Section will illustrate some of them, using as a reference point the EU policies concerning large-scale databases and their interoperability that exist.

Such EU large-scale databases presently include: the second-generation Schengen Information System (SIS II), the Visa Information System (VIS), the European Dactyloscopy (Eurodac), and the more recent Entry-Exit System (EES), European Criminal Records Information System for Third Country Nationals (ECRIS-TCN) and European Travel Information and Authorisation System (ETIAS). The EU established these with the aim of supporting border guards in controlling the external borders of the Schengen Area.[15]

In a nutshell, the SIS allows competent authorities in the EU to issue and consult alerts on missing or wanted objects and people. The VIS supports Member States' consular authorities in the management of applications for short-stay visas to visit or to transit through the Schengen Area. The Eurodac supports competent authorities in determining the responsibility for examining an asylum application. In the near future, the EES will electronically register the time and place of entry and exit of third-country nationals, both those requiring a visa and those who are visa-exempt, admitted for a short stay, other than those refused to entry. The ECRIS-TCN will allow Member States' authorities to identify which other Member States hold criminal records on the third-country nationals or stateless persons being checked. The ETIAS will constitute a pre-travel authorisation system for visa-exempt travellers, the key function of which is to verify if a third-country national meets entry requirements before travelling to the Schengen Area, enabling pre-travel assessment of irregular migration, security or public health risks.[16]

Although each EU large-scale database has its purposes and specificities,[17] their technical architectures are similar. They are composed of a central system, managed by the

European Union Agency for the Operational Management of Large-Scale IT Systems in the Area of Freedom, Security and Justice (eu-LISA), a backup, a national system/interface in each Member State that communicates with the central one, and an (encrypted) communication infrastructure connecting them. National copies of the central system are foreseen for the SIS. All of these databases rely on the extensive processing of personal data, including biometric data (namely, fingerprints, palmprints, facial images, DNA profiles. Note that each database contains different types of biometric data).[18] It has been esteemed that the SIS contains over 70 million alerts, the Eurodac more than 5 million fingerprint datasets, and the VIS over 17 million visa applications.[19]

The official goal of the latest EU policies is that these databases will become interoperable. This interoperability scheme will build upon four components: a European Search Portal (ESP), allowing competent authorities to search multiple EU information systems simultaneously (including certain Europol data and Interpol databases).[20] This common search protocol will use biographical and biometric data; a shared biometric matching service (BMS), enabling the search and comparison of biometric data (fingerprints and facial images) from several systems that store biometric templates; a common identity repository (CIR), containing biographical and biometric data of third-country nationals recorded in the Eurodac, VIS, EES, ETIAS and ECRIS-TCN; and a multiple-identity detector (MID), which checks whether the biographical identity data contained in the search exists in other parts of the shared system, thus allowing the detection of multiple identities linked to the same set of biometric data.[21]

Many fundamental rights are affected by these EU large-scale databases and their interoperability. Various actors, including the European Data Protection Supervisor (EDPS), the EU Agency for Fundamental Rights (FRA), NGOs and academia have noted, *inter alia*, that the processing of large amounts of personal data not only jeopardises the rights to privacy and personal data protection, but may have a larger impact on democracy and society as a whole. In particular, privacy, they argue, is an inherent value in liberal democratic and pluralist societies, in addition to being a cornerstone for the enjoyment of fundamental rights.[22]

However, other fundamental rights, in particular the right to non-discrimination, are affected by these databases and their interoperability. As these databases mainly contain the data of third-country nationals, concerns have been raised over the fairness of EU laws and policies towards third-country nationals. The Court of Justice of the European Union (CJEU), albeit in a different context, highlighted that the coexistence of different data processing practices for nationals and for non-national EU citizens may be discriminatory.[23] Certain analysts even doubt the legality of having different data processing practices for EU and non-EU citizens and whether this respects the essence of the right to personal data protection.[24] Other challenges derive from the technical architecture of the databases, which renders them prone to fragilities (e.g. technical failures, errors in software configurations, discrepancies between the central system and national copies, data quality of the entries, depending mostly on the work practices of their end users).[25] In addition to jeopardising the efficiency of the IT systems, some of these fragilities affect the rights of individuals whose data are stored in them. For instance, inaccuracy of data or discrepancies between information stored national and central systems may lead to unjust administrative decisions against a person. The negative consequences of data inaccuracy are likely to be amplified by the impending interoperability of the EU large-scale databases. When combined with interstate trust, interoperability may legitimise national authorities to blindly rely on data stored in EU data systems, even when not accurate and up-to-date, instead of performing a careful examination of each case.[26]

Furthermore, interoperability entails much more than interconnecting IT systems. It also implicates semantic, social, cultural, economic, organisational and legal issues.[27] Perhaps most importantly, far from being just a technical choice, interoperability entails a political approach that somehow blurs the lines between various policy goals (e.g. asylum, migration management, law enforcement, counterterrorism), risking, for example, a conflation of the notions of "terrorist" or "criminal" used in public discourse with the legally defined notion of "foreigner" or "alien".[28] The interconnection of technologies (and databases) also gives rise to the possibility of function creep, which could imply the expansion of surveillance and data collection functions into areas where they conflict with core data protection principles such as lawfulness, purpose limitation or data minimisation.[29]

EU laws and policies related to EU large-scale databases and interoperability are not alone in facing criticism. Another phenomenon that has been put into question is the externalisation of border control, which refers to a "range of processes whereby European actors and Member States complement policies to control migration across their territorial boundaries with initiatives that realise such control extra-territorially and through other countries and organs rather than their own".[30] The externalisation of border control has been deemed particularly detrimental to the effective exercise of the right to asylum and the principle of non-refoulement.[31]

7.1.3 How border control technologies affect fundamental rights

Just as border management laws and policies embed certain values of a society, so are border control (and digital) technologies unneutral. They can be deployed both to promote the respect of fundamental rights, democracy and the rule of law and, conversely, to advance xenophobic and racially discriminatory ideologies.[32] Border control technologies are multiple and diverse. As a general rule, they may facilitate both border checks and border surveillance activities. Border control technologies aimed at facilitating border checks primarily target individuals and rely on extensive personal data processing, whereas those used for border surveillance purposes focus on detecting events where individuals and groups are involved, which entails different risks for fundamental rights.[33]

For instance, although border control technologies may not always rely on personal data processing, there is a risk that they will jeopardise other fundamental rights, *inter alia*, the right to asylum and to non-refoulement,[34] as well as the rights of minorities, who may inadvertently become the main target groups of border surveillance activities.[35]

One form of border control technology that is particularly challenging from a fundamental rights perspective is the use of algorithmic profiling. In the context of border management, profiling is used mainly to identify known individuals based on previously collected data or as a predictive method to identify unknown individuals who may be of interest to border management authorities,[36] on the basis of risk indicators.[37] EU large-scale databases (in particular, the ETIAS) have come to increasingly incorporate algorithmic decision-making, including profiling functionalities (e.g. to determine whether an individual is to be determined a risk).[38] By analysing existing data derived from past experiences and statistical analysis, correlations between certain characteristics and particular outcomes or behaviours are established and used to draw conclusions, and make decisions about certain individuals.[39] Consequently, whereas profiling can be a useful tool, its use may lead biased outcomes, affecting, *inter alia*, equality, non-discrimination, privacy and data protection.[40]

Equality and non-discrimination are also at stake, considering that the accuracy of certain border control technologies (e.g. facial recognition) relative to parameters such as gender and skin tone, may give rise to discrimination.[41] Border control technologies are, in this sense, prone to perpetuate human rights harms and exacerbate systemic discrimination.[42]

The performance of the integrated impact assessment of border control technologies can help to minimise such negative consequences.

7.2 The historical development of border management law in the EU

As mentioned above, the essential twofold goal of border management (law) is to facilitate the efficient flow of *bona fide* travellers while preventing the entry of irregular travellers.[43] To achieve this objective, multiple approaches are possible.

For centuries, the so-called "nationalist approach" towards border control has been predominant in Europe.[44] In a nutshell, such an approach, typical of modern states, conceives border control as a corollary of sovereignty and therefore a purely domestic matter, for which national governments are the sole responsible actors.[45] The so-called Westphalian (or modern) state system builds upon the idea that sovereign states possess the monopoly of force within their mutually recognised territories, which are delimited by borders.[46] Considering that sovereignty for a state entails having control over the territory, the population and the goods therein, borders function as a kind of "filter", demarcating "a portion of the globe that a centralised authority claims as its own and to protect it from external threats".[47] Centuries after the Treaties of Westphalia (1648), the Montevideo Convention on the Rights and Duties of States (1933) still considers the territory, enclosed within borders, as a statehood criterion, together with population, government, and the capacity to enter into relations with other states.[48]

With the emergence of supranational institutions, the concept of sovereignty transformed. In Europe, with the process of European integration, the Member States of what is today known as the European Union (EU), started to transfer the execution of some of their sovereign competences at a supranational level, including those competences that relate to border management.[49] This conferral of these competences is a direct consequence of the emergence of the Common Market and four freedoms of the EU, namely the freedom of movement of goods, persons, services, capitals (Title IV TFEU), which are, in turn, safeguarded by diverse policies within the Area of Freedom, Security and Justice (AFSJ), pertaining to, for example, migration (Title V TFEU).

In the process of European integration, supranational cooperation has progressively acquired more and more power and competences in the field of border management. The signing of the Schengen Agreement (1985) and of the Convention Implementing the Schengen Agreement (1990) have laid the foundation for the gradual abolition of internal border controls, homogenisation of visa policies, and implementation of a cooperating structure between internal and immigration officers, including the establishment of the Schengen Information System.[50] Yet, the two were international agreements, valid exclusively among the signatory states. The Treaty of Maastricht (1992), establishing the so-called three-pillars structure for the organisation of the competences of the European Union,[51] introduced for the first time the idea of European cooperation in the field of border management, although still based on inter-governmentalism.[52] The Treaty of Amsterdam (1997) went further by incorporating the Schengen rules, previously applicable only to the signatory states of the Schengen Agreement and the Convention implementing it, into the *acquis communautaire*; the body of common rights and obligations that are binding for all EU countries, as EU Member States.[53] With the Treaty of Lisbon (2007) and the abolition of the pillars structure, the intergovernmental approach in the field of border management was overcome, border management being nowadays entirely reconducted to supranational cooperation.[54]

Border management laws and policies in the EU build upon the assumption that, to ensure a high level of security and the freedom of movement within the EU, one of the necessary conditions is the strong and reliable (integrated) management of the movement of persons across external borders.[55] The progressive technologisation and digitalisation that has come to characterise the EU policies of recent decades is precisely intended to better-secure the EU's external borders and streamline border crossing by becoming increasingly reliant on automated information-sharing and self-service.[56]

These developments represent a turning point in comparison to the above-mentioned nationalist approach.[57] Although the EU system still acknowledges the existence of national borders and maintains the rhetoric of borders as filters against external threats, it introduces a key novelty, namely the distinction between internal and external borders. Whereas for the former, the controls are in principle lifted, i.e. these borders may be crossed at any point without a border check on persons – irrespective of their nationality – being carried out,[58] for the latter, controls are in place and – what is perhaps more important – a common policy is established.[59]

This distinction affects also the perception that individuals have about borders and the EU as a whole. From the insider's perspective, the EU may appear open and hospitable, whereas for the rest of the world, it may appear more closed, secure and less permissive.[60] Internal borders are deemed rather inclusive and less visible, while external borders are perceived as exclusive and restrictive, since security and border traffic control are transferred thereto.[61]

7.3 Legal and regulatory instruments governing border management in the EU

Nowadays, border management in the EU is governed by a patchwork of legal and otherwise regulatory instruments, encompassing European primary law sources, namely the Treaties (Treaty on the European Union (TEU) and Treaty on the Functioning of the European Union (TFEU)), and the Charter on Fundamental Rights of the European Union (CFR). While Article 3(2) TEU states the essence thereof – namely that the "Union shall offer its citizens an area of freedom, security and justice without internal frontiers, in which the free movement of persons is ensured in conjunction with appropriate measures with respect to external border controls, asylum, immigration and the prevention and combating of crime", Title V TFEU on the Area of Freedom Security and Justice further specifies a common policy on asylum, immigration and external border control, all of which must conform to the CFR; when implementing EU law, Member States are also bound by the Charter.

Secondary law sources, such as regulations, directives and (implementing) decisions, also play a role in framing EU border management policy. This includes, first and foremost, a legal statute for each border management tool, ranging from Schengen through large-scale databases and their interoperability, the Passenger Name Record (PNR) Directives, the Advanced Passenger Information (API) Directive, the European Border Surveillance System (Eurosur), the rules governing the European bodies and agencies, the rules governing border control of persons crossing the external borders of the Member States of the Union (contained in the Schengen Borders Code (SBC)), to identity cards and passports, unmanned air vehicles, dual-use, etc.[62]

In addition to EU law, Member States are bound by public international law instruments, e.g. bilateral agreements, treaties and conventions, such as the 1950 European Convention on Human Rights, the 1951 Geneva Convention, and the 1967 Protocol Relating to the Status of Refugees. National laws play a role insofar as certain matters, directly or indirectly linked to border management, such as intelligence, military and internal security, are the exclusive competence of Member States.[63]

Eventually, soft law instruments, such as internal policies and practices of border authorities and memoranda of understanding concluded between border control authorities of neighbouring countries, also come into play in the formation of policy. Finally, a number of technical standards fixed for biometric data contained in passports (International Civil Aviation Organisation (ICAO), National Institute of Standards and Technology (NIST)) set certain limitations on the implementation of border management policy.

7.4 Actors involved in border management in the EU

Over recent decades, border management has come to no longer be a prerogative of state actors alone. The actors currently involved, directly or indirectly, in border management activities can be grouped into three main categories, namely national state actors, supra-national state actors (in this context, the EU and its institutions, bodies, offices and agencies) and private actors.

National state actors include the border control authorities entrusted with the actual performance of border checks and border surveillance under national and/or EU law, national law enforcement agencies, insofar as they are assigned border management-related tasks, Passenger Information Units (PIUs) established under the Passenger Name Records (PNR) Directive, and national Data Protection Authorities (DPAs), to the extent that they oversee how nationally competent authorities use EU large-scale databases.

Amongst supranational state actors, apart from the Commission, the European Parliament and the Council, several EU bodies and agencies have been set up and tasked with border management tasks. The European Border and Coast Guard Agency (commonly known as Frontex)[64], together with Member States' responsible authorities, oversees the effective implementation of integrated border management at the external borders of the EU. The European Union Agency for the Operational Management of Large-Scale IT Systems in the Area of Freedom, Security and Justice (eu-LISA) is in charge of the operational management of the SIS, VIS and Eurodac, and of the preparation, development and operational management of EES, ETIAS and ECRIS-TCN.[65] The European Data Protection Supervisor (EDPS) has responsibility for supervising personal data processing in the central units of the databases hosted by eu-LISA (the EDPS and national DPAs form together the Supervision Coordination Groups (SCGs)).[66] The European Asylum Support Office (EASO) contributes to the development of the Common European Asylum System by facilitating, coordinating and strengthening practical cooperation among Member States on the many aspects of asylum.[67] Finally, the European Union Agency for Law Enforcement Cooperation (Europol) will, under certain conditions (e.g. when necessary to fulfil its mandate), have access to the SIS, VIS, Eurodac, EES, ETIAS and ECRIS-TCN.[68]

Private actors include carriers and those private entities that, due to the progressive privatisation of border control, have been tasked with specific border management-related tasks such as sharing passenger-related information with border control authorities or denying boarding.[69] A key group of private actors not mentioned in the legal and otherwise regulatory framework, but that in practice influence border management, are the technology providers themselves.⁷⁰ When public authorities lack the technical capacity for deploying and understanding border control technologies, they may rely, sometimes to a high degree, on technology developers. This has a tendency to enable these private actors to influence the border control agenda and to shape priorities regarding the technologies to be deployed.⁷¹

7.5 Legal requirements enshrining data protection, privacy and ethics in EU border management law

7.5.1 An introduction to the built-in safeguards system of EU border management law

Given the EU's commitment to democracy, the rule of law and fundamental rights, border management law in the EU contains built-in safeguards that protect these values, and in particular data protection, privacy and ethics. Therefore, for the purposes of the process of integrated impact assessment of border control technologies, these requirements enshrining data protection, privacy and ethics have to be evaluated by means of a legal compliance check on the envisaged technology. The adherence to these requirements is further expected to enhance the social acceptance of the technology under assessment.

It should be noted that the sole legal compliance check against data protection, privacy and ethics requirements does not necessarily grant that a border control technology is socially acceptable and respects democracy, the rule of law and fundamental rights. Indeed, as mentioned above, border management laws (and policies) may embed xenophobic and racially discriminatory ideologies. In democratic systems, many safeguards are arguably in place to avoid this happening. For instance, at a procedural level, part of the EU framework governing border management (e.g. regulations, directives) is the outcome of the ordinary legislative procedure,⁷² where the European Parliament is co-legislator with the Council. Yet, this does not automatically ensure the adherence of these laws to superior sources (e.g. Charter of Fundamental Rights of the European Union). The EU legal framework can be challenged in front of the Court of Justice of the European Union and invalidated. In other words, procedural democracy does not necessarily coincide with substantive democracy, which functions with the actual interest of those governed.⁷³ Furthermore, when legislation is adopted specifically to confront emergency situations, using an intergovernmental method,⁷⁴ or has (apparently) more technical content (e.g. EU implementing and delegated acts), the democratic scrutiny is lessened.⁷⁵ Similar considerations are valid, *mutatis mutandis*, for national laws governing border management.

Each type of technology to be implemented corresponds to an applicable legal framework. For example, when border control technologies are used to perform border checks, they may be connected to EU large-scale databases, meaning that rules on EU large-scale databases and the Schengen Borders Code are applicable, and compliance requirements must be extrapolated therefrom. Conversely, when border control technologies are aimed at performing border surveillance activities, other rules (Eurosur) may be relevant. (An inventory of the EU legal framework potentially applicable to border control technologies, grouped into macro-topics, is provided in Annex IV of this textbook.)

As a general rule, the legal framework applicable to border control technologies, and particularly in regard to the exchange of information in border management activities (e.g. EU large-scale databases, interoperability regulations), is governed by its own data protection rules (*lex specialis*). Matters that are not expressly regulated in the framework are referred mainly to the General Data Protection Regulation (GDPR) (*lex generalis*), unless the purpose is "the prevention, detection or investigation of terrorist offences or other serious criminal offences", meaning that the Law Enforcement Directive (LED) is applicable.[76]

For the European institutions, bodies and agencies involved in border management, the *lex generalis* is Regulation (EU) 2018/1725 on the protection of natural persons with regard to the processing of personal data by the Union institutions, bodies, offices and agencies and on the free movement of such data (EUDPR). Chapter IX EUDPR regulates the processing of operational personal data by Union bodies, offices and agencies when carrying out activities falling within the scope of judicial cooperation in criminal matters and police cooperation. Certain regulations establishing EU bodies and agencies contain their own data protection rules that constitute *lex specialis* in relation to the EUDPR (for Frontex, this is, for example, Chapter IV, Section 2 Frontex Regulation). Europol is an exception to this, due to the fact that, at present, it has its own data protection rules.

More specifically, border management law establishes some special rules, especially in relation to data subjects' rights, data transfers, accessibility of personal data and accuracy of biometric data, that specify the *lex generalis*. In addition, border management law gives substance and further specifies certain concepts contained in the GDPR (e.g. allocation of roles of controllers and processors). Regarding other obligations (e.g. the need to appoint a data protection officer (DPO), the requirement for the data controller to perform a DPIA), border management authorities and EU bodies and agencies involved in border management are still bound by the GDPR, the LED and/or the EUDPR.

7.5.2 Summary of the data protection, privacy and ethics requirements of the EU border control system

7.5.2.1 Data Protection Requirements

The following is a cursory overview of the specific regulatory measures current assured by multiple components of EU border management law. This Section needs to be read in conjunction with Chapter 4 on personal data protection, where the concepts under the *lex generalis* are presented.

1. *Roles of controllers and processors*. The responsibilities of controllers and processors are allocated in accordance with the law.

In some cases, border management law expressly allocates the roles of controllers and processors in the entities involved in data processing operations.[77] The distinction is important because data controllers have broader obligations than data processors (e.g. performance of a DPIA).[78]

2. *Lawful processing.* A legal basis grounds the personal data processing performed by the border control technology.

   Border management law may lay down the basis for certain processing operations (e.g. expressly require border control authorities to carry out certain data processing operations), or clarify the legal basis to be used in certain processing (e.g. consent).[79]

3. *Purpose limitation.* Data processed by a border control technology are processed for specified, explicit and legitimate purposes, in line with those specified in the relevant legal and regulatory framework applicable to it.

   Border management law lists the purposes for which a border control activity is carried out and personal data are to be processed (e.g. each EU large-scale IT system has own purposes, whereas the PNR and API directives specify why PNR and API are processed).[80] Therefore, when a border control technology processes personal data, the purposes of processing need to be in-line with those specified in the legal framework applicable to it.

4. *Data minimisation.*

   4.1. The border control technology processes only the personal data that are adequate, relevant and not excessive for the specific border control activity.

   In the context of border management, not all the activities performed by border control authorities require personal data processing. Border management law clarifies that, whereas personal data processing is a core function for border checks,[81] it is conversely exceptional for border surveillance.[82]

   4.2. The border control technology ensures that only certain categories of personal data are processed.

   While a border control technology may have the technical capacity to process multiple categories of personal data, not all of them are necessary for performing a border management activity. For example, border management law provides a closed list of the categories of personal data that can be stored/processed in EU large-scale databases,[83] or collected and transferred by (air) carriers.[84]

5. *Accuracy.* Mechanisms are in place to ensure that data processed by a border control technology are accurate and up-to-date, and that any change in the data is promptly communicated to those (authorities) concerned.

   Keeping data accurate and up-to-date in the context of border management is of utmost importance to effectively take action against those individuals that represent a threat to security and to prevent unjust decisions against *bona fide* individuals.[85] Accordingly, border management law requires border control authorities to set up mechanisms to ensure that inaccurate or outdated information stored in a database is erased or updated within a specific period of time, and that the changes are communicated to those (authorities) concerned.[86]

6. *Accuracy for biometric data.* The border control technology complies with minimum data quality standards for biometric data.

   Border management law adopts a (partially) different approach compared to the *lex generalis* on biometric data. Whereas under the *lex generalis* the processing of biometric data is in principle prohibited, it is conversely the core of the functioning of EU large-scale IT systems and portrayed as a more secure, efficient and reliable solution for identification and verification of the identity of individuals.[87] However, for reliable identification and verification of identities, the accuracy of biometric data is of pivotal importance. For this reason, border management law expressly sets standards for the accuracy of biometric data that border control technologies must comply with.[88]

7. *Storage limitation.*

   7.1. The border control technology ensures that data are automatically deleted once the retention period elapses.

   Border management law expressly defines the data retention period for the information stored in EU large-scale databases and of the personal data processed by Frontex. As a further safeguard for the data subjects, it requires that, once the data retention period elapses, data are automatically deleted.[89]

   7.2. The border control technology ensures that log data are deleted once the retention period elapses.

   Border management law specifies the retention period for logs in relation to both EU large-scale databases and their interoperability. However, since logs are kept for accountability purposes (see *infra*), their deletion is not automatic.[90]

8. *Data security (availability, integrity & confidentiality).* The organisation adopts technical and organisational measures to ensure the security of the data processed by the border control technology.

   Border management law expressly introduces certain technical and organisational measures that that need to be complied with to ensure, to the greatest extent possible, the security and availability of EU large-scale databases. Such organisational measures include the establishment of a security plan, a business continuity plan and a disaster recovery plan, as well as fall-back procedures.[91] The technical measures include the encryption of the communication infrastructure connecting national interfaces and central systems, and measures ensuring the technical compatibility between national interfaces and central systems for the transmission of data.[92]

9. *Accountability.* The border control authority has accountability measures in place.

   Border management law provides for a series of accountability measures that include:
   - maintenance of logs/records of processing activities (which are also made available to supervisory authorities);[93]
   - staff training on data protection and rules and procedures of processing;[94]
   - self-monitoring of the national and EU authorities dealing with EU large-scale databases;[95]

- requirements that that persons working with EU-large scale databases are bound by professional secrecy or equivalent;[96]
- requirements as to what documentation (e.g. records of data subjects' requests, inventories of technical copies of databases, reports of security incidents)[97] is made available to supervisory authorities.

10. *Data subjects' rights.* Data subjects are granted the possibility to exercise their rights. Data subjects' rights have been developed with the aim of mitigating the power imbalances between data controllers and data subjects, to enhance the control of the latter over their personal information.[98] In law enforcement and security-related contexts, they are more limited in scope but still need to be granted.[99] Similarly, border management law poses some limitations, but still ensures that data subjects enjoy the rights to:
    - information;[100]
    - access (also indirect via a DPA);[101]
    - rectification;[102]
    - erasure;[103]
    - restriction of processing (for EES, ETIAS, ECRIS-TCN, MID);
    - to a certain extent, not to be subject to a decision based solely on automated processing that significantly affects them.[104]

    Border control authorities need to keep track of data subjects' requests, reply to them within the deadlines specified in the legal framework applicable to them and, in the event that they are unable to comply with the request, inform data subjects of the reasons for refusal and of their right to lodge a complaint with a DPA. Together with eu-LISA, they are liable for damages suffered by individuals resulting from unlawful data processing.[105]

11. *Data transfers.* Transfers to third countries and/or international organisations of data collected by the border control technology is either not allowed or restricted to very specific cases.
    Border management law adopts a special approach towards data transfer compared to the *lex generalis*. Data transfers to third countries are forbidden or limited to very specific cases. This is due to the fact that the sharing of personal data with third countries could be particularly dangerous for those seeking international protection.[106] Restrictions are also in place regarding transfers to international organisations and private entities.[107]

12. *Accessibility of personal data.*
    12.1. Only specific staff members of pre-defined national competent authorities have access to data processed by the border control technology.
    12.2. Only specific staff members of pre-defined EU agencies have access to data processed by the border control technology insofar as it is necessary for fulfilling their mandate or performing their tasks.
    Preventing unlawful access in the context of border management is a pressing issue considering the possibilities of function creep brought about by the inter-

operability of EU large-scale databases.¹⁰⁸ This is why border management law ensures, on the one hand, that only specific staff members of pre-defined national competent authorities have access to data processed by the border control technology,¹⁰⁹ and, on the other, that only specific staff members of pre-defined EU agencies have access to data processed by the border control technology insofar as it is necessary to fulfil their mandate or perform their tasks.¹¹⁰

7.5.2.2 Privacy and ethics requirements

Border management law sets out provisions neither on ethics nor the protection of privacy or private life are scarce.

It should be noted that privacy and ethics requirements are inferred from the broader requirement to ensure, in the course of border management activities, the protection of fundamental rights. As mentioned above, ethics (and privacy) requirements still remain legal requirements. Yet, ethics requirements have been defined in this way because compliance with them might be requested by ethics committees or similar expert bodies.

Privacy Requirements

1. *Respect of one's private life*. The border control technology ensures that the processing of personal data respects one's private life.
   Border management law requires that the processing of personal data respects one's private life.¹¹¹
2. *Respect of (body) integrity*. The border control technology ensures that the processing of personal data respects the (body) integrity of individuals.
   Border management law requires that processing of personal data respects the (body) integrity of individuals.¹¹²
3. *Privacy by design*. Privacy considerations have been embedded in the border control technology for its entire lifecycle.
   Border management law requires that data privacy considerations are embedded in the border control technology for its entire lifecycle.¹¹³ This requirement derives from the need for eu-LISA to follow the principles of privacy by design and by default throughout the entire lifecycle of the development of the EES.
4. *Privacy by default*. The default settings of the border control technology are the most privacy-friendly possible.
   Border management law requires that the default settings of the border control technology are the most privacy-friendly possible.¹¹⁴ This requirement derives from the need for eu-LISA to follow the principles of privacy by design and by default throughout the entire lifecycle of the development of the EES.

Ethics requirements

1. *Informed consent*.
   1.1. The public is informed about the existence of the border crossing point.¹¹⁵
   1.2. The public is informed of the temporary reintroduction of border controls.¹¹⁶

2. *Freedom of choice.*
   2.1. Persons may opt to not use a border control technology (e.g. e-gate).[117]
   2.2. Persons who opt to not use a border control technology (e.g. e-gate) are not discriminated against for their choice.[118]
3. *Dual-use.*
   Border management law sets restrictions on dual-use border control technologies (e.g. limitations to their export, transit and brokering).[119]
4. *Fairness.*
   The use of the border control technology is fair towards third-country nationals. This requirement derives from the need of EU policies to be fair towards third-country nationals.[120]
5. *Human dignity.*
   5.1. The use of the border control technology does not result in inhuman or degrading treatment. This requirement derives from the need for border control to not result in inhuman or degrading treatment.[121]
   5.2. Fingerprinting is in accordance with safeguards in the CFR.[122]
6. *Non-discrimination and bias.*
   The processing of personal data shall not result in discrimination against persons on any grounds.[123]
7. *Rights of elderly and people with disabilities.*
   Border control technologies are designed to be used by all persons, except for children under 12 years of age.[124]
8. *Rights of children.*
   8.1. Children under a certain age are exempted from providing fingerprints.[125]
   8.2. Border control alerts regarding children are admissible only in restricted cases, and with the aim of safeguarding the best interests of the child.[126]
   8.3. Alerts concerning children are deleted when the child reaches the age of majority.[127]
   8.4. Queries in the CIR against minors of 12 years of age are forbidden unless in the best interests of the child.[128]
9. *Vulnerable persons.*
   9.1. Alerts concerning vulnerable persons are admissible only in restricted cases.[129]
   9.2. Alerts concerning vulnerable persons are deleted in certain circumstances.[130]
   9.3. Border guards have received specialised training for detecting and dealing with situations involving vulnerable persons.[131]
10. *Non-refoulement and right to asylum.*
    10.1. Regardless of the use of a border control technology, individuals are not subject to refoulement and have the possibility to request asylum.[132]
    10.2. Particular attention is to be paid to the rights of people in need of international protection.[133]

Endnotes

1. Berry Tholen, "The Changing Border: Developments and Risks in Border Control Management of Western Countries," *International Review of Administrative Sciences* 76, no. 2 (2010): 259–78, https://doi.org/10.1177/0020852309365673; Evelien Brouwer, "Large-Scale Databases and Interoperability in Migration and Border Policies: The Non-Discriminatory Approach of Data Protection," *European Public Law* 26, no. 1 (2020): 71–92.
2. Nadav Morag, "Border Management in Europe: Is the Paradigm Evolving?," *Homeland Security Affairs* 16, no. 1 (2020). Recital 1 Regulation (EU) 2019/1896 of the European Parliament and of the Council of 13 November 2019 on the European Border and Coast Guard and repealing Regulations (EU) No 1052/2013 and (EU) 2016/1624, OJ L 295, 14.11.2019, 1–131 (Frontex Regulation). See also Recital 6 Regulation (EU) 2016/399 of the European Parliament and of the Council of 9 March 2016 on a Union Code on the rules governing the movement of persons across borders (Schengen Borders Code), OJ L 77, 23.3.2016, p. 1–52.
3. Gloria González Fuster and Serge Gutwirth, "When 'Digital Borders' Meet 'Surveilled Geographical Borders': Why the Future of EU Border Management Is a Problem", in *A Threat against Europe. Security, Migration and Integration*, eds. J. Peter Burgess and Serge Gutwirth (Brussels: VUBPress, 2011), 171–90.
4. Tholen, "The Changing Border: Developments and Risks in Border Control Management of Western Countries."
5. Gloria González Fuster, Paul De Hert, and Serge Gutwirth, "Privacy and Data Protection in the EU Security Continuum," *INEX Policy Brief* 12 (2011).
6. González Fuster and Gutwirth, "When 'Digital Borders' Meet 'Surveilled Geographical Borders': Why the Future of EU Border Management Is a Problem."
7. Petra Molnar, EDRi, and the Refugee Law Lab, "Technological Testing Grounds – Migration Management Experiments and Reflections from the Ground Up," 2020.
8. Tholen, "The Changing Border: Developments and Risks in Border Control Management of Western Countries."
9. Diego Naranjo and Petra Molnar, "The Privatization of Migration Control," 2020.
10. Sergio Carrera, Elspeth Guild, and Nicholas Hernanz, "The Triangular Relationship between Fundamental Rights, Democracy and the Rule of Law in the EU Towards an EU Copenhagen Mechanism", CEPS Paperbacks, 2013.
11. Although the benchmark for the integrated impact assessment is quadripartite, the legal requirements were grouped into the three categories of data protection, privacy and ethics because border management law does not contain provisions enshrining social acceptance.
12. Zaiotti refers to different 'cultures of border control' defined as "relatively stable constellation[s] of background assumptions and corresponding practices shared by a border control community in a given period and geographical location". Ruben Zaiotti, *Cultures of Border Control: Schengen and the Evolution of European Frontiers* (Chicago: University of Chicago Press, 2011).
13. Tendayi Achiume, "Report of the Special Rapporteur on Contemporary Forms of Racism, Racial Discrimination, Xenophobia and Related Intolerance," 2020.
14. Achiume.
15. European Court of Auditors, "Special Report EU Information Systems Supporting Border Control-a Strong Tool, but More Focus Needed on Timely and Complete Data," 2019.
16. The EES, ETIAS and ECRIS-TCN are foreseen to be established by 2023. Diana Dimitrova and Teresa Quintel, "Technological Experimentation Without Adequate Safeguards? Interoperable EU Databases and Access to the Multiple Identity Detector by SIRENE Bureaux," *Data Protection and Privacy, Volume 13, Data Protection and Artificial Intelligence*, eds.,

17. Dara Hallinan, Ronald Leenes, and Paul De Hert (Oxford: Hart Publishing, 2021). See Glossary for further information.
17. For an overview of the main objectives of each EU large-scale database: European Union Agency for Fundamental Rights, *Under Watchful Eyes: Biometrics, EU IT Systems and Fundamental Rights* (Luxembourg: Publications Office of the European Union, 2018), https://doi.org/10.2811/29.
18. Teresa Quintel, "Connecting Personal Data of Third Country Nationals: Interoperability of EU Databases in the Light of the CJEU's Case Law on Data Retention," *University of Luxembourg Law Working Paper* 2 (2018); Simone Casiraghi and Alessandra Calvi, "Biometric Data in the EU (Reformed) Data Protection Framework and Border Management," in *Personal Data Protection and Legal Developments in the European Union*, ed. Maria Tzanou (Hershey: IGI-Global, 2020), 202–23, https://doi.org/10.4018/978-1-5225-9489-5.ch010.
19. European Union Agency for Fundamental Rights, *Under Watchful Eyes: Biometrics, EU IT Systems and Fundamental Rights*.
20. I.e. the Interpol Stolen and Lost Travel Document database (SLTD database) and the Interpol Travel Documents Associated with Notices database (TDAWN database).
21. Katrien Luyten and Sofija Voronova, "Interoperability between EU Border and Security Information Systems," 2019.
22. European Union Agency for Fundamental Rights, *Under Watchful Eyes: Biometrics, EU IT Systems and Fundamental Rights*.
23. González Fuster, De Hert, and Gutwirth, "Privacy and Data Protection in the EU Security Continuum."
24. Brouwer, "Large-Scale Databases and Interoperability in Migration and Border Policies: The Non-Discriminatory Approach of Data Protection."
25. Rocco Bellanova and Georgios Glouftsios, "Controlling the Schengen Information System (SIS II): The Infrastructural Politics of Fragility and Maintenance," *Geopolitics* 24, no. 2 (2020): 1–25, https://doi.org/10.1080/14650045.2020.1830765.
26. Evelien Brouwer, "Interoperability of Databases and Interstate Trust: A Perilous Combination for Fundamental Rights," Verfassungsblog.de, 2019.
27. Paul De Hert and Serge Gutwirth, "Interoperability of Police Databases within the EU: An Accountable Political Choice?," *International Review of Law, Computers & Technology* 20, no. 1–2 (2006): 21–35, https://doi.org/10.1080/13600860600818227.
28. EDPS Opinion 4/2018 on the Proposals for two Regulations establishing a framework for interoperability between EU large-scale information systems, Brussels, 16 April 2018.
29. Tim Dekkers, "Technology Driven Crimmigration? Function Creep and Mission Creep in Dutch Migration Control," *Journal of Ethnic and Migration Studies* 46, no. 9 (2020): 1849–64, https://doi.org/10.1080/1369183X.2019.1674134.
30. Violeta Moreno-Lax and Martin Lemberg-Pedersen, "Border-Induced Displacement: The Ethical and Legal Implications of Distance-Creation through Externalization," *QIL, Zoom-In* 56 (2019): 5–33.
31. Bill Frelick, Ian M. Kysel, and Jennifer Podkul, "The Impact of Externalization of Migration Controls on the Rights of Asylum Seekers and Other Migrants," *Journal on Migration and Human Security* 4, no. 4 (2016): 190–220.
32. Achiume, "Report of the Special Rapporteur on Contemporary Forms of Racism, Racial Discrimination, Xenophobia and Related Intolerance."
33. Rocco Bellanova and Denis Duez, "The Making (Sense) of EUROSUR: How to Control the Sea Borders?," in *EU Borders and Shifting Internal Security: Technology, Externalization and Accountability*, ed. Raphael Bossong and Helena Carrapico (Heidelberg: Springer, 2016), 23–44.
34. European Union Agency For Fundamental Rights, *How the Eurosur Regulation Affects Fundamental Rights* (Luxembourg: Publications Office of the European Union, 2018).

35. Molnar, EDRi, and the Refugee Law Lab, "Technological Testing Grounds – Migration Management Experiments and Reflections from the Ground Up."
36. European Union Agency for Fundamental Rights, *Preventing Unlawful Profiling Today and in the Future: A Guide* (Luxembourg: Publications Office of the European Union, 2018), https://doi.org/10.2811/801635.
37. Gloria González Fuster, "Artificial Intelligence and Law Enforcement" (Brussels, 2020).
38. Fondazione Giacomo Brodolini, "Fundamental Rights Review of EU Data Collection Instruments and Programmes," 2019; González Fuster, "Artificial Intelligence and Law Enforcement."
39. European Union Agency for Fundamental Rights, *Preventing Unlawful Profiling Today and in the Future: A Guide*.
40. European Union Agency for Fundamental Rights.
41. Joy Buolamwini and Timnit Gebru, 'Gender Shades: Intersectional Accuracy Disparities in Commercial Gender Classification', in Proceedings of Machine Learning Research (Conference on Conference on Fairness, Accountability, and Transparency 2018), 2018, 1–15.
42. Molnar, EDRi, and the Refugee Law Lab, "Technological Testing Grounds – Migration Management Experiments and Reflections from the Ground Up."
43. Tholen, "The Changing Border: Developments and Risks in Border Control Management of Western Countries."
44. Zaiotti, *Cultures of Border Control: Schengen and the Evolution of European Frontiers*.
45. Zaiotti.
46. Iain McLean and Alistair McMillan, "Westphalian State System," in *The Concise Oxford Dictionary of Politics* (Oxford University Press, January 2009), https://doi.org/10.1093/acref/9780199207800.001.0001.
47. Mariano Cesar Bartolomé, "The Modern State Facing a Challenging International Security Scenario of Postwestfalian Characteristics," *Defense and Security Studies* 5, no. 5 (2008): 10–15.
48. Archie Simpson, "Nations and States," in *Issues In International Relations*, ed. Trevor C. Salmon, Mark F. Imber, and Trudy Fraser, 2nd ed. (London and New York: Routledge, 2008), 1–258, https://doi.org/10.4324/9780203926598.
49. Nathalie Brack, Ramona Coman, and Amandine Crespy, "Sovereignty Conflicts in the European Union," *Les Cahiers Du Cevipol* 4, no. 4 (2019): 3–30.
50. Saara Koikkalainen, "Free Movement in Europe: Past and Present," 2011.
51. The pillars were the European Communities (EC) pillar, aimed at implementing the single market; the Common Foreign and Security Policy (CFSP) pillar, aimed at defining and implementing a common foreign and security policy; and the Justice and Home Affairs (JHA) pillar, aimed at developing a common action in areas such as the controlling external borders and illegal migration in order ensure a high level of safety for citizens within the JHA. The main difference between the three pillars regarded the decision-making process (for the first pillar, the community method, characterised by the centrality of the role of European Institutions in the decision-making; for the second and third pillar, the intergovernmental method, requiring the consensus of governments of the single Member States and envisaging a limited role for European Institutions). Ina Sokolska, "The Maastricht and Amsterdam Treaties," 2021; General Secretariat of the Council of the European Union, *The Pillars of Europe – The Legacy of the Maastricht Treaty after 25 Years* (Brussels, 2018).
52. Youri Devuyst, "The European Union's Institutional Balance after the Treaty of Lisbon: Community Method and Democratic Deficit Reassessed," *Georgetown Journal of International Law* 2, no. 39 (2008): 247–326. General Secretariat of the Council of the European Union, *The Pillars of Europe – The Legacy of the Maastricht Treaty after 25 Years*.
53. Hilf Meinhard, "Acquis Communautaire," in *Max Planck Encyclopedia of Public International Law* (Oxford University Press, 2009), https://doi.org/10.1093/law:epil/9780199231690/e1717; Koikkalainen, "Free Movement in Europe: Past and Present."

54. Devuyst, "The European Union's Institutional Balance after the Treaty of Lisbon: Community Method and Democratic Deficit Reassessed."
55. Communication from the Commission to the European Parliament and the Council 'Stronger and Smarter Information Systems for Borders and Security' (COM/2016/0205 final)
56. Pinja Lehtonen and Pami Aalto, "Smart and Secure Borders through Automated Border Control Systems in the EU? The Views of Political Stakeholders in the Member States," *European Security* 26, no. 2 (2017): 207–25, https://doi.org/10.1080/09662839.2016.1276057.
57. Zaiotti, *Cultures of Border Control: Schengen and the Evolution of European Frontiers*.
58. Article 22 SBC. It is only exceptionally, and as *extrema ratio*, when there is a serious threat to public policy or internal security in a Member State, that a Member State may reintroduce border control at all or specific parts of its internal borders for a limited period of up to 30 days or for the foreseeable duration of the serious threat if its duration exceeds 30 days (Article 25 SBC).
59. Zaiotti.
60. Mircea Brie and Ioan Horga, "The European Union External Border: An Epistemological Approach," *Romanian Review on Political Geography*, no. 1 (2009): 15–31.
61. Brie and Horga.
62. See Annex 4 in this Volume.
63. Morag, "Border Management in Europe: Is the Paradigm Evolving?"
64. Article 5 Regulation (EU) 2019/1896 of the European Parliament and of the Council of 13 November 2019 on the European Border and Coast Guard and repealing Regulations (EU) No 1052/2013 and (EU) 2016/1624 (hereafter, Frontex Regulation).
65. Regulation (EU) 2018/1726 of the European Parliament and of the Council of 14 November 2018 on the European Union Agency for the Operational Management of Large-Scale IT Systems in the Area of Freedom, Security and Justice (eu-LISA), and amending Regulation (EC) No 1987/2006 and Council Decision 2007/533/JHA and repealing Regulation (EU) No 1077/2011.
66. Article 62 Regulation (EU) 2018/1725 of the European Parliament and of the Council of 23 October 2018 on the protection of natural persons with regard to the processing of personal data by the Union institutions, bodies, offices and agencies and on the free movement of such data, and repealing Regulation (EC) No 45/2001 and Decision No 1247/2002/EC.
67. Regulation (EU) No 439/2010 of the European Parliament and of the Council of 19 May 2010 establishing a European Asylum Support Office.
68. Brouwer, "Large-Scale Databases and Interoperability in Migration and Border Policies: The Non-Discriminatory Approach of Data Protection."
69. Frank Mc Namara, "Externalised and Privatised Procedures of EU Migration Control and Border Management – A Study of EU Member State Control and Legal Responsibility" (European University Institute, 2017).
70. Naranjo and Molnar, "The Privatization of Migration Control."
71. Naranjo and Molnar.
72. Legislative Affairs Unit of the European Parliament (LEGI), *Handbook on the Ordinary Legislative Procedure – A Guide to How the European Parliament Co-Legislates*, 2020.
73. Marc Bühlmann and Hanspeter Kriesi, "Models for Democracy," in *Democracy in the Age of Globalization and Mediatization* (London: Palgrave Macmillan UK, 2013), 44–68, https://doi.org/10.1057/9781137299871_3.
74. Devuyst, "The European Union's Institutional Balance after the Treaty of Lisbon: Community Method and Democratic Deficit Reassessed."
75. Thomas Christiansen and Mathias Dobbels, "Non-Legislative Rule Making after the Lisbon Treaty: Implementing the New System of Comitology and Delegated Acts," *European Law Journal* 19, no. 1 (2013): 42–56, https://doi.org/10.1111/eulj.12012; Molnar, EDRi, and the Refugee Law Lab, "Technological Testing Grounds – Migration Management Experiments and Reflections from the Ground Up."

76. Casiraghi and Calvi, "Biometric Data in the EU (Reformed) Data Protection Framework and Border Management."
77. For example, Article 40 Interoperability Regulation (EU) 2019/817 of (hereafter, Interoperability Regulation 817) and Interoperability Regulation (EU) 2019/818 (hereafter, Interoperability Regulation 818) clarifies that national authorities that are controllers, on the one hand, for the EES, VIS and SIS and, on the other hand, for the Eurodac, SIS and ECRIS-TCN respectively shall be considered controllers in relation to the biometric templates that they enter into the Shared BMS; similarly, for the data *ex* Article 18 Interoperability Regulations that they enter into the CIR. National authorities adding or modifying the data in the identity confirmation file are controllers for the processing of the personal data in the MID. Article 41 Interoperability Regulations specifies that eu-LISA is data processor for the Shared BMS, the CIR and the MID. Article 57 Regulation (EU) 2018/1240 (hereafter, ETIAS Regulation) establishes that: Frontex is considered the data controller in relation to the processing of personal data in the ETIAS Central System; the ETIAS National Unit is considered the data controller in relation to the processing of personal data in the ETIAS Central System by a Member State; eu-LISA is considered the data controller in relation to information security management of the ETIAS Central System but the data processor in relation to the processing of personal data in the ETIAS Information System.
78. Brendan Van Alsenoy, "Liability under EU Data Protection Law: From Directive 95/46 to the General Data Protection Regulation," *JIPITEC* 7, no. 3 (2017).
79. For example, Article 8 SBC establishes against which databases individuals must be controlled during border checks. Article 47 Regulation (EU) 2018/1861 (hereafter, SIS Regulation 1861) requires the consent of the person whose identity has been misused to enter and process in the SIS certain data. Similarly, Article 54 ETIAS Regulation admits that an individual may consent to have their application files stored after the expiry of ETIAS travel authorisation for the purpose of facilitating a new application.
80. Lists of the purposes for which personal data may be processed by a border control technology are contained for instance in: Articles 1, 24, 25, 41, 47, 49 SIS Regulation 1861; Articles 1, 26, 32, 34, 36, 38, 40, 56, 64 Regulation (EU) 2018/1862 (hereafter, SIS Regulation 1862); Article 2 Regulation (EC) No 767/2008 (hereafter, VIS Regulation); Article 1 Regulation (EU) No 603/2013 (hereafter, Eurodac Regulation); Article 1 Regulation (EU) 2017/2226 (hereafter, EES Regulation); Article 4 ETIAS Regulation; Article 2 Regulation (EU) 2019/816 (hereafter, ECRIS-TCN Regulation); Articles 2, 6, 12, 17, 25 Interoperability Regulations 817 and 818; Articles 18 and 87 Frontex Regulation; Article 1 Directive (EU) 2016/681 (hereafter, PNR Directive); Article 6 Council Directive 2004/82/EC (hereafter, API Directive). It must be noted that EU laws and policies related to EU large-scale databases and interoperability have been facing criticism for their clash with certain data protection principles, including purpose limitation. It is uncertain whether such extensive list of purposes will survive the scrutiny of the CJEU in the future.
81. With some differences as to the processing for persons enjoying the right of free movement and third-country nationals, as specified in Article 8(2) and 8(3) SBC.
82. Within Eurosur, processing of personal data other than ship and aircraft identification number is exceptional (Article 89 Frontex Regulation).
83. These categories of personal data are specified in Article 20 SIS Regulations 1861 and 1862, Article 5 VIS Regulation, Article 11 Eurodac Regulation, Articles 17, 18, 19, 20 EES Regulation, Article 17 ETIAS Regulation, Article 5 ECRIS-TCN. Similarly, only certain categories of personal data can be processed/stored in the ESP, Shared BMS, CIR, MID, namely: alphanumeric or biometric data for queries with the ESP (Article 9 Interoperability Regulations 817 and 818), biometric templates for the shared BMS (Article 13 Interoperability Regulations 817 and 818), personal data as from Article 5 VIS Regulation, Article 7 EES Regulation, Article 6 ETIAS Re-

gulation, Article 5 ECRIS-TCN Regulation for the CIR; confirmation files for the MID (Article 25 Interoperability Regulations 817 and 818). Note also that the definition of biometric data in the GDPR, the LED and the EUDPR differs from those contained in border management law. The latter is more restricted, as biometric data encompasses only fingerprints, palmprints, facial images and DNA profiles and not, for example, behavioural characteristics.

84. Annex I PNR Directive and Article 3 API Directive.
85. Brouwer, "Interoperability of Databases and Interstate Trust: A Perilous Combination for Fundamental Rights."
86. See, for example, Article 44 SIS Regulation 1861 and Article 59 SIS Regulation 1862, Articles 24 and 38 VIS Regulation, Article 27 Eurodac Regulation, Article 35 EES Regulation, Article 55 ETIAS Regulation, Article 9 ECRIS-TCN Regulation, Articles 32 and 33 Interoperability Regulations 817 and 818 for the CIR and Article 48 Interoperability Regulations 817 and 818 for the MID.
87. Casiraghi and Calvi, "Biometric Data in the EU (Reformed) Data Protection Framework and Border Management."
88. For instance, border management law requires that: only biometric data of sufficient quality enter the EU large-scale databases (Article 32 SIS Regulation 1861 and Article 42 SIS Regulation 1862, Article 25 Eurodac Regulation); the fingerprint of a third-country national is of sufficient quality when used for automated biometric matching (Article 17 EES Regulation); the facial image of a third-country national is of sufficient quality when used for automated biometric matching (Article 15 EES Regulation); only biometric templates complying with minimum data quality standards are entered in the BMS (Article 13 Interoperability Regulations 817 and 818); performance requirements in terms of the False Positive Identification Rate, False Negative Identification Rate and Failure To Enrol Rate as set in Commission Implementing Acts are complied with (Article 36 EES Regulation).
89. See, for example, Articles 39, 40, 49 SIS Regulation 1861 and Article 53, 54, 55, 64 SIS Regulation 1862, Articles 23 and 25 VIS Regulation, Articles 16 and 18 Eurodac Regulation, Article 34 EES Regulation, Article 54 ETIAS Regulation, Article 8 ECRIS-TCN Regulation, Article 15 Interoperability Regulations 817 and 818 for the Shared BMS, Article 23 Interoperability Regulations 817 and 818 for the CIR, Article 91 Frontex Regulation.
90. See, for example, Article 12 SIS Regulations 1861 and 1862, Article 34 VIS Regulation, Article 28 Eurodac Regulation, Article 46 EES Regulation, Article 69 ETIAS Regulation, Article 31 ECRIS-TCN Regulation, Article 10 Interoperability Regulations 817 and 818 for the ESP, Article 16 Interoperability Regulations 817 and 818 for the Shared BMS, Article 34 Interoperability Regulations 817 and 818 for the CIR, Article 36 Interoperability Regulations 817 and 818 for the MID.
91. See, for example, Article 10 and 16 SIS Regulations 1861 and 1862, Article 32 VIS Regulation, Article 34 Eurodac Regulation, Article 43 EES Regulation, Articles 21, 46, 48 and 59 ETIAS Regulation, Article 19 ECRIS-TCN, Article 11 Interoperability Regulations 817 and 818.
92. See, for example, Articles 4, 9 and 10 SIS Regulations 1861 and 1862, 1.10.3. SIRENE Manual, Article 32 VIS Regulation, Article 3 and 34 Eurodac Regulation, Article 7 and 43 EES Regulation, Article 6 and 59 ETIAS Regulation, Article 19 ECRIS-TCN Regulation, Articles 32 and 33 Interoperability Regulations 817 and 818 for the CIR, Article 42 Interoperability Regulations 817 and 818 for the MID.
93. See Article 12 SIS Regulations 1861 and 1862, Article 34 VIS Regulation, Article 28 Eurodac Regulation, Article 46 EES Regulation, Articles 69 and 70 ETIAS Regulation, Article 31 ECRIS-TCN Regulation; Article 10 Interoperability Regulations 817 and 818 for the ESP, Article 16 Interoperability Regulations 817 and 818 for the Shared BMS, Article 34 Interoperability Regulations 817 and 818 for the CIR, Article 36 Interoperability Regulations 817 and 818 For the MID, Article 89 Frontex Regulation.

94. See, for example, Article 14 SIS Regulations 1861 and 1862, Article 28 VIS Regulation, Recital 19 Eurodac Regulation, Article 38 EES Regulation, Articles 75, 76, 77 ETIAS Regulation, Articles 12, 13 ECRIS-TCN Regulation.
95. See, for example, Article 13 SIS Regulation 1861 and 1862, Article 35 VIS Regulation, Article 36 Eurodac Regulation, Article 47 EES Regulation, Article 61 ETIAS Regulation, Article 21 ECRIS-TCN Regulation.
96. See, for example, Article 11 SIS Regulation 1861 and 1862, Article 26 VIS Regulation, Article 4 Eurodac Regulation, Article 37 EES Regulation, Article 74 ETIAS Regulation, Article 11 ECRIS-TCN Regulation, Article 55 Interoperability Regulations 817 and 818.
97. For instance, in the event(s) of security incidents, Article 45 SIS Regulation 1861 and Article 60 SIS Regulation 1862 require Member States, Europol, Frontex to notify the Commission, eu-LISA, the competent DPA and the EDPS; and eu-LISA to notify the Commission and the EDPS in relation to central system. Article 34 Eurodac Regulation requires Member States to inform eu-LISA and eu-LISA to notify the Commission, Europol and the EDPS in relation to central system. Article 44 EES Regulation requires Member States to notify the Commission, eu-LISA, the competent DPA and the EDPS; and eu-LISA to notify the Commission and the EDPS in relation to central system. Article 60 ETIAS Regulation requires the Member States to notify the Commission, eu-LISA and the EDPS; eu-LISA to notify the Commission and the EDPS in relation to central system; Europol to notify the Commission and the EDPS. Article 43 Interoperability Regulations 817 and 818 requires Member States to notify the Commission, eu-LISA, the competent DPA and the EDPS; eu-LISA to notify the Commission and the EDPS in relation to central system of interoperability components; ETIAS Central Unit and Europol to notify the Commission, eu-LISA, the competent DPA and the EDPS.
98. European Union Agency For Fundamental Rights, European Court of Human Rights, and European Data Protection Supervisor, *Handbook on European Data Protection Law* (Luxembourg: Publications Office of the European Union, 2018), https://doi.org/10.2811/58814.
99. Plixavra Vogiatzoglou et al., "From Theory To Practice: Exercising The Right Of Access Under The Law Enforcement and PNR Directives," *JIPITEC* 11, no. 274 (2020).
100. See, for example, Article 52 SIS Regulation 1861, Article 37 VIS Regulation, Article 47 Interoperability Regulation 817 (for VIS, EES, ETIAS, shared BMS, CIR, MID); Article 29 Eurodac Regulation; Article 64 ETIAS Regulation. Note however that certain authors expressed concerns about the effectiveness of the legal framework at ensuring the exercise of the data subjects' rights, depending, *inter alia*, on its fragmented and complex nature. Diana Dimitrova, "Surveillance at the Borders: travellers and their data protection rights" in *Handbook on Data Protection and Privacy*, eds. Paul De Hert, Rosamunde van Brakel, and Gloria Gonzalez Fuster (Edward Elgar, forthcoming).
101. See, for example, Article 53 SIS Regulation 1861 and Article 67 SIS Regulation 1862, Article 38 VIS, Article 29 Eurodac Regulation, Article 52 EES Regulation, Article 64 ETIAS Regulation, Article 25 ECRIS-TCN Regulation, Article 48 and 49 Interoperability Regulations.
102. Ibid.
103. Ibid.
104. For example, data subjects have the right to request human intervention when using the border control technology (Article 15 SBC); when an automated processing leads to a hit in ETIAS system, the application shall be processed manually by the ETIAS National Unit of the Member State responsible (human in the loop) (Article 26 ETIAS Regulation); when different identities are detected, manual verification is ensured (Article 29 Interoperability Regulations 817 and 818).
105. See, for example, Article 58 SIS Regulation 1861 and 72 SIS Regulation 1862, Article 33 VIS Regulation, Article 37 Eurodac Regulation, Article 45 EES Regulation, Article 63 ETIAS Regulation, Article 20 ECRIS-TCN Regulation, Article 46 Interoperability Regulations 817 and 818.

106. European Union Agency for Fundamental Rights, *Under Watchful Eyes: Biometrics, EU IT Systems and Fundamental Rights*.
107. See, for example, Article 50 SIS Regulation 1861, Article 31 VIS Regulation, Article 35 Eurodac Regulation, Article 41 EES Regulation, Article 65 ETIAS Regulation, Article 18 ECRIS-TCN, Article 50 Interoperability Regulations 817 and 818, Article 89 Frontex Regulation.
108. European Union Agency for Fundamental Rights.
109. For the SIS, national competent authorities responsible for the identification of third-country nationals for the purposes listed in Article 34 SIS Regulation 1861; national competent authorities for the purposes listed in Art. 44 SIS Regulation 1862; national competent authorities responsible for naturalisation for examining an application of naturalisation (Article 34 SIS Regulation 1861 and Art. 44 SIS Regulation 1862); vehicle registration services, boat and aircraft registration services, firearms registration services as specified in Articles 45, 46 and 47 Regulation 1862. Links between alerts do not affect the right to access (Article 48 SIS Regulation 1861). For the VIS, duly authorised staff of the visa authorities as specified in Article 6 VIS Regulation. For the Eurodac, for law enforcement purposes, as specified in Article 6 Eurodac Regulation. For the EES, duly authorised staff of the national authorities of each Member State as specified in Article 9 EES Regulation. For the ETIAS, duly authorised staff of the ETIAS Central Unit and of the ETIAS National Units as specified in Article 9 ETIAS Regulation. For the ECRIS-TCN, only duly authorised staff have access to the data for the performance of their tasks as specified in Article 13 ECRIS-TCN Regulation. For the ESP, see Article 7 Interoperability Regulations 817 and 818. For the CIR, see Articles 18 and 20 Interoperability Regulations 817 and 818. For the MID, see Article 26 Interoperability Regulations 817 and 818. Note however that certain authors criticised the rules on the functionality of the MID, considered ambiguous, *inter alia*, in relation to the access of the SIRENE Bureaux to the links. Diana Dimitrova and Teresa Quintel, "Technological Experimentation Without Adequate Safeguards? Interoperable EU Databases and Access to the Multiple Identity Detector by SIRENE Bureaux."
110. For access by Europol to the SIS, see Article 35 Regulations 1861 and Article 48 SIS Regulation 1862; to the VIS, see Article 3 VIS Regulation; to the Eurodac, see Article 21 Eurodac Regulation; to the EES, see Article 33 EES Regulation; to the ETIAS, see Article 53 ETIAS Regulation; to the ECRIS-TCN, see Article 14 ECRIS-TCN Regulation; to the ESP, see Article 7 Interoperability Regulations 817 and 818; to the CIR, see Article 17 Interoperability Regulations 817 and 818. For access by Eurojust to the SIS, see Article 49 SIS Regulation 1862; to the ECRIS-TCN, see Article 14 ECRIS-TCN Regulation. For access by Frontex to the SIS, see Article 36 Regulations 1861 and Article 50 SIS Regulation 1862.
111. See, for example, Article 5 Interoperability Regulations 817 and 818, Article 14 ETIAS Regulation, Recital 13 Eurodac Regulation.
112. See, for example, Article 5 Interoperability Regulations 817 and 818, Article 14 ETIAS Regulation.
113. See, for example, Article 37 EES Regulation.
114. Ibid.
115. See, for example, Article 5 SBC.
116. See, for example, Article 34 SBC.
117. See, for example, Articles 8a and 8b SBC.
118. Ibid.
119. See Regulation (EC) No. 428/2009 of 5 May 2009 setting up a Community regime for the control of exports, transfer, brokering and transit of dual-use items (Dual-use Regulation).
120. See, for example, Article 67 TFEU.
121. See, for example, Article 8c SBC, Article 5 Interoperability Regulations 817 and 818, Article 14 ETIAS Regulation.
122. See, for example, Article 3 Eurodac Regulation.

123. See, for example, Article 7 SBC, Article 14 ETIAS Regulation, Article 5 Interoperability Regulations 817 and 818.
124. See, for example, Article 8c SBC.
125. See, for example, Article 17 EES Regulation, Article 9 Eurodac Regulation.
126. See, for example, Articles 32 and 55 SIS Regulation 1862.
127. Ibid.
128. See, for example, Article 20 Interoperability Regulation 818.
129. See, for example, Article 32 SIS Regulation 1862.
130. See, for example, Article 55 SIS Regulation 1862.
131. See, for example, Article 16 SBC.
132. See, for example, Article 4 SBC.
133. See, for example, Article 5 Interoperability Regulations 817 and 818.

8 A tailored method for the process of integrated impact assessment on border control technologies in the European Union and the Schengen Area

Nikolaos IOANNIDIS,* Simone CASIRAGHI,** Alessandra CALVI*** and Dariusz KLOZA****

* Vrije Universiteit Brussel. E-mail: Nikolaos.Ioannidis@vub.be.
** Vrije Universiteit Brussel. E-mail: Simone.Casiraghi@vub.be.
*** Vrije Universiteit Brussel. E-mail: Alessandra.Calvi@vub.be.
**** Vrije Universiteit Brussel. E-mail: Dariusz.Kloza@vub.be.

Introduction

The purpose of this Chapter is to provide sufficiently detailed explanations to enable the completion of the Template for reporting the integrated impact assessment process (Annex 1). The assessors consult this Chapter's instructions in conjunction with Annex 1, whose structure firmly corresponds to the structure herein.

The Template for reporting the integrated impact assessment process in Annex 1 is organised into tables and matrices. Following the 11-step method, consecutive steps are marked in brown and the ongoing steps in orange, as presented in the diagram below. The assessors are to fill in only the fields coloured in light brown or light orange. A field for any further remarks or comments, if necessary, is provided at the end of each step. The assessors fill in, in an easily understandable language, the empty rows in the tables and/or other fields assigned to each step. To the greatest extent possible, each answer is exhaustive and sufficiently motivated (described, explained, justified, etc.), as is equally the case for the criteria/explanations 'fulfilled' and 'not fulfilled'. Further rows can be added in each table, should there be a need, or, should the space be insufficient, each element can be moved to attachments. Alternatively, any of the tables and/or fields may be removed, and the same information presented in some other format if the assessors deem it appropriate. Provision of an explanation is required whether the box is ticket or not. After the receipt of the filled-in report, the sponsoring organisation, in turn, fills in the light green fields only, facilitating the final decision (of whether or not to proceed with the envisaged initiative).

The Template assumes the team of assessors is familiar with the legal framework for personal data protection and privacy in the European Union, as well as the principles of ethics and social acceptance. (References to legal provisions without any further specification pertain to the General Data Protection Regulation [GDPR].) It also assumes minimum familiarity with the process of risk appraisal and with the criteria limiting the enjoyment of human rights, in particular those of necessity and proportionality. Furthermore, it is expected that all relevant stakeholders, be they the data controller(s), the data protection officer (DPO), the pertinent EU agencies and border control authorities, among others, are involved in the entirety of the assessment process. As the assessment process concerns an as-yet-unimplemented initiative, the assessors may have to rely on estimations and, at times, incomplete information.

Overview of the method

Start

	Steps	Data Protection	Ethics	Social Acceptance	Privacy
ONGOING PHASE → ←					
	PHASE I: PREPARATION OF THE ASSESSMENT PROCESS				
	[1] Screening	[1a] Preliminary description			
		[1ba] Data protection screening	[1bb] Ethics and social acceptance screening		[1bc] Privacy screening
	[2] Scoping	[2aa] Personal data protection benchmark	[2ab] Ethics benchmark	[2ac] Social acceptance benchmark	[2ad] Privacy benchmark
		[2b] Stakeholders and their consultation techniques			
		[2c] Appraisal techniques			
		[2d] Other evaluation techniques			
→ ←	[3] Planning and preparation	Objectives ♦ criteria for acceptability of negative impacts ♦ resources ♦ procedures and timeframes of the assessment process ♦ assessors ♦ stakeholders ♦ continuity of the assessment process ♦ criteria triggering a revision			
	PHASE II: ASSESSMENT				
	[4] Systematic description of the initiative				
→ ←	[5] Appraisal of impacts	[5aa] Data protection: Necessity and proportionality of the processing operations [5ab] Data protection: Risk to the rights and freedoms of natural persons	[5b] Ethics assessment	[5c] Social acceptance assessment	[5d] Privacy impact assessment
		[5e] Legal compliance check			
	[6] Recommendations				
	PHASE III: EX-POST (EVENTUAL) STEPS				
	[7] Prior consultation with supervisory authority				
	[8] Revisiting				

The end

[A] Stakeholder involvement — Identify, define the level of involvement and involve stakeholders at different phases of the process

[B] Quality control — Check the quality of the IIA process (internally or externally)

[C] Documentation — Document the IIA process

PHASE I: PREPARATION OF THE ASSESSMENT PROCESS

Step 1: Screening (threshold analysis)

> The goal of this Step is to determine if the impact assessment process is required in the first place. Conducting the impact assessment process is necessary when one or more criteria set forth by law (for data protection and privacy) or by other principles (ethics and social acceptance) are met, or, alternatively, it is not required when a pertinent exemption is provided. This is preceded by the preliminary description of the initiative, which provides a contextual and a technical overview thereof.

Step 1a: Preliminary description
In this part, the assessors briefly expose the most critical aspects of the envisaged initiative, answering questions about the context and technical aspects thereof. The overview is quadripartite, comprising the assessment benchmark, namely: i) the right to data protection; ii) the right to privacy; iii) ethics; and iv) social acceptance. Although little information is usually available at the early stages, the preliminary description is kept short (approx. one page), while still being sufficiently detailed to allow the assessors to determine whether or not the threshold criteria are satisfied. General statements are avoided. If, in Step 1b, it is determined that the assessment process is required, this preliminary description will be expanded in Step 4.

Step 1b: Screening
Step 1ba: *Data protection*: The assessors analyse whether the envisaged data processing operations satisfy any of the threshold criteria prescribed by law. As a prerequisite, the assessors determine if personal data would be processed within the envisaged initiative. The threshold criteria are based on the concept of risk, and are either positive or negative. The negative criteria take precedence over positive ones. If any of the positive criteria are satisfied, the assessment process for the right to personal data protection will then be required by law. By contrast, if any of the negative criteria are satisfied, the data controller is exempted from conducting such an assessment process.

Step 1bb: *Ethics and social acceptance*: The assessors determine whether the envisaged initiative raises any ethical or social acceptance challenges by answering a set of questions. If *any* of them is answered affirmatively, the ethics assessment and social acceptance assessment are required. Conversely, if *all* are answered negatively, there is no need for an ethics and social acceptance assessment. The assessors proceed to this Step in order to complement the data protection element (Step 1b), when this is required.

Step 1bc: *Privacy*: The assessors determine if the envisaged initiative interferes with any of the 9 dimensions of privacy, i.e. bodily, spatial, communicational, proprietary, intellectual, decisional, associational, behavioural and informational privacy. If *at least one* type of privacy is interfered with, then a privacy impact assessment is required. Conversely, if *none* is interfered with, there is no need for a privacy impact assessment.

If no integrated impact assessment process is required or warranted, the assessors prepare a reasoned statement of no significant impact.

Step 2: Scoping

> The goal of this Step is to identify, with a reasonable degree of precision:
> - the benchmark of the integrated impact assessment, in which case, four elements are examined in particular: i) the right to data protection; ii) the right to privacy; iii) ethics; and iv) social acceptance (Step 2a)
> - the categories of stakeholders, that is, those to involve in the assessment process and how to involve them in each Step (Step 2b)
> - appraisal techniques, other than the necessity and proportionality assessment, and risk assessment, to be used in the assessment process (Step 2c)
> - other evaluation techniques that may be warranted or necessary (Step 2d).

Step 2a: Benchmark

Step 2aa: *Data protection*: The assessors first map the aspects that the envisaged data processing operations would touch upon by checking the applicable laws and regulations. The assessors list all legal (national, European, international) and regulatory instruments applicable to the initiative, including by-laws (e.g. policies, codes of conducts, technical standards) applicable within the organisation. This also constitutes the legal and regulatory framework for border management, from which compliance requirements are inferred and checked against in Step 5.

Step 2ab: *Ethics*: The assessors identify the ethical arguments that are mobilised to support or criticise the initiative in the public debate. Each set of arguments is assigned an ID that will be used in the subsequent phases of the assessment. This task requires that the assessors perform some preliminary desk research (if necessary, they can ask external researchers to provide support in this regard). The assessors fill in the relevant table in the template by ticking the arguments that apply to the initiative, with the help of the examples provided and explained in Chapter 5. The assessors may add extra arguments through the addition of extra rows, as indicated in '1.x …', '2.x …' etc.

Step 2ac: *Social acceptance*: The assessors identify three aspects: the perspective to assess social acceptance, the categories of stakeholders and the acceptance assessment techniques. Regarding the perspective of social acceptance, the assessors choose between (at least) one of the three levels indicated in Chapter 6 (i.e. socio-political, community or market perspective) and tick the chosen level. An assessment of all three perspectives is not required, yet, the focus *must not* be exclusively on the market perspective. The assessors identify a list of stakeholders that is specific for the social acceptance assessment. Stakeholders are understood in the broadest sense, and their range and the number to be involved is commensurate to the processing operations. Stakeholders are *not* assessors; the former provide input, which the latter subsequently take into account or reject. This activity can be performed in parallel with the identification of stakeholders for the 'stakeholder involvement phase' (Step 2b), which will provide the assessors with a broader list to be consulted throughout the whole impact assessment process. The sample chosen, especially for travellers, is to be as representative as possible. The assessors choose at least one technique of stakeholder involvement, without relying too heavily on questionnaires, especially if they are close-ended and require a quantitative analysis. Finally, the responses from the questionnaires can be made more robust by informing the respondents about the initiative under assessment with, for example, informational meetings or technology demonstrations.

Step 2ad: *Privacy*: The assessors identify which types of privacy will form part of the benchmark, and justify why these identified types are interfered with. To do so, they will briefly describe the interference, the circumstances and the vulnerability that is produced due to the contact of a natural person with a specific technology, using the same types of privacy that they included in the previous step. Additionally, they will determine the appraisal techniques that they deem most pertinent (usually the privacy impact assessment) and the stakeholders, who may be the same as those involved in the data processing operations.

Step 2b: Stakeholders and their consultation techniques

In this step, the assessors identify the categories of stakeholders to be consulted throughout the impact assessment process, namely internal and external stakeholders. The list is broader than the one compiled for Step 2a (social acceptance scoping). Possible techniques to involve stakeholders are provided in Annex 2 of this Volume. Critical external stakeholders in the context of border management law are EU agencies and bodies, carriers, Passenger Information Units (PIUs) and technology providers, among others.

Step 2c: Appraisal techniques

Six appraisal techniques are foreseen, corresponding to the quadripartite benchmark: (a) necessity and proportionality, and (b) risk assessment for data protection; ethics assessment for ethics; privacy impact assessment for privacy; social acceptance assessment for social acceptance; legal compliance check against data protection, privacy, ethics requirements, inferred from border management law as identified in Step 2a (the legal compliance check is expected to enhance social acceptance, too). Should these six appraisal techniques prove to render insufficient information for decision-making purposes, other appraisal techniques should be employed, as listed in Annex 3, e.g. scenario analysis (planning), technology foresight or cost–benefit analysis (CBA).

Step 2d: Other evaluation techniques

The assessors can resort to other evaluation techniques, which may be warranted or even required by law. For example, if the envisaged initiative *also* affects the natural and/or human environment, then a standalone process of environmental impact assessment (EIA) may be needed alongside the integrated impact assessment process.

In addition, for the reasons of comprehensiveness and efficiency, various types of impact assessment and other evaluation techniques can be integrated, provided the benchmark and/or appraisal techniques are coherent, not subordinate to one another, and not internally contradictory. Results of such an integrated assessment process must then be synthesised.

Step 3: Planning and Preparation

> The goal of this Step is to set the terms of reference of a given impact assessment process, constituting a written manual therefor, which may possibly be updated throughout the assessment process. For all parts of the benchmark, the assessors can devise a common approach since the resources and the timeframes of each separate assessment should align with each other.

Specific objectives of a given process: On the one hand, the substantive goal of an impact assessment process is to ensure informed decision-making by comprehensively examining the elements of the benchmark. On the other, its formal goal is to comply with the law and ethical or social norms. The impact assessment process aims to ensure both goals are achieved by aiding the decision-making process as to the deployment of the initiative; however, the assessors may clarify in greater detail the specific objectives of a given assessment process.

Acceptability criteria of negative impacts: The criteria are set and justified for each element of the benchmark and for each appraisal technique employed (cf. Step 2c). For instance, the element of data protection requires that the data controller set and justify a threshold below which a processing operation would be deemed unnecessary and/or disproportionate. Furthermore, it requires that the controller set a threshold above which a risk to a right would no longer be deemed acceptable (e.g. risk-prone, or risk-adverse). The data controller defines both the likelihood and severity scales beforehand. The same exercise can be repeated for each element of the benchmark, with respect to the nature and specificities of each. Jurisprudence in border control, relevant legislation and common practices are, among others, ideal sources for setting the acceptability criteria of negative impacts.

Resources to be committed: The assessors list and ensure the resources which they need for conducting the impact assessment process, which include time, money, workforce, knowledge, know-how, premises and infrastructure. Assessors might resort to the help of software that facilitates the impact assessment process by automating parts thereof. Lastly, the choices of locations (e.g. a venue for a workshop or for a facility tour) or setup (e.g. of a technology demonstration) further contribute to the selection of resources.

Procedures and timeframes: The assessors establish the timeframes for an impact assessment process, specifying, for example, milestones and deadlines, assigning responsibilities and specifying who is answerable to whom within the organisational structure. For example, the ethics assessment is connected to the preparation of paperwork required in order to obtain the ethical approval and/or opinion from the relevant ethics committee or competent authority of the country hosting the study. The latter applies especially if (sensitive) personal data of people are processed during the assessment.

Team of assessors, and their roles and responsibilities: The assessment process requires multiple types of expertise. The organisation responsible for the initiative chooses the assessors on the basis of transparent criteria, either internal or external (outsourced), spelling out their roles and responsibilities, and ensures their professional independence (e.g. assessors do not seek nor receive instructions; their bias is explicitly marked as such).

Stakeholders: Based on the pre-defined categories in Step 2b, the assessors identify a list of stakeholders (e.g. a minimum number of people interviewed, number of participants in the workshop, etc.), taking into account and ensuring diversity (e.g. gender balance, geographic diversity, age diversity or multidisciplinarity). For large-scale consultations, a consultation plan may be necessary. Personal data of identified stakeholders is appropriately protected. The planning includes:
- dates and timespan of the assessment (e.g. duration of interviews);
- setup (e.g. of a technology demonstration);
- questionnaire or interview design;
- number and modality of stakeholders to involve (e.g. a minimum number of people interviewed, number of participants in the workshop, etc.).

Continuity: The organisation specifies the continuity of the assessment process in the event of, for example, changes in the actors involved in the assessment process (e.g. assessors, data controller, data processors, etc.), or disruption, natural disasters, or utility failures.

Revision: The organisation specifies the criteria that would trigger the revision of the impact assessment process. For instance, with regards to the data protection element, a change in the level of risk could be enough to trigger the revision of the whole process. The level of risk depends on the technological advancements, on the users' perception of a technology, or on a landmark court decision that re-interprets a legal provision. The decision as to whether to revise the entire process or just a part of it is dependent on the degree to which the elements of the benchmark are intertwined with each other.

PHASE II: ASSESSMENT

Step 4: Systematic (detailed) description of the initiative

> The goal of this Step is, by expanding the preliminary description (cf. Step 1a), to systematically describe the envisaged initiative both contextually and technically.

A long list of factors is to be taken into consideration in relation to the right to data protection. As an illustration, contextual aspects include the nature, scope, internal and external context, and purposes of the envisaged processing operations and, when applicable, the legitimate interest pursued by the data controller. Technical aspects include diagrams of data flows and/or other visualisations, which might be appended. Such a description can also be based on the records of processing operations. Continuing the systematic description with regards to the right to privacy, the assessors identify, for example, the actors and parties involved in the initiative, the scope of the right based on the nine aforementioned types of privacy, and the level and nature of intrusiveness, among others. Lastly, a detailed description relevant to the ethics and social acceptance of the initiative may involve a description of the broader ethical and societal impact of the initiative, beyond those of the right to privacy and data protection.

The critical difference in the systematic description, compared to the preliminary one, is that it must expand the latter (cf. Step 1a), and hence needs to be much lengthier and more comprehensive. It shall be sufficiently complete, accurate and reliable so as to constitute the basis for the analysis and assessment of impacts in Step 5.

Step 5: Appraisal of Impacts

> The goal of this Step is to analyse and assess the impacts of the envisaged initiative, appraised in accordance with the pre-selected techniques. These impacts pertain to the societal concern(s) that might be touched on by the planned initiative, and to the positioning of the stakeholders, who might be external to the sponsoring organisation. Typically, the assessment consists of a detailed identification, analysis, and evaluation of the impacts.

Step 5a: Data protection

Step 5aa: *Necessity and proportionality of the processing operations:* The assessors use specific appraisal techniques pre-defined in Step 2c and base their analysis on the results of Step 4. The assessors can use any of the numerous suitable methods made available thus far, or they can employ the one proposed in Annex 1. Contrary to methods for assessing risk (e.g. international standards, such as ISO 31000:2018 or ISO 27005:2018), methods for assessing proportionality and necessity in the context of personal data protection are rather scarce.

The assessment of necessity and proportionality can occur at two levels. First, each data processing operation is assessed against personal data protection principles (Level 1). These are: lawfulness, fairness and transparency, purpose limitation, data minimisation, accuracy, storage limitation, integrity, and confidentiality, including security of processing and data protection by design and by default. Each data processing operation is assessed in a specific table, with this table needing to be replicated for each data processing operation.

Given the fact that a fundamental right is at stake and that an assessment process of the envisaged processing operations against solely personal data protection principles (Level 1) might not always be sufficiently complete, to the detriment of the level of protection and the quality of the decision-making process it is intended to advise, the assessors may decide to expand their appraisal to the entirety of human rights limitation criteria (Level 2).

As the right to personal data protection and many related fundamental rights are not absolute but rather relative ones (i.e. an interference with the right can only be justified under certain conditions), the following five limitation criteria derived from Article 52 of the CFR can be applied:

- legality (i.e. if a basis for a data processing operation is 'provided for by law' of a sufficient quality, for example, clarity, accessibility, precision, foreseeability, conformity with the rule of law);
- the respect for the essence of a right (i.e. if the interference with a fundamental right does not make it impossible to exercise a right);
- legitimacy (i.e. if a processing operation serves a given 'general interest' (cf. e.g. Article 3 Treaty on European Union (TEU)) or 'protect[s] the rights and freedoms of others');
- necessity (i.e. if a processing operation is 'necessary and [if it] genuinely meet[s]' legitimate objectives); and
- proportionality *sensu stricto* (e.g. balancing) (i.e. if the least intrusive option has been chosen).

Step 5ab: *Risk to the rights and freedoms of natural persons:* On the grounds of data protection law, risk is understood as a negative consequence arising from processing operations that might or might not occur in the future. Such a consequence, if it materialised, would give rise to physical, material or non-material damage for natural persons (largely, data subjects) and not solely for the data controllers or data processors. Risk assessment is meant to be as objective as possible; this is, however, not always achievable in practice, due to ambiguities about assignable likelihoods and possible types of damage, and the subjectivity of perceptions of risk by stakeholders.

Risk is typically assessed by combining two measurements, namely its likelihood or probability (i.e. chance of happening) and its severity (i.e. magnitude of consequences).

Risk can be assessed qualitatively, quantitatively or through a combination of both. There are aspects of personal data protection that fit into the former (i.e. risk to rights and freedoms) and the latter (e.g. data security). Quantitative risk assessment measures the probability of occurrence of a risk and combines this with its severity. Probability is expressed on a scale ranging from 0 to 1. In turn, qualitative risk assessment instead uses levels of likelihood (e.g. a quadripartite descriptive scale of negligible, low, medium, and high) to be combined with its severity. Eventually, severity of a risk indicates a magnitude of damage should a risk materialise. It can be equally expressed on a quadripartite descriptive scale. Both scales – likelihood and severity – are predefined and justified in Step 3b. A typical method for risk assessment requires, first, the identification of a risk. In the second step, the risk is analysed, for example by multiplying the likelihood (probability) of its occurrence by the severity of its consequences. In the third step, the risk is evaluated, in order to determine whether the risk and its level are acceptable, if any mitigation measure is to be recommended, and if any risk(s) should be prioritised.

Step 5b: Ethics

Analysis: The assessors analyse the recurrent arguments in the debate with specific reference to the technology under assessment, by answering the guiding questions with elaborated open answers. Along with the preliminary examples provided under the respective column, the assessors shall look into arguments:
- Appearing in newspapers, policy discourses, academic literature on the initiative (or similar initiatives), and/or
- Used by the company that produces the technology (or similar technologies), and/or
- Used by civil society organisations (e.g. activists, human rights NGOs).
- The assessors adapt each generic argument to the context of the assessment and include any relevant variations of the argument under the column 'explanation'. For every explanation, the assessors refer to the specific ID assigned in Step 2a. The assessors complete only the parts (IDs) that were ticked in Step 2a.

Assessment: The assessors determine whether the arguments identified and analysed in the analysis are sound or inconsistent. It is not necessary to complete both sub-columns under 'assessment', but at least one of them must be completed. Under the column 'assessment', the assessors might indicate:
- Whether there is any conflict between the arguments identified. For example, whether one argument contradicts another, or whether one argument is usually preferred over another (e.g. consequentialist arguments preferred to deontological or distributive justice ones). To indicate the conflicts, the assessors should use the ID numbers assigned in the previous phases.
- Whether there can be counter-arguments or fallacies to the arguments identified. The assessors use Section 5.2.3 as a guide, where for each argument possible criticisms or a list of fallacies are provided.

Step 5c: **Social acceptance**
Analysis: After having executed one or more social acceptance assessment techniques identified in Step 3, the assessors analyse the data collected during the previous phase, for example, if the chosen technique is a questionnaire, the assessors collect a number of completed questionnaires, be these in person or online. If the technique chosen is a workshop, participants are invited, the event is held, and minutes and/or are taken by the assessors during the event. If the technique is an interview or an observation, the assessors/interviewers take field notes and/or recordings of the discussion, and so on. which are reported again in the first column and ascribed an ID number. The 'type of analysis' can be qualitative or quantitative, or a mixture of the two, depending on the types of technique chosen. Answers obtained through close-ended questions (with scales or multiple choices) can be analysed quantitatively, using, for example, pie charts or percentages. Answers to open-ended questions involve qualitative analysis (discussion and critical analysis) *without* the use of digits and calculations.

The assessors find patterns and report a summary of findings in the final column. The findings include results that are exceptional and stand out, whereby the analysis does not simply reveal data that confirm the assessors' initial hypothesis. In the case of interviews and questionnaires, the assessors may find patterns in the replies to certain questions (e.g. some categories of travellers find the technology invasive, or the majority of interviewees find it convenient).

Assessment: The assessors assess the data analysed in the previous phase. Depending on the results, they come up with a list of (envisaged) positive and negative consequences stemming from the initiative, and specify which stakeholders are affected, and the extent to which the initiative affects them positively or negatively, by listing their names in the appropriate column.

Step 5d: **Privacy**
An explanatory representation of the assessment of privacy is illustrated in an 8x7 matrix, where on the vertical axis the eight types of privacy are listed (excluding informational privacy, which is equalised to data protection), and on the horizontal axis are listed the human rights limitations criteria against which these are assessed.

The assessors tick the appropriate box in the first column of the matrix (under: *Applicability* – ticking the box signifies that a certain type of privacy is assessed), and briefly describe the envisaged impact on each applicable type of privacy using factual and theoretical substantiation. Following this, and only for the applicable types of privacy under assessment, the assessors analyse each interference against human rights limitation criteria (i.e. legality, essence, necessity, proportionality, legitimacy); these criteria were elaborated in Step 5aa (cf. *supra*).

Step 5e: **Legal compliance check against border management law**
Analysis: The assessors evaluate whether or not the requirements listed in the table are applicable to the initiative under assessment; they may also include other requirements extracted from the legal framework applicable to the initiative, as identified in Step 2aa. An ID number (and sub-ID, when relevant) is assigned to each requirement. It is probable that not all requirements listed in the table (as extracted from the rules on EU large-scale databases, interoperability, Schengen Borders Code and Frontex Regulation) are applicable. Conversely, in cases where other rules are applicable (e.g. national laws), it may be necessary to complement the list with other requirements.

Assessment: Only if a requirement is applicable do the assessors evaluate the compliance of the initiative with the said requirement. The result of the assessment is binary (ticking or not ticking the box) because an initiative is either compliant or non-compliant with the requirement. Partial compliance is to be considered as non-compliance. In both situations, they motivate their assessment by specifying, *inter alia*, the legal and regulatory provisions from which the requirements were extracted. Reference to the legal provisions can be found in Chapter 7, in particular Section 7.5 Legal Requirements enshrining data protection, privacy and ethics in EU border management law.

Step 6: Recommendations

> The goal of this Step is to provide concrete, detailed measures (controls, safeguards, solutions, etc.), their addressees and their timeframes in order to minimise the negative impacts and, if possible, to maximise the positive ones. The assessors justify their distinction between 'negative' and 'positive' impacts since this distinction is contextual and subjective. The assessor takes stock of the measures already implemented. Particularly, in the process of this integrated impact assessment, recommendations for data protection are embedded in Step 5, while for the other elements of the benchmark, a separate Step is introduced (Step 6). This choice is warranted due to the level of granularity, which is formally required by law in the case of data protection.

Data protection: By recommending possible mitigating measures, the assessors address the risks, and non-necessity and disproportionality of the processing operations in order to protect individuals and to demonstrate compliance with law. Assessors might also suggest measures to maximise positive impacts. They recommend and describe mitigation measures for each negative impact (risks, disproportionate and unnecessary interferences) identified in Step 5. Each risk is mitigated by manipulating either its likelihood (probability) – by, for example, limiting the exposure to a risk – or its severity – by, again for example, preparing a response plan should the risk materialise – or both. Risks can be avoided, mitigated, transferred (to another entity, e.g. outsourcing, insurance, etc., or in delayed in time) or accepted. Residual risks are those that remain if there is no measure available to mitigate them and trigger a prior consultation with a supervisory authority (SA) (cf. Step 7). For both risk and non-necessity and disproportionality, mitigation measures can be of a regulatory (legal), technical, organisational or behavioural nature.

Ethics: The assessors provide recommendations on the basis of the critical evaluation of the ethical arguments identified, either to suggest how to identify (recurring) fallacies or to highlight some arguments that are side-tracked or overlooked in current policy and academic debates. For example, if an argument is not sound or is fallacious, what can be done to criticise it? What channels can be used to provide criticisms in the public debate and raise awareness? How can the public be informed of the possible risks? If two (or more) arguments are in contrast, is there a way to balance them? Which of the two arguments in contrast is the more convincing? Why? Are there any arguments that are side-tracked, suppressed, or marginalised? If so, why and by whom? If necessary, how can these 'hidden' arguments be brought to the attention of the public? If an argument is sound, and the initiative is beneficial, how can this be disseminated more effectively? Can similar initiatives be proposed in other contexts? How can this be translated into policy or new design ideas? If an argument is sound, and the initiative is harmful, how can the risks be mitigated? Are there alternative solutions in place that would be less harmful? How can this be translated into policy or new design ideas?

Social acceptance: Through the recommendations, the intention is not that the assessors ensure that the initiative is accepted, but rather that they suggest how to address the reasons of discomfort or resistance. If the assessors conclude, by contrast, that there are few reasons of discomfort or resistance, they might recommend some steps to develop or to deploy the initiative further. The assessors choose the scope and length of the recommendations, but below are some suggestions depending on the outcome of the assessment:
- If (some) travellers find the initiative acceptable and beneficial, how can these results be communicated? How can they be translated into policy initiatives?
- If (some) travellers find the initiative unacceptable and harmful, how can these harms be avoided? Is it possible to achieve the same results through less harmful means?
- If (some) travellers show different attitudes, how can these attitudes be reconciled to distribute harms and benefits more fairly?

Privacy: Given that in the previous Steps the assessors have already identified which types of privacy are applicable and to what extent they are interfered with, in this Step they introduce reverse mechanisms. Their objective is to compensate for the limitations to the right, depending on the scope of the assessment and the nature of interference (i.e. the level of intrusiveness). Such remedies could take the form of additional safeguards, transparency modalities, right of access and information forms, and explicit consent mechanisms, to be applied both before and after the use of the technology. When proposing the recommendations, the assessors shall ensure that the involved parties, including the users of the technology, are able to be appropriately informed (at least in high-level) about the technology under assessment, its explicability, and also the meaning and function of each privacy type. There is no standard mathematical formula for assessing the risks to the right to privacy. Among best practices, it would be appropriate for the assessors to report a misalignment of the envisaged initiative and the technology involved therein, if at least one of the privacy types is unnecessarily and/or disproportionately interfered with.

Legal compliance check against border management law: When a requirement is not met, the assessors provide recommendations to ensure that the initiative is adjusted, and compliance with the requirement is achieved. The assessors use the ID and sub-ID numbers identified in the previous Step to classify the measures to be taken. The measures recommended can be technical or organisational. For example, an organisation may set up accountability measures (e.g. self-monitoring, staff-training). If the default settings of an e-gate do not respect the right to privacy, the recommendation would be to change them; if a border control technology could not be used by visually impaired persons, the recommendation would be to modify the design of the technology to make it more inclusive. The assessors conclude this Step with an implementation plan in which the responsible person, in a separate process, lists the measures and their deadline.

Upon receipt of the report, the leadership of the organisation makes a decision as to the deployment of an envisaged initiative and under what conditions.

PHASE III: EX POST (EVENTUAL) STEPS

Step 7: Prior Consultation with a Supervisory Authority

> The goal of this Step is to seek advice from an SA in the event that an impact assessment process indicates the existence of high residual risk(s) in the absence of measures taken by the data controller to mitigate such risk. Since this legal requirement is found only in data protection legislation, it essentially concerns only the first element of the benchmark pertaining to data protection.

The process of integrated impact assessment, to the extent that it incorporates a data protection impact assessment, is observed by the domestic SA. In this case, the parts on privacy, ethics and social acceptance would not be subject to review and consultation from an SA.

The communication with the SA is mainly in written form; frequently, the SA will require specific forms (templates) to request a prior consultation; the European Data Protection Board (EDPB) maintains an up-to-date contact list of its Member SAs. Insofar as an SA considers that the envisaged processing operations could infringe the law, it may provide a written notice to the data controller within a reasonable time, depending on the complexity of the request. An SA might also use its investigative and advisory powers in order to scrutinise the impact assessment process formally and substantially.

Step 8: Revisiting

> The goal of this Step is to decide whether and when to perform the impact assessment process again, in its entirety or in part, under the condition that the envisaged initiative has been deployed.

Following the criteria defined in Step 3 (under 'Criteria triggering the revision of the assessment process'), the assessors perform a review of the impact assessment process when necessary. Regarding the case of data protection, this Step is performed when there is a change in the risk represented by the processing operations, i.e. if the nature, scope, context, or purpose of the processing operations have changed, and hence so has the level of risk. An impact assessment process then has to be conducted again, in total or in part.

Apart from the change in the level of risk due to a modification of a data processing operation, other factors triggering the revision process are the circumstances of the initiative's deployment, such as extending the accessibility of EU large-scale databases to more actors, the perception of social acceptance and ethics vis-à-vis a specific technology, and possibly the public pressure exercised.

ONGOING PHASE

Step A: Stakeholder involvement

> The goal of this ongoing Step, which runs in parallel to each phase, is to consult (typically, seek views), throughout the entire process, if practicable, of anybody who holds a stake (interest) in the initiative, regardless of whether or not they are aware of this and of whether or not the interest is directly articulated.

Stakeholders are typically identified, informed, involved (consulted) and, eventually, have their views considered. Stakeholders whose categories have been stipulated in the Scoping Step (Step 2b) are now further identified in this Step. Their involvement is continuous, and they are asked about their views on the subject matter of each Step. Information given to stakeholders is robust, accurate, inclusive and meaningful, in plain (understandable) language, and may require the preparation of specific documentation, e.g. technical briefings. Having gathered the viewpoints of the stakeholders, the assessors consider and take a stance on their views, i.e. whether they accept them or not; if the latter, the assessors provide exhaustive justification for this. Among information, consultation, and co-decision, the choice is set at consultation, yet other levels are not excluded, should assessors deem it necessary.

Data protection: The goal of the stakeholder involvement is to consult (seek views), throughout the entire process, of data subjects and/or of their representatives as to the envisaged processing operations and privacy interferences. The exact meaning of this legal requirement is not – and cannot be – delineated, due to the subjectivity of the term 'involvement' and the 'appropriateness' of involvement. These, in turn, depend on the degree of explicability of a given technology, on the number of relevant parties, and on the size of the project, among others.

Privacy: Beyond the formalities required by data protection legislation, a considerable number of stakeholders, with interdisciplinary backgrounds, participate in the public discourse surrounding the right to privacy. Stakeholders that are usually consulted include non-governmental organisations (NGOs) that incorporate the protection of fundamental and digital rights within the scope of their mission, the government, political parties, the police, and other authorities such as the border control authority or the ministry of internal affairs, to name a few.

Ethics: The assessors involve stakeholders in any of the previous Steps, if deemed necessary. In Step 1c, in the event that the threshold analysis questionnaire evokes a negative result (i.e. no ethics assessment is needed), the assessors consult stakeholders to confirm or oppose this outcome, to make the result of the screening more robust. In Step 2a, the assessors involve stakeholders (e.g. researchers or policy makers) to provide input as to the type of arguments present in the public debate, especially if the team of assessors does not possess enough knowledge or skills on the topic. In Step 5, the assessors involve stakeholders to carry out the analysis or to integrate or validate its results. Lastly, the assessors involve stakeholders to critically assess the arguments, support them in this task, or corroborate/criticise the assessment executed.

Social acceptance: The assessors may opt to involve additional stakeholders throughout the whole acceptance assessment process. In particular, stakeholders may provide their opinion on the validation of the results of the acceptance assessment. An example of this would be the involvement of experts (e.g. social scientists) to provide an alternative analysis of the data collected (Step 5).

Step B: Quality control

> The goal of this ongoing Step, which runs in parallel to each phase, is to check, internally and/or externally, throughout the entire assessment process, whether or not an impact assessment process adheres to a given standard of performance and to remedy, if necessary, any irregularities.

Quality control can be internal, external or both, and take the form of monitoring, review, audit, etc. The team of assessors might be required to be updated on the progress of the assessment process on a regular or *ad hoc* basis, or might establish a progress monitoring tool or an internal advisory board. The external quality control may be performed by an audit organisation hired by the data controller or, alternatively, by an SA, either upon request of the data controller or of its own volition (e.g. when required by law). The quality control can be structured, permanent or performed on an *ad hoc* basis; it can be formal (e.g. concerning the compliance with the procedures for an impact assessment process) or substantive (e.g. if the risks were appropriately assessed). In case of judicial claims, courts of law may review an impact assessment process, either as to its form, its substance or both.

Step C: Documentation

> The goal of this ongoing Step, which runs in parallel to each phase, is to maintain intelligible records in writing or another permanent format (analogue or digital) of all activities undertaken within a given assessment process, with due respect for legitimate secrecy.

Documentation consists of the report and the attachments listed within it, both in draft and final form. Assessors also list all the activities undertaken in a given assessment process, e.g. draft versions of the report or interactions with data subjects, SAs, etc. It is best practice to make (parts of) the present report from an impact assessment process, as well as all appendices, publicly available (e.g. on the website of the data controller), with due respect for legitimate secrecy. Once the assessment process is revisited, a new version is to also be made publicly available, with reference being made within this to any previous version(s).

Annexes

Annex 1: A template for a report from the process of integrated impact assessment on border control technologies in the European Union and the Schengen Area[1]

Nikolaos IOANNIDIS,* Simone CASIRAGHI,** Alessandra CALVI*** and Dariusz KLOZA****

Vrije Universiteit Brussel. E-mail: nikolaos.ioannidis@vub.be.
**Vrije Universiteit Brussel. E-mail: simone.casiraghi@vub.be.*
***Vrije Universiteit Brussel. E-mail: alessandra.calvi@vub.be.*
****Vrije Universiteit Brussel. E-mail: dariusz.kloza@vub.be.*

Cover page

Name of the initiative under assessment	
Name, contact details and other identifying details of:	
• border control authority deploying the initiative	
• data controller(s)	
• data processor(s), if applicable	
• person(s) in charge of the initiative	
• assessor(s)	
• data protection officer(s) (DPO), if appointed	
• chief information security officer, if appointed	

DOI: 10.46944/9789461171375.a1

• quality control body supervising the assessment process, if appointed	
• data protection authority/ies (DPA)	
• research ethics committees at public or private organisations	
• national ethics committees or councils	
• groups of *ad hoc* recruited ethics experts	
• anyone else involved, as practicable	
Version of the assessment report	
Level of confidentiality of the assessment report	☐ Public ☐ Confidential ☐ Specific *[explain]*
Date and place of compilation of the report	

[Any other details, as practicable]

Executive summary

[Summarise the most significant information concerning the outcomes of each step of the integrated impact assessment process.]

Annex 1 – Step 1: Screening (threshold analysis)

Phase I: preparation of the assessment process
Step 1: Screening (threshold analysis)
Step 1a: Preliminary description of the envisaged initiative

Overview of data protection aspects	*Contextual description*	What?	
		How much/how many?	
		Where?	
		Why?	
	Technical description	Overview of personal data and processing operations	
		Infrastructure	
		Actors	
Overview of privacy aspects			
Overview of ethical aspects			
Overview of social acceptance aspects			
[other, explain]			

Step 1ba: Personal data protection screening (threshold analysis)

Positive criteria	Legal provision	Applicable?	Explanation
Criterion 1: The envisaged processing operations are likely to result in a high risk to the rights and freedoms of natural persons (general)	35(1)	☐	
Criterion 2: Processing operations deemed highly risky			
2a. Processing operations entailing systematic and extensive evaluation of personal aspects relating to natural persons which is based on automated processing, including profiling, and on which decisions are based that produce legal effects concerning the natural person or similarly significantly affect the natural person	35(3)(a)	☐	
2b. Processing operations regarding special categories of data, or personal data relating to criminal convictions and offences on a large scale	35(3)(b)	☐	
2c. Processing operations entail a systematic monitoring of a publicly accessible area on a large scale	35(3)(c)	☐	
Criterion 3: Processing operations included in the public list of processing operations that require a data protection impact assessment compiled by the DPA(s) to which jurisdiction(s) the data controller is subject	35(4)	☐	
Criterion 3bis: Processing operations that require a DPIA as included in a code of conduct to which the data controller is subject	40	☐	
[other, cf. Step 2a: Benchmark; explain]		☐	
DECISION		☐	required
		☐	not required

Annex 1 – Step 1: Screening (threshold analysis)

Negative criteria	Legal provision	Applicable?	Explanation
Criterion 4: Processing operations included in the public list of processing operations that DO NOT require a data protection impact assessment compiled by the DPA(s) to which jurisdiction(s) the data controller is subject	35(5)	☐	
Criterion 5: Whereas the legal basis for the processing operations is the compliance with a legal obligation to which the controller is subject or the performance of a task carried out in the public interest, on the basis of EU or member state's law, and an impact assessment satisfying the conditions of DPIA under the GDPR has already been performed	35(10)	☐	
Criterion 6: Processing operations concerning personal data from patients or clients performed by an individual physician, other health care professional or lawyer	Recital 91	☐	
Criterion 6bis: Processing operations exempted from a DPIA by a code of conduct to which the data controller is subject	40	☐	
[other, cf. Step 2a: Benchmark; *explain]*		☐	
DECISION		☐	exempted
		☐	not exempted

Step 1bb: Ethics and social acceptance screening

Could the initiative result in the development and/or use of technologies and/or processing activities that:

		Applicable?	Explanation
1.	Would produce excessive costs in comparison to the advantages they bring?	☐	
2.	Would fail to ask for the users' consent in a plain understandable language, allowing space for questions, when it is needed?	☐	
3.	Could be misused (e.g. for terrorism purposes)?	☐	
4.	Would involve vulnerable individuals or groups?	☐	
5.	Would involve children and/or minors?	☐	
6.	Would increase risk of discrimination of certain groups (e.g. third-country nationals)?	☐	
7.	Would divide users into categories (e.g. low risk and high risk)?	☐	
8.	Would not be accessible for certain categories of people?	☐	
9.	Could have potential for military applications?	☐	
10.	Would increase chances of identity theft?	☐	
RESULT		☐	required
		☐	not required

Annex 1 – Step 1: Screening (threshold analysis)

Step 1bc: Privacy screening

	Applicable?	*Explanation*
Could the initiative result in the development and/or use of technologies and/or processing activities that:		
1. Would interfere with *bodily privacy*?	☐	
2. Would interfere with *spatial privacy*?	☐	
3. Would interfere with *communicational privacy*?	☐	
4. Would interfere with *proprietary privacy*?	☐	
5. Would interfere with *intellectual privacy*?	☐	
6. Would interfere with *decisional privacy*?	☐	
7. Would interfere with *associational privacy*?	☐	
8. Would interfere with *behavioural privacy*?	☐	
9. Would interfere with *informational privacy*? [overlapping]	☐	
RESULT	☐	required
	☐	not required

Comments

[Explanation]

Step 2: Scoping
Step 2a: Benchmark
Step 2aa: Personal data protection

Applicable laws and regulations		Applicable?	Explanation
lex generalis	General Data Protection Regulation (GDPR)	☐	
	National law(s) supplementing/implementing the GDPR	☐	
	National data protection laws (extra-EEA)	☐	
	National exclusion/inclusion list(s) (Art. 35(4)-(5) GDPR)	☐	
	Codes of conduct	☐	
	Certificates (Art. 42 GDPR)	☐	
	Technical standards	☐	
	Laws from extra-EU jurisdictions	☐	
	[other, general sources for personal data protection, explain]	☐	
lex specialis	Regulation 1725/2018 (EU Institutions)	☐	
	Europol Regulation	☐	
	ePrivacy Directive [as transposed in national law]	☐	
	Law Enforcement Directive (LED) [as transposed in national law]	☐	
	SIS framework	☐	
	VIS framework	☐	
	Eurodac framework	☐	
	EES framework	☐	
	ETIAS framework	☐	
	ECRIS-TCN framework	☐	
	Interoperability framework	☐	
	Eurosur framework	☐	
	API framework	☐	
	PNR framework	☐	
	[other, specific sources for personal data protection, explain]	☐	

Annex 1 – Step 2: Scoping

	Applicable laws and regulations		Applicable?	Explanation
by-laws	Data protection policies		☐	
	[other, explain]		☐	

	Scope of the assessment process	Legal provision	Applicable?	Explanation
	Personal data protection principles	Art. 5	☐	
	Legal basis for processing	Art. 6	☐	
	Data subject rights	Art. 15-22	☐	
	Obligations of data controller and processor	Art. 24-39	☐	
	Data transfers outside EU/EEA	Art. 46	☐	
	Specific processing situations	Art. 85-91	☐	
Other fundamental rights	Private and family life, home and communications	Recital 4	☐	
	Freedom of thought, conscience and religion		☐	
	Freedom of expression and information		☐	
	Freedom to conduct business		☐	
	Right to an effective remedy and to a fair trial		☐	
	Cultural, religious and linguistic diversity		☐	
[other, explain]			☐	

Step 2ab: Ethics

ID	Theory	Argument	Examples	Applicable?
1		Universality of principles and/or values	1.1 The initiative is (not) based on universal principles	☐
			1.2 The initiative is (not) based on universal values	☐
			1.x …	☐
2		Technological determinism	2.1 The initiative is presented as a panacea for long-lasting social problems	☐
			2.2 It is inevitable that the initiative will become ubiquitous in society	☐
			2.3 It is inevitable that "traditional" border checks will disappear	☐
			2.4 The initiative is the *only* way to solve problems of security and improve efficiency	☐
			2.x …	☐
3		Neutrality of technology	3.1 The initiative is (not) neutral	☐
			3.2 The initiative is (not) biased	☐
			3.x …	☐
4		Arguments from precedent	4.1 The initiative is likely to propose problems that have happened in the past	☐
			4.2 The initiative is likely to solve problems that have happened in the past	☐
			4.3 The initiative is likely to promote benefits that have happened in the past	☐
			4.x …	☐
5		Change of ethical values arguments	5.1 The initiative will change people's ethical values (such as autonomy)	☐
			5.2 The initiative will change/improve people's ethical behaviour	☐
			5.3 The initiative will change/improve people's ethical judgements	☐
			5.4 The initiative affects the autonomy of border guards' decision-making	☐
			5.x …	☐

Annex 1 – Step 2: Scoping

ID	Theory	Argument	Examples	Applicable?
6		Slippery slope	6.1 The initiative, if developed on a large scale, can give rise to uncontrollable effects	☐
			6.2 If we do not implement T now, we will suffer uncontrollable effects	☐
			6.3 The initiative bears the risk of "function creep"	☐
			6.x …	☐
7	Deontology	Principles/rights/duties before consequences	7.1 The initiative will respect principle X, regardless of the consequences	☐
			7.2 The initiative is designed respecting the principle/value X	☐
			7.3 There is a categorical prohibition (e.g. "red line") for certain uses of the initiative	☐
			7.4 The initiative (does not) respect the human right X	☐
			7.5 The initiative is not in line with the Code of conduct X	☐
			7.x …	☐
8	Consequentialism	Benefits will outweigh costs	8.1 The initiative brings about (economic) benefits that will outweigh the costs	☐
			8.2 The initiative will increase security despite an infringement of privacy	☐
			8.3 The initiative will make border crossing/control more efficient	☐
			8.4 The initiative can be misused or used for military purposes	☐
			8.x …	☐

ID	Theory	Argument	Examples	Applicable?
9	Distributive justice	(Un)equal distribution of benefits and risks	9.1 The initiative is (not) equally accessible to everyone (e.g. people in wheelchairs, third-country nationals)	☐
			9.2 Only/mostly *some* people will benefit from the initiative (e.g. *bona fide* travellers)	☐
			9.3 Some people are more prone to be considered high-risk travellers (e.g. third country nationals)	☐
			9.4 There are risks of bias or stigmatisation when using the initiative	☐
			9.5 The accuracy of the initiative is unreliable for certain categories of people	☐
			9.x …	☐

Step 2ac: Social acceptance scoping

Perspective	Applicable?	Stakeholders considered for acceptance assessment		Acceptance assessment technique	Explanation
Socio-political	☐	EU/EEA/CH citizens	☐		
		Non-EU/EEA/CH citizens, and sub-categories	☐		
		Border control authorities	☐		
		[other, explain]	☐		
Market	☐	Industrial stakeholders	☐		
		Scientific experts	☐		
		Policy makers	☐		
		[other, explain]	☐		
Community	☐	Local stakeholders	☐		

Step 2ad: Privacy

Would it affect...?		Applicable?	Explanation
Informational privacy	Bodily privacy	☐	
	Spatial privacy	☐	
	Communicational privacy	☐	
	Proprietary privacy	☐	
	Intellectual privacy	☐	
	Decisional privacy	☐	
	Associational privacy	☐	
	Behavioural privacy	☐	

Step 2b: Stakeholders and their consultation techniques

Internal stakeholders

Category of stakeholder	Involved?	Level of involvement	Stakeholder involvement techniques	Explanation
Data processor(s)	☐			
Data protection officer(s) (DPO)	☐			
Recipient(s) (Article 4(9))	☐			
Third parties (Article 4(10))	☐			
Representative(s) (Article 27)	☐			
Information security officer(s)	☐			
Legal service	☐			
Employees, trade unions, contractors, etc.	☐			
[other, specify]				

External stakeholders

	Category of stakeholder	Involved?	Level of involvement	Stakeholder involvement techniques	Explanation
Individuals whose rights and freedoms are affected by the initiative and their representatives	Data subjects, including: • Minors • Vulnerable people • [*other, specify*]	☐			
	Representative(s) of data subject(s)	☐			
	Individuals who are not data subjects	☐			
	Representative(s) of individuals who are not data subjects	☐			
Public sector stakeholders	Supervisory authority(ies) (DPA)	☐			
	Policy makers	☐			
	Local stakeholders	☐			
Private sector stakeholders	Technology providers	☐			
	Transportation companies	☐			
Experts	Research Ethics Committees, at public or private organisations	☐			
	National ethics committees or councils, at EU or Member State level	☐			
	Groups of *ad hoc* recruited ethics experts	☐			
	Scientific experts	☐			
	[*Anybody else affected, etc., specify*]				

Step 2c: Appraisal techniques

Element of the benchmark	Technique	Applicable?	Explanation
Data Protection	Necessity and proportionality assessment	☐	
Data Protection	Risk assessment	☐	
Privacy	Necessity and proportionality assessment (as per human rights)	☐	
Privacy	Risk assessment	☐	
Ethics	Ethics assessment	☐	
Social acceptance	Social acceptance assessment	☐	
Border management	Legal compliance with border management law	☐	
Supplementary	Scenario planning	☐	
Supplementary	Cost-Benefit Analysis (CBA)	☐	
Supplementary	Strengths, Weaknesses, Opportunities, Threats (SWOT)	☐	
Supplementary	[other, specify]	☐	

Step 2d: Other evaluation techniques

Technique	Applicable?	Explanation
Environmental impact assessment	☐	
Health impact assessment	☐	
Risk assessment	☐	
[other, specify]	☐	

Comments

[Explanation]

Step 3: Planning and Preparation

Specific objectives of the assessment process

Objective	Applicable?	Explanation
Protection of individuals	☐	
Compliance with the law	☐	
[other, specify]	☐	

Criteria for the acceptability of negative impacts

Objective		Applicable?	Explanation
Necessity and proportionality (Article 35(7)(b))		☐	
Human rights limitation criteria (Article 52(1) CFR)		☐	
Risk assessment (qualitative, quantitative) (risk criteria)	Likelihood scale	☐	
	Severity scale	☐	
	Point of acceptability	☐	
[other, specify]		☐	

Resources

	Value(s)	Explanation
Time (how long?)		
Money (how much?)		
Workforce (how many people?)		
Knowledge (what expertise?)		
Know-how (what experience?)		

	Value(s)	Explanation
Premises (where?)		
Infrastructure (by what means?)		
[other, specify]		

Procedures and timeframes for the assessment process

	Milestone	Deadline	Responsibility	Supervision
1	[Specify]			
2				

Assessor(s)

	Name	If external: organisation	Contact details	Expertise	Roles and responsibilities	Other information
1	[Specify]				[Leader]	
2						

Stakeholders

[Provide contact details of all stakeholders to involve in the present impact assessment process and a consultation plan, if necessary.]

Continuity of the assessment process

[How would the present assessment process be continued in the event of a disruption, reorganisation, etc. of the sponsoring organization?]

Annex 1 – Step 3: Planning and Preparation

Criteria triggering the revision of the assessment process

Criterion	Applicable?	Explanation
Change of likelihood and/or severity of a risk	☐	
[Other, specify]	☐	

Comments

[Explanation]

Ongoing Steps for Phase I

Step A: Stakeholder involvement

Internal stakeholders

Category of stakeholders	What information has been communicated to stakeholders?	What input have the stakeholders provided (e.g. opinion)?	How was their input included? Why was it rejected?
Data processor(s)			
Data protection officer(s) (DPO)			
Recipient(s) (Article 4(9))			
Third parties (Article 4(10))			
Representative(s) (Article 27)			
Information security officer(s)			
Legal service			
Employees, trade unions, contractors, etc.			

[*other, specify*]

External stakeholders

	Category of stakeholders	What information has been communicated to stakeholders?	What input have the stakeholders provided (e.g. opinion)?	How was their input included? Why was it rejected?
Individuals whose rights and freedoms are affected by the initiative and their representatives	Data subjects, including: • Minors • Vulnerable people • [*other, specify*]			
	Representative(s) of data subject(s)			
	Individuals who are not data subjects			
	Representative(s) of individuals who are not data subjects			

Annex 1 – Ongoing Steps for Phase I

Public sector stakeholders	Supervisory authority(ies) (DPA)	
	Policy makers	
	Local stakeholders	
Private sector stakeholders	Technology providers	
	Transportation companies	
Experts	Research Ethics Committees, at public or private organisations	
	National ethics committees or councils, at EU or Member States' level	
	Groups of *ad hoc* recruited ethics experts	
	Scientific experts	
	[*Anybody else affected, etc., specify*]	

Lack of stakeholder involvement in the present phase

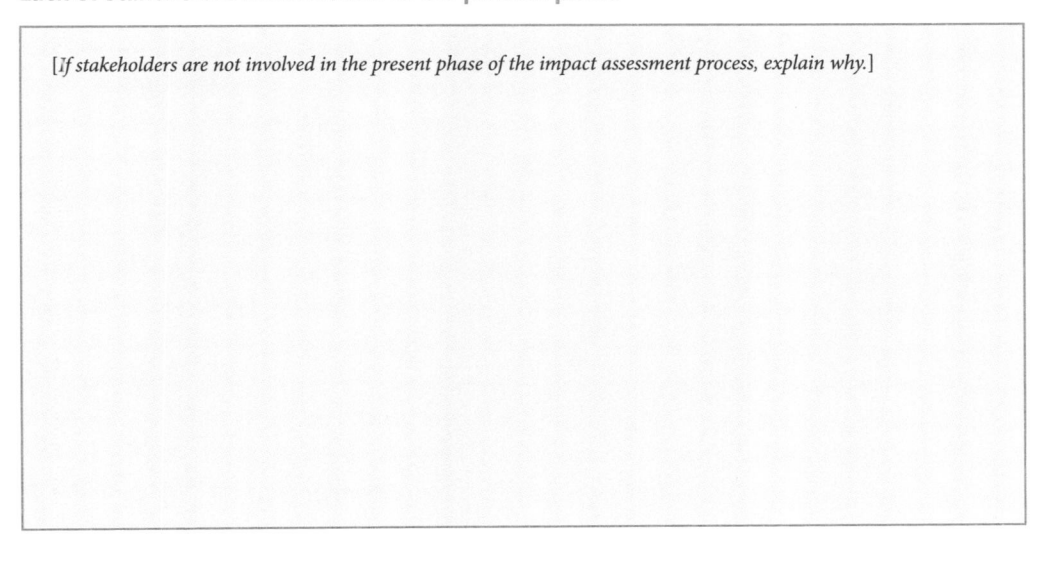

[*If stakeholders are not involved in the present phase of the impact assessment process, explain why.*]

Step B: Quality control

Quality control body	What feedback was received?	How was the feedback implemented? Why was it rejected?
Data protection officer(s) (DPO)		
Supervisory authority (DPA)		
[Other, specify]		

Comments

[Explanation]

Annex 1 – Step 4: Systematic (detailed) description of the initiative

Phase II: Assessment
Step 4: Systematic (detailed) description of the initiative

a) A succinct description of the envisaged initiative

> [Explanation]

b) Personal data protection

Overview

			Explanation
Contextual description	**Nature** (what types of processing operations? e.g. collection, storage, erasure, etc.)		1
			2
			...
	Scope	**Scale** (how much? how many? how far?)	
		Time (when? how long?)	
	Context (in what circumstances?)	**Internal** (concerning the controller)	
		External (concerning individuals, groups, society, etc.)	
	Purpose of processing operations, including, where applicable, legitimate interest (why?)		
	Benefits of processing operations	for individuals, including data subjects	
		for the data controller	
		for society as a whole	
	Drawbacks of processing operations	for individuals, including data subjects	
		for the data controller	
		for society as a whole	

Explanation

Technical description	
Categories of personal data (what?) • special categories of personal data • personal data of vulnerable people (e.g. children) • data of a highly personal nature	
Means of processing (infrastructure) (by what means?)	
Envisioned data flows (where to where? whom to whom?)	
Data security (how is it ensured?)	
Jurisdiction/market (where?)	
Actors in the 'supply chain' (who?)	

[Other, explain]

Diagram of personal data flows and/or other visualisations

[Insert a diagram]

Annex 1 – Step 4: Systematic (detailed) description of the initiative

c) Privacy

	Explanation
Bodily privacy	
Spatial privacy	
Communicational privacy	
Proprietary privacy	
Intellectual privacy	
Decisional privacy	
Associational privacy	
Behavioural privacy	
Informational privacy	

Comments

[Explanation]

Step 5: Appraisal of Impacts & Step 6: Recommendations

Step 5aa: Data protection : Necessity and proportionality of the processing operations

i) Level 1: Personal data protection principles

STEP 5 Appraisal of impacts

ID of a processing operation

Type of a processing operation

STEP 6 Recommendations

Response plan, if principle not satisfied

Principle			Legal provision	Applicable?	Satisfied?	Explanation	Measures in place	Measures to introduce	Responsible person	Priority	Deadline
	Lawfulness	Consent	6(1)(a)	☐	☐						
		Contract	6(1)(b)	☐	☐						
		Legal compliance	6(1)(c)	☐	☐						
		Vital interests	6(1)(d)	☐	☐						
		Public interest	6(1)(e)	☐	☐						
		Legitimate interests	6(1)(f)	☐	☐						

Annex 1 – Step 5: Appraisal of Impacts

Fairness		5(1)(a)	☐		
Transparency			☐		
Purpose limitation	Specific		☐		
	Explicit		☐		
	Legitimate	5(1)(b)	☐		
	Not processed further		☐		
	(*Exceptions*)	89(1)	☐		
Data minimisation	Adequate		☐		
	Relevant	5(1)(c)	☐		
	Limited		☐		
Accuracy	Accurate	5(1)(d)	☐		
	Up-to-date		☐		
Storage limitation	Necessary	5(1)(e)	☐		
	(*Exceptions*)	89(1)	☐		
Data security	Integrity and confidentiality	5(1)(f)	☐		
	Security of processing	32	☐		
Data protection by design		25(1)	☐		
Data protection by default		25(2)	☐		

ii) Level 2: Human rights limitation criteria (Article 52(1) CFR)

Criterion	Satisfied?	Explanation	STEP 6 Recommendations — Response plan, if principle not satisfied				
			Measures in place	Measures to introduce	Responsible person	Priority	Deadline
STEP 5 Appraisal of impacts							
LEGALITY — Is the envisaged initiative provided for by law of a sufficient quality?	☐						
ESSENCE — Does the envisaged initiative still make it possible to exercise a fundamental right or freedom?	☐						
PROPORTIONALITY							
LEGITIMACY — Does the envisaged initiative serve a legitimate aim?	☐						
SUITABILITY — Is the envisaged initiative suited (ever capable) to achieving this aim?	☐						
NECESSITY — Is the envisaged initiative necessary to achieve this aim?	☐						
PROPORTIONALITY SENSU STRICTO (BALANCING) — Is the interference with the right justified in light of the gain in protection for the competing right or interest?	☐						

Step 5ab: Data protection: Risk to the rights and freedoms of natural persons

STEP 5 APPRAISAL OF IMPACTS

STEP 6 RECOMMENDATIONS

		RISK IDENTIFICATION	RISK ANALYSIS				RISK EVALUATION					
						Risk response			Response plan			
ID	Risk	Description (risk source, risk owner, etc.)	Likelihood [probability] of occurrence	Severity of consequence(s) if risk materialises	Risk level (score)	Explanation	Type	Description	Revised risk level (score) (Any residual risk?)			Measures in place	Measures to introduce	Responsible person	Priority	Deadline
			L[P]	S	R = L[P] * S				L[P]	S	R				
	[Specify]														
1															
2															
3															
4															

Annex 1 – Step 5: Appraisal of Impacts

Risk matrix

Before recommendations

[Insert a diagram]

After recommendations

[Insert a diagram]

Step 5b: Ethics assessment

Stage 1: Analysis

ID	Questions	Answers
1	How is the initiative (not) in line with universal values or principles?	
2	How is the initiative presented in a deterministic way? Is it a positive or negative picture?	
3	Why is the initiative (not) neutral?	
4	Is the initiative legitimised by similar technologies that already worked in the past? Or is it legitimised by reference to a dystopian future?	
5	How is the initiative said to change our values or ethical principles?	
6	How does the use (or lack of use) of the initiative cause uncontrollable effects?	
7	How does the initiative protect principles/rights/duties before consequences? Which principles/rights/duties are respected, and which are infringed?	
8	Why is the initiative said to produce more benefits than costs? How is the argument justified?	
9	How are the risks and benefits of the initiative distributed between different groups? Which groups are discriminated and how?	

Stage 2: Assessment

IDs	Questions	Assessment	
		Conflict	Counterarguments or fallacies
1	Are the values/principles invoked universal? Or are they instead local?		
2	Will the initiative materialise independently of what people think and decide? Or is there some room for alternatives?		
3	Is the initiative neutral or biased?		
4	Does the parallel with the past/future hold?		

IDs	Questions	Assessment	
		Conflict	Counterarguments or fallacies
5	To what extent does the initiative change our morality?		
6	Can more and more similar initiatives ultimately lead to a dystopian future if used on a larger scale, although it seems innocuous at first?		
7	Do the principles/rights/duties invoked actually justify the initiative? Are invocations to principles/rights/duties side-tracked by consequentialist arguments? Can one principle/right/duty be outweighed by another? If so, how do you balance competing principles?		
8	Are the promises of the initiative plausible? Is there a better alternative to the initiative (e.g. less invasive) that is technically and economically feasible? What are the possible unintended side effects? Do costs outweigh benefits? Or are the costs and risks downplayed?		
9	Is (the access to) the initiative distributed equally between travellers? Is (the access to) the initiative distributed on the basis of the needs of the travellers? Are distributive justice arguments side-tracked by consequentialist ones? Are discriminatory issues sufficiently addressed?		

Annex 1 – Step 5: Appraisal of Impacts

Step 5c: Social acceptance assessment
Stage 1: Analysis

ID	Acceptance assessment technique	Type of analysis		Findings and patterns (summary)
1	...	Quantitative	☐	
		Qualitative	☐	
		Mix	☐	

Stage 2: Assessment

ID	Positive or negative consequences	Stakeholders affected
1	1x ...	
	1y ...	
	1z ...	

Step 5d: Privacy assessment

Technology implemented (repeat and justify for each)	Applicable?	Description of impact	Legality	Essence	Legitimacy	Necessity	Proportionality
Bodily privacy	☐						
Spatial privacy	☐						
Communicational privacy	☐						
Proprietary privacy	☐						
Intellectual privacy	☐						
Decisional privacy	☐						
Associational privacy	☐						
Behavioural privacy	☐						

Step 5e: Legal compliance requirements

ID	Description		Applicable?	Compliance?	Explanation
		Data Protection			
1	Roles of controllers and processors	Have the responsibilities of controllers and processors been allocated in accordance with the law?	☐	☐	
		[*other, specify*]			
2	Lawful processing	Has a legal basis grounding the personal data processing been identified?	☐	☐	
		[*other, specify*]			
3	Purpose limitation	Are the purposes for which a border control technology processes personal data in line with those specified in the relevant legal and otherwise regulatory framework applicable to it?	☐	☐	
		[*other, specify*]			
4	Data minimisation	1. Does the border control technology process only the personal data that is adequate, relevant and not excessive for the specific border control activity?	☐	☐	
		2. Does the border control technology ensure that only specific categories of personal data are processed?	☐	☐	
		[*other, specify*]			

Annex 1 – Step 5: Appraisal of Impacts

ID	Description		Applicable?	Compliance?	Explanation
		Data Protection			
5	Accuracy	Where inaccurate or outdated information is stored in a database, are mechanisms place to ensure that the information is erased or updated within a specific period of time, and that the changes are communicated to those (authorities) concerned?	☐	☐	
		[*other, specify*]			
6	Accuracy of biometric data	Does the border control technology comply with minimum data quality standards for biometric data?	☐	☐	
		[*other, specify*]			
7	Storage limitation	1. Does the border control technology ensure that data is automatically deleted once the retention period elapses?	☐	☐	
		2. Does the border control technology ensure that logs are deleted once the retention period elapses?	☐	☐	
		[*other, specify*]			
		Data Protection			
8	Availability, integrity and confidentiality	Has the organisation adopted technical and organisational measures to ensure the security of the data processed by the border control technology? • security, business continuity and disaster and recovery plan • fall-back procedures • encryption • etc.	☐	☐	
		[*other, specify*]			

ID	Description		Applicable?	Compliance?	Explanation
9	Accountability	Does the border control authority have accountability measures in place? • logs/records of processing activities • staff training • self-monitoring • professional secrecy • reports of security incidents • etc. [*other, specify*]	☐	☐	
		Data Protection			
10	Data subjects' rights	1. Are data subjects granted the possibility to exercise their rights? • information • access • rectification • erasure • restriction of processing • to not be subjected to a decision solely based on automated decision making • etc. [*other, specify*]	☐	☐	
11	Data transfers	Are personal data transfers to third countries and/or international organisations and/or private entities either not allowed or restricted to very specific cases? [*other, specify*]	☐	☐	

Annex 1 – Step 5: Appraisal of Impacts

ID	Description		Applicable?	Compliance?	Explanation
		Data Protection			
12	Accessibility of data:	1. Do only specific staff members of pre-defined national competent authorities have access to data processed by the border control technology?	☐	☐	
		2. Do only specific staff members of pre-defined EU agencies have access to data processed by the border control technology insofar as it is necessary to fulfil their mandate or exercise their tasks?	☐	☐	
		[*other, specify*]			
	Other / specify				
		Privacy			
1	Respect for private life	Does the border control technology ensure that the processing of personal data respects one's private life?	☐	☐	
		[*other, specify*]			
2	Respect of (bodily) integrity	Does the border control technology ensure that the processing of personal data respects the (bodily) integrity of individuals?	☐	☐	
		[*other, specify*]			
		Privacy			
3	Privacy by design	Have privacy considerations been embedded in the border control technology for its entire lifecycle?	☐	☐	
		[*other, specify*]			

ID	Description		Applicable?	Compliance?	Explanation
4	Privacy by default	Are the default settings of the border control technology the most privacy-friendly possible?	☐	☐	
		[other, specify]			
	Other / specify				
		Ethics			
1	Informed consent	1. Is the public informed about the existence of the border crossing point?	☐	☐	
		2. Is the public informed of the temporary reintroduction of border controls?	☐	☐	
		[other, specify]			
2	Freedom of choice	1. May a person opt to not use a border control technology (e.g. e-gate)?	☐	☐	
		2. Are persons who opt to not use the border control technology not discriminated against for their choice?	☐	☐	
		[other, specify]			
		Ethics			
3	Dual-use	Are restrictions in place for dual-use items?	☐	☐	
		Other / specify			
4	Fairness	Is the use of the border control technology fair towards third-country nationals?	☐	☐	
		[other, specify]			

Annex 1 – Step 5: Appraisal of Impacts

ID	Description		Applicable?	Compliance?	Explanation
5	Human dignity	1. Does the use of the border control technology not result in inhuman or degrading treatment?	☐	☐	
		2. Is the procedure of taking fingerprints in accordance with safeguards in CFR?	☐	☐	
		[*other, specify*]			
6	Non-discrimination and bias	Has the technology been developed in such a way that the processing of personal data will not result in discrimination against persons on any grounds, such as gender, race, colour, ethnic or social origin, genetic features, language, religion or belief, political or any other opinion, membership of a national minority, property, birth, disability, age or sexual orientation?	☐	☐	
		[*other, specify*]			
Ethics					
7	Rights of elderly and persons with disabilities	Has the border control technology been designed in such a way to be used by all persons, except for children under 12 years of age, to the fullest extent possible?	☐	☐	
		[*other, specify*]			

ID	Description			Applicable?	Compliance?	Explanation
8	Rights of children	1.	Are children under a certain age exempted from giving fingerprints?	☐	☐	
		2.	Are alerts regarding children admissible only in restricted cases and to safeguard the best interest of the child?	☐	☐	
		3.	Are alerts concerning children deleted when the child reaches the age of majority and in the circumstances specified in Article 55 SIS Regulation 1862?	☐	☐	
		4.	Are queries in the CIR against minors of 12 years or under allowed, except when in the best interest of the child?	☐	☐	
			[other, specify]			
			Ethics			
9	Vulnerable persons	1.	Are alerts concerning vulnerable persons admissible only in restricted cases?	☐	☐	
		2.	Are the alerts concerning vulnerable persons deleted in the circumstances specified in Article 55 SIS Regulation 1862?	☐	☐	
		3.	Have border guards received specialised training for detecting and dealing with situations involving vulnerable persons?			
			[other, specify]			

Annex 1 – Step 5: Appraisal of Impacts

ID	Description			Applicable?	Compliance?	Explanation
10	Non-refoulement and right to asylum	1.	Are the individuals not subject to refoulement? Do they have the possibility to ask for asylum?	☐	☐	
		2.	Are the rights of people in need of international protection taken into special account?	☐	☐	
		[other, specify]				
	Other / specify					

Other evaluation techniques

Assessment	Recommendations
[Explanation]	[Explanation]

Comments

[Explanation]

Step 6: Recommendations

Recommendations concerning ethics

ID	Conflicts	Counter-arguments	Fallacies	Response plan		
				Measure	Responsible	Deadline
1						

Recommendations concerning social acceptance

ID	Users	Critical points	Response plan		
			Measure	Responsible	Deadline
1					

Recommendations concerning privacy

Technology	Aspect(s) of privacy	Interference	Response plan		
			Measure	Responsible	Deadline

Recommendations concerning legal compliance

ID	Response plan		
	Measure	Responsible	Deadline
	Data protection		
1			
	Privacy		
1			
	Ethics		
1			

Annex 1 – Step 6: Recommendations

Other evaluation techniques

[Explanation]

Recommendations

	Synthesis of recommendations	Decision of the sponsoring organisation and its justification
1	[Explanation]	
2		

	Overall recommendation		Decision of the sponsoring organisation and its justification
☐	to deploy the initiative without changes		
☐	to modify the initiative	[Specify how]	
☐	to cancel the initiative	[Specify why]	

Comments

[Explanation]

Ongoing Steps for Phase II
Step A: Stakeholder involvement
Internal stakeholders

Category of stakeholder	What information has been communicated to stakeholders?	What input have the stakeholders provided (e.g. opinion)?	How was their input included? Why was it rejected?
Data processor(s)			
Data protection officer(s) (DPO)			
Recipient(s) (Article 4(9))			
Third parties (Article 4(10))			
Representative(s) (Article 27)			
Information security officer(s)			
Legal service			
Employees, trade unions, contractors, etc.			

[*other, specify*]

External stakeholders

	Category of stakeholder	What information has been communicated to stakeholders?	What input have the stakeholders provided (e.g. opinion)?	How was their input included? Why was it rejected?
Individuals whose rights and freedoms are affected by the initiative and their representatives	Data subjects, including: • Minors • Vulnerable persons • [*other, specify*]			
	Representative(s) of data subject(s)			
	Individuals who are not data subjects			
	Representative(s) of individuals who are not data subjects			

Annex 1 – Ongoing Steps for Phase II

	Category of stakeholder	What information has been communicated to stakeholders?	What input have the stakeholders provided (e.g. opinion)?	How was their input included? Why was it rejected?
Public sector stakeholders	Supervisory authority(ies) (DPA)			
	Policymakers			
	Local stakeholders			
Private sector stakeholders	Technology providers			
	Transportation companies			
Experts	Research Ethics Committees, within public or private organisations			
	National ethics committees or councils, at EU or Member State level			
	Groups of *ad hoc* recruited ethics experts			
	Scientific experts			
	[Anybody else affected, etc., specify]			

Lack of stakeholder involvement in the present phase

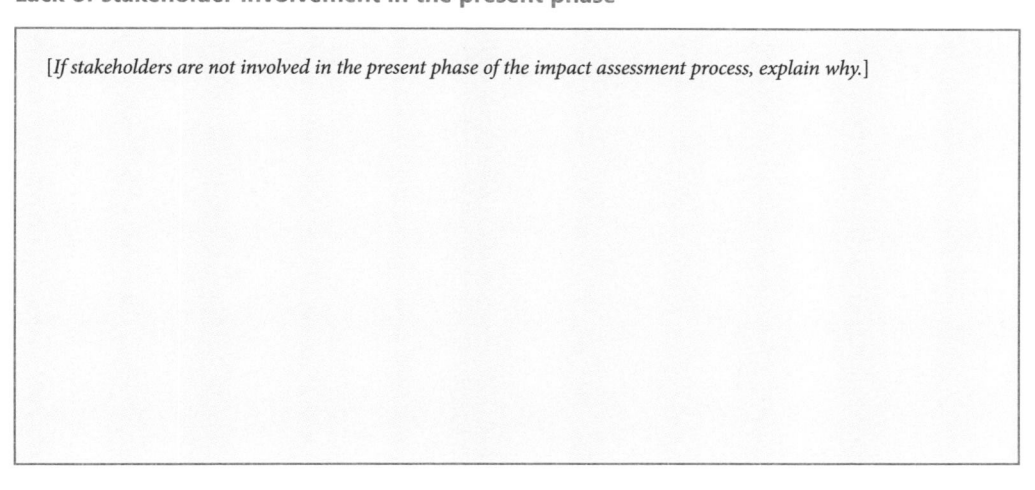

[*If stakeholders are not involved in the present phase of the impact assessment process, explain why.*]

Step B: Quality control

Quality control body	What feedback was received?	How was the feedback implemented? Why was it rejected?
Data protection officer(s) (DPO)		
Supervisory authority (DPA)		
[Other, specify]		

Comments

[Explanation]

Phase III: *Ex post* (eventual) steps
Step 7: Prior Consultation

Data protection	Competent DPA(s)	
	Date of submission	
	Date of receipt of the response	
	Inquiry (summary)	
	Response (summary)	
	Decision of the controller after consultation	
Ethics	Ethics committee and/or competent authority	
	Date of submission of application for approval	
	Date of receipt of the response	
	Response (summary)	
	Decision of the sponsoring organisation after consultation	
[other, explain]		

Comments

[Explanation]

Step 8: Revisiting

	Criterion		Change?	Explanation
Contextual description	**Nature** *(what types of processing operations? e.g. collection, storage, erasure, etc.)*		☐	
	Scope	**Scale** *(how much? how many? how far?)*	☐	
		Time *(when? how long?)*	☐	
	Context *(in what circumstances?)*	**Internal** *(concerning the controller)*	☐	
		External *(concerning individuals, groups, society, etc.)*	☐	
	Purpose *of processing operations, including, where applicable, legitimate interest (why?)*		☐	
	Benefits of processing operations	for individuals, including data subjects	☐	
		for the data controller	☐	
		for society as a whole	☐	
	Drawbacks of processing operations	for individuals, including data subjects	☐	
		for the data controller	☐	
		for society as a whole	☐	
Technical description	Categories of personal data (what?) • special categories of personal data • personal data of vulnerable persons (e.g. children) • data of a highly personal nature		☐	
	Means of processing (infrastructure) (by what means?)		☐	
	Envisioned data flows (where to where? whom to whom?)		☐	
	Data security (how is it ensured?)		☐	
	Jurisdiction/market (where?)		☐	
	Actors in the 'supply chain' (who?)		☐	
	[Other, explain]		☐	

Annex 1 – Step 8: Revisiting

Overall suggestion

What should be done with the assessment process?		When?	Decision of the sponsoring organisation and its justification
☐ revise	☐ entirely	*[Specify]*	
	☐ in part *[Specify]*	*[Specify]*	
☐ do not revise	*[Specify why]*		

Ongoing Steps for Phase III

Step A: Stakeholder involvement

Internal stakeholders

Category of stakeholder	What information has been communicated to stakeholders?	What input have the stakeholders provided (e.g. opinion)?	How was their input included? Why was it rejected?
Data processor(s)			
Data protection officer(s) (DPO)			
Recipient(s) (Article 4(9))			
Third parties (Article 4(10))			
Representative(s) (Article 27)			
Information security officer(s)			
Legal service			
Employees, trade unions, contractors, etc.			
[other, specify]			

External stakeholders

	Category of stakeholder	What information has been communicated to stakeholders?	What input have the stakeholders provided (e.g. opinion)?	How was their input included? Why was it rejected?
Individuals whose rights and freedoms are affected by the initiative and their representatives	Data subjects, including: • Minors • Vulnerable persons • [other, specify]			
	Representative(s) of data subject(s)			
	Individuals who are not data subjects			
	Representative(s) of individuals who are not data subjects			

Annex 1 – Ongoing Steps for Phase III

	Category of stakeholder	What information has been communicated to stakeholders?	What input have the stakeholders provided (e.g. opinion)?	How was their input included? Why was it rejected?
Public sector stakeholders	Supervisory authority(ies) (DPA)			
	Policymakers			
	Local stakeholders			
Private sector stakeholders	Technology providers			
	Transportation companies			
Experts	Research Ethics Committees, within public or private organisations			
	National ethics committees or councils, at EU or Member State level			
	Groups of *ad hoc* recruited ethics experts			
	Scientific experts			
	[*Anybody else affected, etc., specify*]			

Lack of stakeholder involvement in the present phase

[*If stakeholders are not involved in the present phase of the impact assessment process, explain why.*]

Step B: Quality control

Quality control body	What feedback was received?	How was the feedback implemented? Why was it rejected?
Data protection officer(s) (DPO)		
Supervisory authority (DPA)		
[Other, specify]		

Comments

[Explanation]

Annex 1 – Ongoing Steps for Phase III

Step C: Documentation

		Attachment	Confidentiality level	Appended?	Comments
Step 1 Step 4	Data protection	Record of processing activities		☐	
				☐	
Step 2		Approved codes of conduct		☐	
		Certificates		☐	
		Binding corporate rules (BCRs)		☐	
		Standard contractual clauses (SCCs)		☐	
		Data protection policies		☐	
		Professional codes of conduct		☐	
		Data sharing agreement(s)	confidential	☐	
Step 3	Stakeholder involvement	A copy of a service contract (in the event that the impact assessment is outsourced)		☐	
		A list of stakeholders to consult and their contact details		☐	
		Stakeholder consultation plan	confidential	☐	
Step 7	Data protection	Request for prior consultation with a supervisory authority		☐	
		Response from a supervisory authority		☐	
		Response from a supervisory authority		☐	

		Attachment	Confidentiality level	Appended?	Comments
Step A	Stakeholder involvement	Technical briefing(s) for stakeholder consultation		☐	
		Stakeholder consultation (reports)		☐	
	Data protection	DPO opinion (report)		☐	
[Reports from other evaluation techniques; specify]				☐	
[other, explain]				☐	

Comments

[Explanation]

Closing Page

Endorsements

Responsibility	Name	Remarks	Date	Signature
Assessor(s)				
Data protection officer				
Data controller(s)				
[other, explain]				

Endnotes

1. Based on: Dariusz Kloza et al., "Data Protection Impact Assessment in the European Union: Developing a Template for a Report from the Assessment Process," d.pia.lab Policy Brief (Brussels: VUB, 2020), https://doi.org/10.31228/osf.io/7qrfp.

Annex 2: Inventory of stakeholder involvement techniques

Simone Casiraghi
Vrije Universiteit Brussel. E-mail: simone.casiraghi@vub.be.

Category	Participation method type	Type and size of stakeholder group	Selection process	Description	Time/scale duration
Problem-solving meetings	(Citizen) Advisory group or task force[1]	10-25 stakeholders (including, but not limited to, citizens with specialised knowledge or representing specific interests of a community).	Selected by the assessors on the basis of expertise and to ensure a balance of different interests. A public notice or targeted invitation is sent out.	Examination of some significant issues to provide advice, e.g. to policy makers or border authorities. Its mission can vary depending on the responsibilities it is assigned. For instance, it can provide an official voice for a group of travellers affected by an initiative.	The meetings take place over an extended period of time, e.g. several weeks. Advisory groups can perform several tasks and be involved throughout the whole assessment process (including its possible revisions) or be involved for only a single task.
	Charrette[2]	20-60 stakeholders (including, but not limited to, citizens with various skills and interests, including a facilitator).	Selected by the assessors on the basis of expertise and to ensure a balance of different interests. A public notice or targeted invitation is sent out.	Cooperation in solving a problem or advising on a controversial issue before a given deadline, with an experienced facilitator. This usually takes place in design fields like land use or urban planning, at the beginning of a decision process, to address contrasts that might arise between competing interests. It can be a powerful, cost-efficient way to come up with creative solutions	An intensive and collective effort over a short period of time (usually one day).
	Citizens' panel/jury or consensus conferences[3]	A panel of 10-20 citizens that represent lay knowledge and a local population, with different backgrounds.	Selected through a lottery system, from a sample of a local population.	Method used to incorporate the opinions and values of citizens into decisions about an initiative. A dialogue takes place within a panel composed of "lay" public knowledge as opposed to the technical expertise of other stakeholders. The purpose is not necessarily to reach a final decision, but also to gain information on the public awareness of the initiative.	A first phase of education of the panel (1-2 weekends) followed by a number of meetings of a few days (3 to 10).

Category	Participation method type	Type and size of stakeholder group	Selection process	Description	Time/scale duration
	Delphi method[4]	A panel of stakeholders with different backgrounds, including a facilitator. The size of the group is bigger if the method is performed remotely (e.g. online).	Selected by the assessors to avoid methodological weaknesses and to ensure the soundness of the results.	Interactive and structured forecasting method to achieve consensus through a series of questionnaires (without requiring face-to-face meetings, either by electronic or traditional correspondence). Each questionnaire is alternated with feedback on individual contributions. Usually, the input of participants remains anonymous.	Iterative; it can have multiple rounds of interaction over a single day or multiple days.
	Public meetings[5]	Speakers (e.g. experts or politicians) and interested citizens, with a moderator. The meetings are open to anyone, but the number of citizens involved depends on the size of the venue.	Announcement (e.g. via social media, newspapers or mailing lists) at least 30 days before the scheduled date.	Open and flexible ways of sharing information and discussing issues, not necessarily making decisions. They differ from public hearings, which are more formal, and they can also be a legal requirement (see below).	Meetings can last weeks or months, and usually take place over a number of working days.
	Public hearings[6]	Speakers (e.g. experts or politicians) and interested citizens, with a moderator. The number of citizens involved depends on the size of the venue.	Announcement (e.g. via social media, newspapers or mailing lists) at least 30 days before the scheduled date.	Sometimes regulated by law, presentations by an agency on an initiative in open forums. The citizens have a formal (i.e. recorded in the public record) chance to voice their opinions but have no direct impact on the recommendations. Transcripts of the comments will be available for review.	Hearings can last several hours or days and usually take place over a number of working days.

Category	Participation method type	Type and size of stakeholder group	Selection process	Description	Time/scale duration
	Roundtables[7]	A small group of 10-15 stakeholders, including a moderator.	Selected by the assessors on the basis of expertise and to ensure a balance of different interests. A public notice or targeted invitation is sent out. The number of participants is limited to those who registered though a registration form.	A form of (academic) discussion in which participants agree on a specific topic to discuss. Each person is given *equal* opportunity to express their view, e.g. by allocating the same time slot for each participant to make comments on the initiative under discussion.	Usually over one or two days.
	(Scenario) Workshop[8]	A small group of 10-30 stakeholders, including a moderator and/or chair.	Announcement well in advance (about 3 weeks before) and notification or invitation of experts via e-mail. The number of participants is limited to those who registered though a registration form.	A gathering or seminar led by a specialist to express a wide range of viewpoints and confront one another. If scenario-based, the participants themselves carry out the assessment with the use of scenarios, i.e. mental views about possible future outcomes.	Usually over one or two days.
	Study Circles[9]	A small group of 5-10 stakeholders with similar interests and background.	Selected by the assessors on the basis of expertise and to ensure a balance of different interests. A targeted invitation is sent out.	Physical or online gatherings to discuss a shared topic or find solutions to a common problem. The group can be self-sufficient or supported by government or community officials. Minutes can be taken during the meetings to monitor the evolution of the thinking of the group regarding particular issues of the assessment process.	The group meets a defined number of times, usually up to five, on a regular basis (weekly or monthly).

Annex 2

Category	Participation method type	Type and size of stakeholder group	Selection process	Description	Time/scale duration
Information-sharing meetings	Informational meeting[10]	A large group of stakeholders with various or similar backgrounds. The size of the group depends on the size of the venue of the meeting.	Invitation sent out by the assessors on the basis of interest, background and/or affiliation.	A gathering of a group of stakeholders to be merely informed about a given initiative e.g. through presentation, videos or infographics. The format is not very interactive, and the stakeholders predominantly have the passive role of listeners.	Usually over one or two days.
	Q&A sessions[11]	Stakeholders that also took part in an event e.g. an exhibition, presentation or meeting.	Announcement of the Q&A session after an event. Anyone that was present at the event can participate.	Staff are available to stakeholders to answer questions, typically after an exhibition, a presentation or a meeting. Sessions can be either formal or informal.	Usually from 30 minutes to two hours, depending on the number of questions.
	Facility tours or technology demonstration[12]	A large group of stakeholders with various or similar backgrounds. The size of the group depends on the size of the venue for the tour or demonstration.	Participants are either recruited *in loco* (e.g. travellers at a border crossing point) or via a targeted invitation.	Stakeholders are gathered to assist a demonstration of the initiative under assessment, e.g. via video presentations or a simulation of a technology. Staff are available to offer further explanations and to answer questions.	Usually over one or two days, it can be repeated multiple times throughout the assessment process.
Information-sharing platforms	Hotline[13]	Any stakeholder, especially minorities and vulnerable populations that might be affected by a given initiative but nonetheless are difficult to engage through other techniques.	Anyone can call the number. The phone number is widely advertised to collect as many diverse inputs as possible.	A toll-free phone number that people can reach to ask questions about a given initiative.	The duration of the phone calls varies depending on the number of people who call, and the type of questions asked. It is possible to decide upon fixed call slots (e.g. four hours per day) beforehand.

Category	Participation method type	Type and size of stakeholder group	Selection process	Description	Time/scale duration
	Online forums and social media[14]	Any stakeholder, especially minorities and vulnerable populations that might be affected by a given initiative but nonetheless are difficult to engage with other techniques.	Anyone can participate and post comments, although creation of an account may be required. The forum or social media page is widely advertised to collect as many diverse inputs as possible. The content is usually approved by a moderator before it is made public.	Online discussion sites to allow general discussions or post comments on specific questions or issues. A platform can also be used to host questionnaires or polls and provide the results to participants.	A forum or social media page can remain active for the entire duration of the assessment process.
	On-scene information office[15]	Any stakeholder that passes through the site, e.g. travellers that pass through a border crossing point.	Anyone can voluntarily go to the information office to gather extra information.	A small office, desk or trailer at a border crossing point where staff respond to inquiries.	Staff should be available at the office up to 40 hours a week.
Surveys	Focus groups[16]	Small groups of 5-10 stakeholders with specific interests or expertise.	Selected by the assessors either randomly or to approximate the demographics of an affected community.	Small discussion groups, with the help of one or more facilitators, to gather in-depth insights and reactions of people to a given initiative e.g. on values, concerns and perspectives involved in the given initiative.	Single meeting, usually up to two hours.

Annex 2

Category	Participation method type	Type and size of stakeholder group	Selection process	Description	Time/scale duration
	Interviews[17]	The number and types of interviewees depend on the time and resources available to the assessors. Only interviewing a small sample of people is appropriate only if these people are considered representative of a particular community or interest group.	Selected by the assessors on the basis of expertise and to ensure a balance of different interests. A targeted invitation is sent out.	Participants are asked specific questions on a given initiative, in a more-or-less structured manner, face-to-face or via telephone. The in-depth inputs gathered from the answers are used to identify gaps, problems or potential solutions to a given initiative.	Approximately one hour per interview.
	Door-to-door canvassing[18]	Potentially all members of a pre-selected local population, or at least a significant proportion of these.	Assessors select staff (i.e. canvassers) to conduct the canvassing activity. Canvassers need to identify the area to be canvassed beforehand and notify local residents.	A method to collect and distribute information by engaging with community members individually. Canvassers ask questions, discuss issues and/or provide informative material related to the initiative under assessment.	Canvassing is a time- and resource-intensive activity, although the time spent canvassing depends on the area to be canvassed.

225

Category	Participation method type	Type and size of stakeholder group	Selection process	Description	Time/scale duration
	Opinion polls[19]	Very large sample (up to several thousand), in particular (potential) travellers at border crossing points.	An online link for a poll is advertised and made available by the assessors. Alternatively, respondents can be contacted via telephone or door-to-door. In the latter case, the assessors select a sample of respondents (random or representative) beforehand.	An assessment of public opinion on a certain topic by questioning a representative sample. Polling can be performed online, door-to-door or by telephone. Opinion polls differ from questionnaires (below) insofar as usually they contain only one multiple choice question to which the respondents give one answer. Therefore, results are immediately known, and no analysis is required.	They can take very little time to be completed by each stakeholder (e.g. one minute). Polls can be available to the public for several weeks.
	Questionnaires[20]	Very large sample (up to several thousand), in particular (potential) travellers at border crossing points.	Assessors distribute the questionnaires in person or online (e.g. via e-mail or on a website). In case specific information is needed, representatives of certain groups of stakeholders are targeted. Alternatively, all travellers crossing borders in a given timeslot are addressed.	Participants are asked to answer a list of various question types (structured or semi-structured, multiple choice, rating), either in person or online. The length and depth of the questionnaire depends on the phase of the assessment and the envisaged level of involvement. As a rule of thumb, a longer questionnaire can give more nuanced input than a shorter one.	Depending on the type of questions and the modality for answering them, questionnaires generally take from 5 to 20 minutes to be completed.
	Referenda[21]	Potentially all members of a national or local population, or at least a significant proportion of these.	Everyone in a given area or community is given the opportunity to vote.	A popular vote to decide on a specific issue that requires a binary yes/no input. The participants have an equal influence, and the outcome can be legally binding.	The vote is cast at a single point in time. This is a cost-efficient way to involve a large amount of people in a decision.

Endnotes

1. James L. Creighton, *The Public Participation Handbook: Making Better Decisions through Citizen Involvement* (San Francisco: Jossey-Bass, 2005), 183; Gene Rowe and Lynn J. Frewer, "Public Participation Methods: A Framework for Evaluation," *Science Technology and Human Values* 25, no. 1 (2000): 3–29, https://doi.org/10.1177/016224390002500101; US Environmental Protection Agency, *RCRA Public Participation Manual*, 1996.
2. James A. Segedy and Bradley Johnson, *The Neighbourhood Charrette Handbook*, 2004, https://www.michigantownships.org/downloads/charrette_handbook_2.pdf; Gail Lindsey, Joel Ann Todd, and Sheila J. Hayter, *A Handbook for Planning and Conducting Charrettes for High-Performance Projects*, 2009, https://www.nrel.gov/docs/fy03osti/33425.pdf; Organization for Economic Co-operation and Development (OECD), *Stakeholder Involvement Techniques: Short Guide and Annotated Bibliography*, Nuclear Energy Agency, 2004, 40.
3. Ned Crosby, Janet M. Kelly, and Paul Schaefer, "Citizens Panels: A New Approach to Citizen Participation," *Public Administration Review* 46, no. 2 (1986): 170; Simon Joss and John Durant, *Public Participation in Science. The Role of Consensus Conference in Europe* (London: Science Museum, 1995).
4. Harold Linstone and Murray Turoff, *The Delphi Method: Techniques and Applications* (Boston, MA: Addison Wesley Publishing Company, 1975); Gene Rowe and George Wright, "The Delphi Technique as a Forecasting Tool: Issues and Analysis," *International Journal of Forecasting* 15, no. 4 (1999): 353–75.
5. US Environmental Protection Agency, *RCRA Public Participation Manual*, 117; Creighton, *The Public Participation Handbook : Making Better Decisions through Citizen Involvement*, 130.
6. Rowe and Frewer, "Public Participation Methods: A Framework for Evaluation"; US Environmental Protection Agency, *RCRA Public Participation Manual*, 123; Creighton, *The Public Participation Handbook: Making Better Decisions through Citizen Involvement*, 130.
7. Organization for Economic Co-operation and Development (OECD), *Stakeholder Involvement Techniques: Short Guide and Annotated Bibliography*, 31; Stefan Taschner and Matthias Fiedler, "Stakeholder Involvement Handbook," 2009, 20; Organization for Economic Co-operation and Development (OECD), *Stakeholder Involvement Techniques: Short Guide and Annotated Bibliography*, http://www.aeneas-project.eu/docs/AENEAS_StakeholderInvolvementHandbook.pdf.
8. Gill Ringland, "The Role of Scenarios in Strategic Foresight," *Technological Forecasting and Social Change* 77, no. 9 (2010): 1493–98, https://doi.org/10.1016/j.techfore.2010.06.010; US Environmental Protection Agency, *RCRA Public Participation Manual*, 134.
9. Organization for Economic Co-operation and Development (OECD), *Stakeholder Involvement Techniques: Short Guide and Annotated Bibliography*, 31.
10. Taschner and Fiedler, "Stakeholder Involvement Handbook," 20.
11. US Environmental Protection Agency, *RCRA Public Participation Manual*, 106.
12. US Environmental Protection Agency, 56.
13. Creighton, *The Public Participation Handbook: Making Better Decisions through Citizen Involvement*, 118; US Environmental Protection Agency, *RCRA Public Participation Manual*, 100.
14. Creighton, *The Public Participation Handbook: Making Better Decisions through Citizen Involvement*, 119.
15. US Environmental Protection Agency, *RCRA Public Participation Manual*, 103.

16. Jay Klagge, *Guidelines for Conducting Focus Groups*, 2018, https://doi.org/10.13140/RG.2.2.33817.47201; Gloria E. Bader and Catherine A. Rossi, Focus Groups. *A Step by Step Guide* (San Diego, CA: The Bader Group, 2002); US Environmental Protection Agency, *RCRA Public Participation Manual*, 77.
17. Creighton, *The Public Participation Handbook: Making Better Decisions through Citizen Involvement*, 190; US Environmental Protection Agency, *RCRA Public Participation Manual*, 70.
18. US Environmental Protection Agency, *RCRA Public Participation Manual*, 80.
19. Louis M. Rea and Richard A. Parker, *Designing and Conducting Survey Research. A Comprehensive Research Guide* (Jossey-Bass, 2005); US Environmental Protection Agency, *RCRA Public Participation Manual*, 90; Creighton, *The Public Participation Handbook: Making Better Decisions through Citizen Involvement*, 128.
20. Rea and Parker, *Designing and Conducting Survey Research. A Comprehensive Research Guide*, 90; US Environmental Protection Agency, *RCRA Public Participation Manual*; Creighton, *The Public Participation Handbook: Making Better Decisions through Citizen Involvement*, 128.
21. Rowe and Frewer, "Public Participation Methods: A Framework for Evaluation," 19.

Annex 3: Inventory of appraisal techniques

Nikolaos IOANNIDIS
Vrije Universiteit Brussel. E-mail: Nikolaos.Ioannidis@vub.be.

3.1 Introduction

There are multiple 'recipes' for a proper impact assessment process. The purpose of this Annex is to provide a reference point and a knowledge base for conducting the process of integrated impact assessment of border control technologies. The Annex provides an overview of the appraisal and evaluation techniques, categorised as follows:

1) appraisal techniques that are explicitly referred in the General Data Protection Regulation (GDPR) and hence legally required to be used in the process of data protection impact assessment (DPIA) in the EU;
2) supplementary appraisal techniques that are compatible with the GDPR as far as the processes of DPIA and integrated impact assessment is concerned; and
3) evaluation techniques that are stand-alone, borrowed from other areas of practice, and can be integrated within the process of impact assessment; these evaluation techniques employ one or more appraisal techniques.

Under the first category are the appraisal methods explicitly stipulated in the GDPR. For the process of DPIA, the assessors use the following appraisal techniques: (i) assessment of necessity and proportionality of the personal data processing operations in relation to the purposes of the technology and (ii) assessment of the risks to the rights and freedoms of data subjects. The second category comprises closely related appraisal methods, which could be used more broadly on different types of assessments, not exclusively for DPIA. For example, cost-benefit analysis belongs to this category and can be used to supplement risk assessment legally required by the GDPR. Finally, the third category comprises stand-alone evaluation techniques with a view of their possible integration, such as technology foresight and environmental impact assessment (EIA).

Several appraisal or evaluation techniques can be combined in order to conduct a process of integrated impact assessment, depending on the benchmark under assessment and the context in which the impact assessment process is utilised. Using one technique does not usually exclude or render obsolete the others. On the contrary, such a combination is frequently considered as best practice. There clearly exist many appraisal and evaluation techniques, of various levels of quality and applicability. Their abundance is due to the need for tailored solutions, adapted to the specific context of assessment. Additionally, the fact that impact assessment is an adaptable 'living instrument' results in existence of numerous versions and adaptations of the final impact assessment process.

Due to the evolving character of the concept of impact assessment, this Annex cannot be considered exhaustive. Although it extends as far as bringing together the well-established EIA with the newly conceived and relatively unclear concept of artificial intelligence impact assessment, there is no 'silver bullet' for selecting and combining the appraisal techniques that will be best adapted for an integrated impact assessment process.

This Annex is structured as follows: under each appraisal or evaluation technique, a list follows with corresponding sources prominent in the field (either academic or from the area of policymaking) (Sections 2-4). For instance, for DPIA, numerous methods and templates have been developed; however it is impossible to list each and every one of them. The scope of this Annex does not extend to the matter of combining several appraisal and evaluation techniques, although the list of sources under each technique indicates its affinity with others. In addition, Section 5 is dedicated to attempts to develop techniques for ranking technologies as to their invasiveness into societal values.

3.2 Appraisal techniques explicitly required by the General Data Protection Regulation

3.2.1 Assessment of necessity and proportionality

3.2.1.1 Overview
The necessity and proportionality assessment refers first and foremost to the observance of the personal data protection principles. In particular, it is connected to the principle of purpose limitation. It first asks about the purpose of the data processing operation, whether 'the processing could not be reasonably fulfilled by other means' and whether the personal data would be 'collected for specified, explicit and legitimate purposes and not further processed' in a way that is inconsistent with those purposes.[1]

This assessment further pertains to the principle of lawfulness of processing, alongside the principles of data minimisation, accuracy and storage limitation, security of processing, and also data protection by design and by default. In other words, it asks whether the personal data would be 'processed lawfully, fairly and in a transparent manner', whether it would be 'adequate, relevant and limited to what is necessary in relation to the purposes', whether it would be 'accurate and, where necessary, kept up to date' or whether it would be stored for any longer than necessary.[2]

Often, the envisaged initiative under assessment may voluntarily be additionally examined against the entirety of human rights limitation criteria. In other words, while the entirety of the provisions of the GDPR, and especially the personal data protection principles, is meant to observe human rights limitation criteria, there might be instances that would give rise to the questioning of such an assumption. This scenario could happen in the provisions about a national exemption or derogation from the GDPR (Article 85). The five limitation criteria, following the Charter of Fundamental Rights, are:

- *legality*, i.e. if a basis for a data processing operation is provided for by law of a sufficient quality, e.g. clarity, accessibility, precision, foreseeability, conformity with the rule of law;
- *the respect for the essence of a right*, i.e. if the interference with a fundamental right does not make it impossible to exercise a right;
- *legitimacy*, i.e. if a processing operation serves a given general interest or protects the rights and freedoms of others;
- *necessity*, i.e. if a processing operation is necessary and if it genuinely meets legitimate objectives; and
- *proportionality sensu stricto* (e.g. balancing), e.g. if the least intrusive option has been chosen.

3.2.1.2 Assessment techniques

Article 29 Data Protection Working Party
- Article 29 Data Protection Working Party, *Guidelines on Data Protection Impact Assessment (DPIA) and determining whether processing is "likely to result in a high risk" for the purposes of Regulation 2016/679* (Brussels: 2017), https://www.cnil.fr/sites/default/files/atoms/files/20171013_wp248_rev01_enpdf_4.pdf.

European Data Protection Supervisor (EDPS)
- European Data Protection Supervisor [EDPS], *Accountability on the ground. Part II: Data Protection Impact Assessments & Prior Consultation* (Brussels: 2018), https://edps.europa.eu/sites/edp/files/publication/18-02-06_accountability_on_the_ground_part_2_en.pdf.
- EDPS, *Assessing the necessity of measures that limit the fundamental right to the protection of personal data: A Toolkit* (Brussels: 2017), https://edps.europa.eu/sites/edp/files/publication/17-04-11_necessity_toolkit_en_0.pdf.
- EDPS, *Guidelines on assessing the proportionality of measures that limit the fundamental rightsto privacy and to the protection of personal data* (Brussels: 2019), https://edps.europa.eu/sites/edp/files/publication/19-12-19_edps_proportionality_guidelines2_en.pdf.

> *Commission Nationale de l'Informatique et des Libertés (CNIL)*
> - CNIL, *Privacy Impact Assessment (PIA). Templates* (Paris, 2018), https://www.cnil.fr/sites/default/files/atoms/files/cnil-pia-2-en-templates.pdf.
> - CNIL, *Privacy Impact Assessment (PIA). Methodology* (Paris, 2018), https://www.cnil.fr/sites/default/files/atoms/files/cnil-pia-1-en-methodology.pdf.

3.2.2 Assessment of a risk to the rights and freedoms of data subjects

3.2.2.1 Risk assessment: an overview

Risk assessment is the overall process of risk identification, risk analysis and risk evaluation. In particular, the purpose of risk analysis is to comprehend the nature of risk and its characteristics, including the level of risk. Risk analysis involves a detailed consideration of uncertainties, risk sources, consequences, likelihoods, events, scenarios, controls, and their effectiveness.

Risk analysis can be undertaken with varying degrees of detail and complexity, depending on the purpose of the analysis, the availability and reliability of information, and the resources available. Analysis techniques can be qualitative, quantitative or a combination of these, depending on the circumstances and intended use.

Consequent to risk analysis is the evaluation of the risks. This step involves comparing the results of the risk analysis with the established risk criteria to determine where additional action is required.

3.2.2.1.1 Qualitative risk analysis

Qualitative risk analysis uses a scale of qualifying attributes to describe the magnitude of potential consequences (e.g. low, medium and high) and the likelihood that those consequences will occur. An advantage of qualitative analysis is its ease of understanding by all relevant personnel, while a disadvantage is the dependence on the subjective choice of the scale. These scales can be adapted or adjusted to suit the circumstances, and different descriptions can be used for different risks. Qualitative analysis should use factual information and data, where available, and can be used:

1. as an initial screening activity to identify risks that require more detailed analysis;
2. where this kind of analysis is appropriate for decisions;
3. where numerical data or resources are inadequate for a quantitative risk analysis.

3.2.2.1.2 Quantitative risk analysis

Quantitative risk analysis uses a scale with numerical values (rather than the descriptive scales used in qualitative risk analysis) for both consequences and likelihood. The quality of the analysis depends on the accuracy and completeness of the numerical values and the validity of the models used.

Quantitative risk analysis, in most cases, uses historical incident data, providing the advantage that they can be related directly to the information security objectives and concerns of the organisation. A disadvantage of the quantitative approach can occur where factual, auditable data are not available, thus creating an illusion of worth and accuracy of the risk assessment. The way in which consequences and likelihood are expressed and the ways in which they are combined to provide a level of risk, will vary according to the type of risk and the purpose for which the risk assessment output is to be used. The uncertainty and variability of both consequences and likelihood should be considered in the analysis and communicated effectively.

3.2.2.2 Risks to the rights and freedoms in data protection law: an overview

The concept of risk assessment within the scope of data protection law is understood to refer to the risks to the rights and freedoms of data subjects. On the grounds of the GDPR, risk is understood as a negative consequence arising from processing operations, which may or may not occur in the future. Such a consequence, if materialised, would produce physical, material, or non-material damage to natural persons (largely, data subjects) and not solely to the controllers or processors. Such risk includes, for example, discrimination, identity theft or fraud, financial loss or damage to reputation, loss of confidentiality, unauthorised reversal of pseudonymisation, any significant economic or social disadvantage, loss of control over personal data, and processing of unauthorised sensitive data or data from vulnerable natural persons, in particular children.

The classic method for assessing risk typically combines two measurements, namely its likelihood (or probability) and its severity. Risk can be assessed qualitatively, quantitatively or through a combination of these.[3] There are aspects of personal data protection that fit into the former (i.e. risk to rights and freedoms) and the latter (e.g. data security).

Quantitative risk assessment measures the probability of occurrence of a risk, and combines this with its level of severity. Probability is expressed on a scale ranging from 0 to 1. In turn, qualitative risk assessment instead uses levels of likelihood (e.g. a four-partite descriptive scale of negligible, low, medium and high) to be combined with its severity. Eventually, severity of a risk indicates a magnitude of damage should a risk materialise. It can be equally expressed on a 4-partite descriptive scale. Both scales – likelihood and severity – are pre-defined and justified.

3.2.2.3 Assessment techniques

International Organization for Standardization (ISO)
- ISO 31000:2018 *Risk management – Guidelines,* https://www.iso.org/standard/65694.html.
- ISO 27005:2018 *Information technology – Security techniques – Information security risk management,* https://www.iso.org/standard/75281.html.
- ISO 22301:2019 *Security and resilience – Business continuity management systems – Requirements,* https://www.iso.org/standard/75106.html.

National Institute of Standards and Technology (NIST)
- SP 800-37 Rev. 2 *Risk Management Framework for Information Systems and Organizations: A System Life Cycle Approach for Security and Privacy,* https://doi.org/10.6028/NIST.SP.800-37r2.

3.3 Supplementary appraisal techniques compatible with the General Data Protection Regulation

3.3.1 Scenario analysis (planning)

3.3.1.1 Overview

Scenario analysis is conducted with the aim of analysing the impacts of possible future events on the system performance by taking into account several alternative outcomes, i.e. scenarios, and presenting different options for future development paths, resulting in varying outcomes and corresponding implications.

It is the process of forecasting the expected value of a performance indicator, given a time period, occurrence of different situations, and related changes in the values of system parameters under an uncertain environment. Scenario analysis can be used to estimate the behaviour of the system in response to an unexpected event, and may be utilised to explore the changes in system performance, in a theoretical best-case (optimistic) or worst-case (pessimistic) scenario.

Key steps in scenario analysis are: a) identification of the scenario field, b) identification of key factors, c) analysis of key factors, d) scenario generation, and e) scenario transfer.

3.3.1.2 Assessment techniques

> - Celeste Amorim Varuma and Carla Meloa, "Directions in Scenario Planning Literature - A Review of the Past Decades," Futures 42, no. 4 (2010): 355–69, https://doi.org/10.1016/j.futures.2009.11.021.
> - Hannah Kosow and Robert Gaßner, *Methods of Future and Scenario Analysis. Overview, Assessment, and Selection Criteria* (2008), https://www.econstor.eu/bitstream/10419/199164/1/die-study-39.pdf.
> - M.S. Reed, J. Kenter, A. Bonn, K. Broad, T.P. Burt, I.R. Fazey, E.D.G. Fraser, K. Hubacek, D. Nainggolan, C.H. Quinn, L.C. Stringer, F. Ravera, "Participatory scenario development for environmental management: A methodological framework illustrated with experience from the UK uplands," *Journal of Environmental Management* 128 (2013): 345-362, https://doi.org/10.1016/j.jenvman.2013.05.016.
> - Philip Notten, *Scenario Development: A Typology of Approaches, Think Scenarios, Rethink Education* (2006), https://www.oecd.org/site/schoolingfortomorrowknowledgebase/futuresthinking/scenarios/scenariodevelopmentatypologyofapproaches.htm.
> - Yousra Tourki, Jeffrey Keisler, and Igor Linkov, I., "Scenario analysis: a review of methods and applications for engineering and environmental systems", *Environment Systems & Decisions* 33 (2013): 3–20, https://doi.org/10.1007/s10669-013-9437-6.

3.3.2 Technology foresight

3.3.2.1 Overview

Foresight is a systematic, participatory, future-intelligence-gathering, and medium-to-long-term vision-building process aimed at present-day decisions and mobilising joint actions.

Research foresight is "the process involved in systematically attempting to look into the longer-term future of science, technology, the economy and society with the aim of identifying the areas of strategic research and the emerging generic technologies likely to yield the greatest economic and social benefits.

Technology foresight is a systematic means of assessing those scientific and technological developments, which could have a *strong impact* on industrial competitiveness, wealth creation and quality of life.

Future-oriented technology analysis methods include, among others: creativity approaches, monitoring and intelligence, descriptive methods, matrices, statistical and trend analyses, road mapping, economic analyses, modelling and simulation.[4]

3.3.2.2 Assessment techniques

- Cinzia Battistella and Alberto F. De Toni, "A methodology of technological foresight: A proposal and field study," *Technological Forecasting and Social Change* 78, no. 6 (2011): 1029-1048, https://doi.org/10.1016/j.techfore.2011.01.006.
- M. Hussain, E. Tapinos, and L. Knight, "Scenario-Driven Roadmapping for Technology Foresight," *Technological Forecasting and Social Change* 124 (2017): 160–77, https://doi.org/10.1016/j.techfore.2017.05.005.
- Alan L. Porter, "Technology foresight: types and methods," *International Journal Foresight and Innovation Policy* 6, no. 1/2/3 (2010): 36–45, https://www.foresightfordevelopment.org/sobipro/download-file/46-590/54.

3.3.3 Cost-benefit analysis

3.3.3.1 Overview

Cost-benefit analysis (CBA) is a tool for the allocation of resources and the selection of economically efficient policies, monetising all involved costs and benefits. It asks the question of whether a single initiative or more "should be undertaken and, if investable funds are limited, which one, two or more among these specific projects that would otherwise qualify for admission should be selected".[5] Put simply, it is "a mathematical tool used by decision-makers to determine if the perceived program benefits outweigh expected costs".[6]

CBA guides decision-making by making a reference predominantly to profitability,[7] in this way promoting efficiency understood as effectiveness as the least waste of resources. In the context of human rights, even values, if these could be translated into monetary terms, they might be better protected, taking into account the costs that occur when rights are violated. This approach could provide decision-makers with a more accurate methodology when human rights are affected. Yet, a criticism of this approach is that it might be unsuitable in certain contexts, as placing a monetary value on human life and suffering is morally illegitimate.[8]

3.3.3.2 Assessment techniques

- Stephanie Riegg Cellini and James Edwin Kee, "Cost-Effectiveness and Cost-Benefit Analysis," in *Handbook of Practical Program Evaluation*, eds. Kathryn E. Newcomer, Harry P. Hatry, and Joseph S. Wholey (New Jersey: John Wiley & Sons, 2015), https://doi.org/10.1002/9781119171386.ch24.
- Ezra J. Mishan and Euston Quah, *Cost-Benefit Analysis* (Taylor & Francis, 2007).
- European Commission, *Guide to Cost-Benefit Analysis of Investment Projects, Economic appraisal tool for Cohesion Policy 2014-2020* (2014), https://ec.europa.eu/regional_policy/sources/docgener/studies/pdf/cba_guide.pdf.
- Michael D. Makowsky and Richard E. Wagner, "From Scholarly Idea to Budgetary Institution: The Emergence of Cost-Benefit Analysis," *Constitutional Political Economy* 20, no. 1 (2009), https://doi.org/10.1007/s10602-008-9051-7.
- Pamela Misuraca, "The Effectiveness of a Costs and Benefits Analysis in Making Federal Government Decisions: A Literature Review," *Igarss* no. 1 (2014), https://doi.org/10.1007/s13398-014-0173-7.2.
- Robert H. Frank, "Why Is Cost-Benefit Analysis so Controversial?," *The Journal of Legal Studies* 29, no. S2 (2000): 913, https://doi.org/10.1086/468099.

3.3.4 Strengths, Weaknesses, Opportunities, Threats

3.3.4.1 Overview

The analysis of strengths, weakness, opportunities and threats (SWOT) is a technique that provides the foundation for realisation of the desired alignment of organisational variables or issues. By listing favourable and unfavourable, internal and external issues in four quadrants of a grid, planners can better understand how strengths can be leveraged to realise new opportunities and how weaknesses can slow progress or magnify organisational threats,[9] and hence act to remedy the latter.

However, other similar types of analyses exist, e.g. that of value, rarity, imitability and organisation (VRIO), which is designed to analyse the competitive implications of a firm's internal strengths and weaknesses, making it possibly useful at the micro-level within an organisation.[10] At a more macro level, other analyses, e.g. PEST analysis (political, economic, socio-cultural and technological), with its derivatives (e.g. adding related societal concerns, such as legal or environmental ones), as well as the STEPE Framework (Social, Technical, Economic, Political, and Ecological) have been developed.[11]

3.3.4.2 Assessment techniques

- Hsu-Hsi Chang and Wen-Chih Huang "Application of a Quantification SWOT Analytical Method," *Mathematical and Computer Modelling* 43, no. 1-2 (2006): 158–69.
- Jay B. Barney, "Looking inside for Competitive Advantage", *Academy of Management Executive* 9, no. 4 (1995): 49–61.
- John V. Richardson, "A Brief Intellectual History of the STEPE Model or Framework (i.e., the Social, Technical, Economic, Political, and Ecological)" (Los Angeles: 2016).
- Marilyn M. Helms and Judy Nixon, "Exploring SWOT Analysis – Where Are We Now?," *Journal of Strategy and Management* 3, no. 3: 215–16, https://doi.org/10.1108/17554251011064837.
- A. Paschalidou, M. Tsatiris, K. Kitikidou, C. Papadopoulou, "Methods (SWOT Analysis)," in *Using Energy Crops for Biofuels or Food: The Choice. Green Energy and Technology* (Springer, 2018), https://doi.org/10.1007/978-3-319-63943-7_6.

3.4 Standalone evaluation techniques

3.4.1 Environmental impact assessment

3.4.1.1 Overview

Environmental Impact Assessment (EIA) is the process of identification, description and assessment of the direct and indirect effects of a project on: human beings, fauna and flora; soil, water, air, climate and the landscape; the interaction of these factors; and on material assets and cultural heritage.[12]

It is used as a tool to identify the environmental, social, and economic impacts of a project prior to decision-making. It aims to predict environmental impacts at an early stage in project planning and design, find ways and means to reduce adverse impacts, shape projects to suit the local environment, and present the predictions and options available to decision-makers. Through use of an EIA, both environmental and economic benefits can be achieved, such as reduced cost and time of project implementation and design, avoidance of treatment/clean-up costs and a better understanding of the impacts of laws and regulations.

The assessment consists of consecutive steps, namely scoping and screening of key issues, identification of impacts and analysis of their significance, impact mitigation, and monitoring and review. Public participation is highly encouraged.[13]

3.4.1.2 Assessment techniques

- National Environmental Policy Act *(NEPA)* [United States]
  - Council on Environmental Quality, *Regulations for Implementing the Procedural Provisions of the National Environmental Policy Act*, Washington 2005, https://ceq.doe.gov/laws-regulations/regulations.html.
  - Council on Environmental Quality, *Collaboration in NEPA. A Handbook for NEPA Practitioners*, Washington 2005, https://www.energy.gov/sites/prod/files/CEQ_Collaboration_in_NEPA_10-2007.pdf.
- A. Lantieri, Z. Lukacova, J. McGuinn, and A. McNeill, *Environmental Impact Assessment of Projects. Guidance on the preparation of the Environmental Impact Assessment Report* (Brussels: 2007), https://ec.europa.eu/environment/eia/pdf/EIA_guidance_EIA_report_final.pdf.
- Bram F. Noble, Bram F. *Introduction to Environmental Impact Assessment. A Guide to Principles and Practice* (Toronto: Oxford University Press, 2015).
- Randall J., Jowett E. *Environmental impact assessment tools and techniques*, World Wildlife Fund, Inc. and American National Red Cross (2010), https://www.sheltercluster.org/resources/documents/grrt-3-environmental-impact-assessment-tools-and-techniques.
- SISSON project, *Final environmental impact assessment (EIA) report, Chapter 5, Methods* (2015), https://iaac-aeic.gc.ca/050/documents_staticpost/63169/93967/Sisson_EIA_July2013_Section_5-0_EIA_Methods.pdf.
- UNESCO, *Environmental Assessment Method*, http://www.unesco.org/new/fileadmin/MULTIMEDIA/HQ/CLT/pdf/ucha_Environmental_Assessment_Method_Southampton.pdf.

3.4.2 Regulatory impact assessment

3.4.2.1 Overview

A regulatory impact assessment (or analysis) (RIA) is a systemic approach to critically identify, assess and evaluate the positive and negative effects of proposed and existing regulations and non-regulatory alternatives. The process of RIA, for example, serves as a tool for the European Commission to estimate the economic, social, and environmental impacts of legislative proposals, non-legislative initiatives (e.g. financial programs) or implementing and delegating acts. It promotes informed decision-making and contributes to better regulation, but does not substitute policy-making *per se*.

The purpose of RIA is at least twofold: on the one hand, for policy-makers to support their reasoning as to why a policy option is preferable in terms of necessity, subsidiarity, proportionality, and objectives pursued compared to other options, and, on the other, for stakeholders (or the general public) to be able to provide feedback during the inception of the legislative process.

3.4.2.2 Assessment techniques

- OECD, "Regulatory Impact Analysis: A Tool for Policy Coherence," in *Regulatory Impact Analysis: A Tool for Policy Coherence* (Paris: OECD Publishing, 2009), https://doi.org/10.1787/9789264067110-1-en.
- OECD, "Best Practice Principles for Regulatory Impact Analysis," in *Regulatory Impact Assessment* (2020), https://www.oecd-ilibrary.org/sites/663f08d9-en/index.html?itemId=/content/component/663f08d9-en.
- European Commission, "Guidelines on impact assessment," in *Better regulation guidelines* (2017), https://ec.europa.eu/info/sites/info/files/better-regulation-guidelines-impact-assessment.pdf.
- World Bank Group, *Global Indicators of Regulatory Governance: Worldwide Practices of Regulatory Impact Assessments* (2018), http://documents1.worldbank.org/curated/en/905611520284525814/pdf/Global-Indicators-of-Regulatory-Governance-Worldwide-Practices-of-Regulatory-Impact-Assessments.pdf.
- Colin Kirkpatrick and David Parker "Regulatory Impact Assessment: An Overview," in *Regulatory Impact Assessment: Towards Better Regulation?* (Cheltenham: Edward Elgar Publishing, 2007), https://doi.org/10.4337/9781847208774.00007.

3.4.3 Strategic niche management

3.4.3.1 Overview

Strategic niche management is a tool supporting the "societal introduction of radical sustainable innovations".[14] In other words, it is a technique designed to "facilitate the introduction and diffusion of new sustainable technologies through societal experiments. Its ultimate aim is to contribute to a broad shift to more sustainable economic development, through an integral combination of technological progress and system-wide social-institutional transformation".[16]

3.4.3.2 Assessment techniques

- Marjolein C.J. Caniëls and Henny A. Romijn, "Strategic Niche Management: Towards a Policy Tool for Sustainable Development," *Technology Analysis & Strategic Management* 20, no. 2 (2008): 245–66, https://doi.org/10.1080/09537320701711264.
- R. Mourik and Rob Raven, *A Practioner's View on Strategic Niche Management Towards a Future Research Outline* (Energy research Centre of the Netherlands, 2006), https://publicaties.ecn.nl/PdfFetch.aspx?nr=ECN-E--06-039.

3.4.4 Privacy impact assessment

3.4.4.1 Overview

Privacy impact assessment (PIA) is the 'process for assessing the impacts on the fundamental right to privacy of a project, policy, program, service, product or other initiative and, in consultation with stakeholders, for taking remedial actions as necessary in order to avoid or minimise the negative impacts'.[17] It usually complements the DPIA process, compensating for the gaps identified where personal data are not processed, but the privacy of individuals is interfered with by a particular technology.[18]

Before the GDPR, and hence before the legal requirement to conduct, in detail, the DPIA process, PIA was the only type of assessment pertaining to processing personal data, while its scope would extent to all kinds of processing operations and technical and organisational measures. For instance, the scope of a PIA included the description of how personal data flowed within a project, analysing the possible impacts on individuals' privacy, identifying and recommending options for avoiding, minimising, or mitigating negative privacy impacts, building privacy considerations into the design of a project, etc. All these steps are nowadays embedded in the DPIA process, which lists in detail all the obligations of the data controller, while the PIA process is employed as a tool for assessing the impacts on the fundamental right to privacy.

3.4.4.2 Assessment techniques

- CNIL, *Privacy Impact Assessment (PIA). Templates* (Paris: 2018), https://www.cnil.fr/sites/default/files/atoms/files/cnil-pia-2-en-templates.pdf.
- CNIL, *Privacy Impact Assessment (PIA). Methodology* (Paris: 2018), https://www.cnil.fr/sites/default/files/atoms/files/cnil-pia-1-en-methodology.pdf.
- EL. Makri, Z. Georgiopoulou, and C. Lambrinoudakis, "A Proposed Privacy Impact Assessment Method Using Metrics Based on Organizational Characteristics," in *Computer Security. CyberICPS 2019, SECPRE 2019, SPOSE 2019, ADIoT 2019. Lecture Notes in Computer Science, vol 11980*, eds. S. Katsikas et al., (Springer, 2020), https://doi.org/10.1007/978-3-030-42048-2_9.
- Marie Caroline Oetzel and Sarah Spiekermann, "A systematic methodology for privacy impact assessments: a design science approach," *European Journal of Information Systems* 23, no. 2 (2014): 126–150, https://doi.org/10.1057/ejis.2013.18.
- Office of the Privacy Commissioner of Canada's, *Guide to the Privacy Impact Assessment Process* (2020), https://www.priv.gc.ca/en/privacy-topics/privacy-impact-assessments/gd_exp_202003/.

- Konstantina Vemou and Maria Karyda, "An evaluation framework for privacy impact assessment methods," Conference: 12th Mediterranean Conference on Information Systems (MCIS2018) (2018), https://www.researchgate.net/publication/326723199_An_evaluation_framework_for_privacy_impact_assessment_methods.
- David Wright and Paul Hert, "Introduction to Privacy Impact Assessment," in *Privacy Impact Assessment* (Dordrecht: Springer, 2012), 3–32, https://doi.org/10.1007/978-94-007-2543-0.

3.4.5 Health impact assessment

3.4.5.1 Overview

A health impact assessment (HIA), or, increasingly frequently, health technology assessment, is a 'systematic study of the consequences of the (introductory or continued) use of a technology in a particular context'. Health impact assessment owes its emergence to gaps in existing mechanisms for the promotion of health in institutional decision-making.[19] A health impact assessment seeks to improve the quality of policy decisions by evaluating any positive or negative health impacts and making recommendations to maximise those deemed positive and mitigate those deemed negative. When properly utilised, health impact assessments recommend options for alternative decisions and mitigation strategies, with the aim of ensuring that any decisions made will protect and promote the population's health.

3.4.5.2 Assessment techniques

- Björn Hofmann, "On Value-Judgements and Ethics in Health Technology Assessment," *Poiesis & Praxis* 3, no. 4 (2005): 278, https://doi.org/10.1007/s10202-005-0073-1.
- Jennifer S. Mindell, Anna Boltong, and Ian Forde, "A Review of Health Impact Assessment Frameworks," *Public Health* 122, no. 11 (2008): 1177–87, https://doi.org/10.1016/j.puhe.2008.03.014.
- World Health Organization. "WHO | Impact Assessment - Directory of References/Resources" (2010), http://www.who.int/heli/impacts/impactdirectory/en/index1.html.
- David Banta, Finn Børlum Kristensen, and Egon Jonsson, "A History of Health Technology Assessment at the European Level," *International Journal of Technology Assessment in Health Care* 25, no. 1 (2009): 68–73. https://doi.org/10.1017/S0266462309090448.

3.4.6 Ethics impact assessment

3.4.6.1 Overview

An ethics impact assessment (eIA) is a process during which an organisation, together with stakeholders, considers the ethical issues or impacts posed by a new project, technology, service, program, piece of legislation, or other initiative, in order to identify risks and solutions.

The steps for conducting an ethics impact assessment could be: a) a decision on which methods should be used, b) a contingency analysis to evaluate the likelihood of ethical impacts, c) assessment of the relative importance of ethical impacts, including identification of potential or actual value conflicts, and e) clarification of the ethical impacts and the related ethical values/principles and formulation of workable conceptualisations.[20]

In addition, Reijers et al. has recently identified, through a systematic literature review, thirty-five different methods to "practice ethics in research and innovation" and arranged them into three groups: "(1) *ex ante* methods, dealing with emerging technologies, (2) intra methods, dealing with technology design, and (3) *ex post* methods, dealing with ethical analysis of existing technologies".[21]

Amongst these, the following are worthy of special mention:
- *Value-Sensitive Design.* Since the revelation that ethical values can be embedded into the process of design of, for example, a technology,[22] many methods to do so have surfaced. One of them is the Value-Sensitive Design, which is a method of "design of a future system in which values of ethical importance are systematically explored throughout the design process to be included in the technical content of the system".[23]
- *Care-Centred Value-Sensitive Design.* A variant thereof, applicable to products and services for medical care, it "provides both an outline of the components demanding ethical attention as well as a step-by-step manner in which such considerations may proceed throughout the design process of a robot: beginning from the moment of idea generation and throughout the design of various prototypes".[24]
- *Responsible Research and Innovation.* This is a "transparent, interactive process by which societal actors and innovators become mutually responsive to each other with a view on the (ethical) acceptability, sustainability and societal desirability of the innovation process and its marketable products (in order to allow a proper embedding of scientific and technological advances in our society)"[25]. This concept is built on "six distinct dimensions termed as follows: engagement, gender equality, science education, ethics, open access and governance".[26] Since its inception, the concept of Responsible Research and Innovation has become an underlying concept for all European Union funding for research and innovation.[27]

3.4.6.2 Assessment techniques

- Aimee van Wynsberghe, "A Method for Integrating Ethics into the Design of Robots," *Industrial Robot: An International Journal* 40, no. 5 (2013): 438, https://doi.org/10.1108/IR-12-2012-451.
- Asle H. Kiran, Nelly Oudshoorn, and Peter-Paul Verbeek, "Beyond Checklists: Toward an Ethical-Constructive Technology Assessment," *Journal of Responsible Innovation* 2, no. 1 (2015): 5–19, https://doi.org/10.1080/23299460.2014.992769.
- Batya Friedman, Peter Kahn, and Alan Borning, *Value Sensitive Design: Theory and Methods* (University of Washington Technical, 2002), https://faculty.washington.edu/pkahn/articles/vsd-theory-methods-tr.pdf.
- Elin Palm and Sven Ove Hansson, "The Case for Ethical Technology Assessment (ETA)," *Technological Forecasting and Social Change* 73, no. 5 (2006), https://doi.org/10.1016/j.techfore.2005.06.002.
- Gill Ringland, "The Role of Scenarios in Strategic Foresight," *Technological Forecasting and Social Change* 77, no. 9 (2010), https://doi.org/10.1016/j.techfore.2010.06.010.
- High-Level Expert Group on Artificial Intelligence, *The Assessment List for Trustworthy Artificial Intelligence* (2020), https://ec.europa.eu/newsroom/dae/document.cfm?doc_id=60419.
- Tsjalling Swierstra and Arie Rip, "Nano-Ethics as NEST-Ethics: Patterns of Moral Argumentation about New and Emerging Science and Technology," *NanoEthics* 1, no. 1 (2007), https://doi.org/10.1007/s11569-007-0005-8.
- Wessel Reijers et. al, *A Common Framework for Ethical Impact Assessment*, Stakeholders Acting Together on the Ethical Impact Assessment of Research and Innovation (SATORI Project, 2016), https://satoriproject.eu/media/D4.1_Annex_1_EIA_Proposal.pdf.

3.4.7 Human rights impact assessment

3.4.7.1 Overview

A human rights impact assessment (HRIA) can be defined as a continuous process for identifying, comprehending, evaluating and addressing the adverse effects emerging from a business project or from activities on the enjoyment of human rights enjoyment by impacted rights-holders, such as workers and community members. It is a relatively new field of impact assessment, compared to the environmental impact assessment or the social impact assessment.

3.4.7.2 Assessment techniques

- Business for Social Responsibility, *Conducting an Effective Human Rights Impact Assessment Guidelines, Steps, and Examples* (2013), http://www.bsr.org/reports/BSR_Human_Rights_Impact_Assessments.pdf.
- James Harrison, "Measuring Human Rights: Reflections on the Practice of Human Rights Impact Assessment and Lessons for the Future," *Warwick School of Law Research Paper No. 2010/26* (2010), http://dx.doi.org/10.2139/ssrn.1706742.
- Nora Götzmann, Tulika Bansal, Elin Wrzoncki, Cathrine Poulsen-Hansen, Jacqueline Tedaldi, and Roya Høvsgaard, *Human rights impact assessment guidance and toolbox* (The Danish Institute for Human Rights, 2016), https://www.humanrights.dk/sites/humanrights.dk/files/media/dokumenter/business/hria_toolbox/hria_guidance_and_toolbox_final_feb2016.pdf.
- Nordic Trust Fund and The World Bank, *Study on Human Rights Impact Assessments: A Review of the Literature, Differences with other Forms of Assessments and Relevance for Development* (2013) https://documents1.worldbank.org/curated/en/834611524474505865/pdf/125557-WP-PUBLIC-HRIA-Web.pdf.
- Alessandro Mantelero, "AI and Big Data: A Blueprint for a Human Rights, Social and Ethical Impact Assessment," *Computer Law & Security Review* 34, no. 4 (2018): 754-772, https://ssrn.com/abstract=3225749.

3.4.8 Social impact assessment

3.4.8.1 Overview

Social impact assessment (SIA) is the process of identifying and managing the social impacts of envisaged projects. It includes the processes of analysing, monitoring, and managing the intended and unintended social consequences, both positive and negative, of planned interventions (including, but not limited to, policies, programs, plans and projects) and any social change processes invoked by those interventions. It is used to predict and mitigate negative impacts and identify opportunities to enhance benefits for local communities and broader society.

The process of an SIA might be both quantitative (statistical) and qualitative (observation, interviews, case studies etc.). It begins with the identification of needs and social problems, participants, and beneficiaries. It continues with the description of action and the initial conditions. It then establishes methods of interaction with affected groups and gauges each alternative. Furthermore, it measures the direct impact of the project, as well as indirect and cumulative impacts. It concludes with recommendations and a plan to counter the impact of undesirable social effects.[28]

3.4.8.2 Assessment techniques

- Raluca Antonie, "Social Impact Assessment Models," *Transylvanian Review of Administrative Sciences* 29E (2010), https://rtsa.ro/tras/index.php/tras/article/view/39.
- Leon Hempel, Lars Ostermeier, Tobias Schaaf, and Dagny Vedder, "Towards a Social Impact Assessment of Security Technologies: A Bottom-up Approach," *Science and Public Policy* 40 (2013): 740–54, https://doi.org/10.1093/scipol/sct086.
- Henk Becker and Frank Vanclay, *The International Handbook of Social Impact Assessment* (Cheltenham: Edward Elgar, 2003), https://doi.org/10.4337/9781843768616.
- Frank Vanclay, Ana Maria Esteves, Ilse Aucamp, and Daniel M. Franks. *Social Impact Assessment: Guidance for Assessing and Managing the Social Impacts of Projects* (Fargo: International Association for Impact Assessment 2015), https://espace.library.uq.edu.au/view/UQ:355365.

3.4.9 Technology assessment

3.4.9.1 Overview

Technology assessment (TA) is defined as a class of policy studies that systematically examine the effects on society that may occur when a technology is introduced, extended or modified. It places an emphasis on those consequences that are unintended, indirect or delayed.[29]

Technology assessment follows the same pattern, with identification of the technology under assessment and affected stakeholders. It continues with an analysis of the precise functionality of the technology and the extent to which it serves its purpose, and finishes with appropriate documentation and a review.

Among the modes of understanding and performing a TA, four approaches are prominent: the classical TA (informing the political sphere about a technology), the participatory TA (enabling the interaction between politicians and society), the argumentative TA (informing about the core values driving science and technology), and the constructive TA (bridging the gap between society and science and technology).[30]

3.4.9.2 Assessment techniques

- Armin Grunwald, "Technology Assessment: Concepts and Methods," in *Philosophy of Technology and Engineering Sciences*, ed. Anthonie Meijers (Amsterdam: Elsevier, 2009), 1103–46, https://doi.org/10.1016/B978-0-444-51667-1.50044-6.
- Joseph F. Coates, "Some methods and techniques for comprehensive impact assessment," *Technological Forecasting and Social Change* 6 (1974): 341-57, https://doi.org/10.1016/0040-1625(74)90035-3.
- Rinie van Est, "The Rathenau Institute's approach to participatory Technology Assessment," *TA-Datenbank Nachrichten* 9, no. 3 (2000): 13-20, https://research.tue.nl/en/publications/the-rathenau-institutes-approach-to-participatory-technology-asse.
- Jan Van Den Ende, Karel Mulder, Marjolijn Knot, Ellen Moors, Philip Vergragt, "Traditional and Modern Technology Assessment: Toward a Toolkit," *Technological Forecasting and Social Change* 58, no. 1–2 (1998): 5-21, https://doi.org/10.1016/S0040-1625(97)00052-8.
- Richard Sclove, *Reinventing Technology Assessment: A 21st Century Model* (Washington: Science and Technology Innovation Program, WoodrowWilson International Center for Scholars, 2010), https://doi.org/10.13140/RG.2.1.3402.5364.

3.4.10 Artificial intelligence impact assessment

3.4.10.1 Overview

Algorithms are increasingly being adopted for the purpose of decision-making, at the expense of human agency. This is already visible in online advertising, social media, and welfare distribution, to name but a few spheres. Such algorithms work by means of data processing, profiling, and inference-drawing, supported by the utilisation of artificial intelligence (AI) and machine learning.

A tool for assessing the impact of artificial intelligence might be warranted in order to cover aspects that have not been taken into consideration by the DPIA. Both instruments are complementary, but not interchangeable, as the artificial intelligence impact assessment (AIIA) is a broader instrument, which focuses on all possible ethical and legal issues that can be associated with the deployment of AI, including the processing of personal data.

Policy developments in the area of AI conclude in the obligation to conduct a process of conformity assessment for high-risk AI systems, with a view to demonstrating their conformity with requirements, such as documentation, record keeping, human oversight, transparency, and provision of information to users.

3.4.10.2 Assessment techniques

- ECP – Platform for the Information Society, *Artificial Intelligence Impact Assessment* (2018), https://ecp.nl/wp-content/uploads/2019/01/Artificial-Intelligence-Impact-Assessment-English.pdf.
- Margot E. Kaminski and Gianclaudio Malgieri, "Algorithmic Impact Assessments under the GDPR: Producing Multi-layered Explanations," *International Data Privacy Law* (2020): ipaa020, https://doi.org/10.1093/idpl/ipaa020.
- Dillon Reisman, Jason Schultz, Kate Crawford, and Meredith Whittaker, *Algorithmic impact assessments: A practical framework for public agency accountability* (AI Now Institute, 2018), https://ainowinstitute.org/aiareport2018.pdf.

3.5 Technology ranking techniques

3.5.1 Overview

With the increased use of quantification (metrification, numerification) and actuarial techniques for decision-making (e.g. probability theory, insurance, statistics) over the last century, a plethora of assessment techniques (e.g. SURVEILLE,[31] DETECTER[32] and HECTOS[33]) have been developed in order to rank the maleficence or, alternatively, beneficence of given technologies, including surveillance and border control technologies. By assigning a numerical grade or a ranking of intrusiveness (interference, invasiveness, etc.) or conformity with a given standard, these assessment techniques allow for an easy comparison of two or more such technologies with a view to making a decision as to their deployment. Such rankings have the benefit of increasing efficiency and eventually granting legitimisation to decision-making processes. Yet, despite their benefits, such ranking techniques are too simplistic and reductionist, assuming the commensurability of the technologies under analysis, and over-simplifying the complexities involved in decision-making.

3.5.2 Literature

- Siddharth Sareen, Andrea Saltelli, and Kjetil Rommetveit, "Ethics of quantification: illumination, obfuscation, and performative legitimation," *Palgrave Communications* 6, no. 1 (2020): 20, https://doi.org/10.1057/s41599-020-0396-5.
- Andrea Saltelli, "Ethics of quantification or quantification of ethics?" *Futures* 116 (2020): 102509, https://doi.org/10.1016/j.futures.2019.102509.
- Zora, Kovacic, "Conceptualizing Numbers at the Science–Policy Interface," *Science, Technology, & Human Values* 43, no. 6 (2018): 1039–65, https://doi.org/10.1177/0162243918770734.

Endnotes

1. Dariusz Kloza et al., 'Towards a Method for Data Protection Impact Assessment: Making Sense of GDPR Requirements', d.pia.lab Policy Brief (Brussels: VUB, 2019), 1, https://doi.org/10.31228/osf.io/es8bm.
2. Ibid.
3. ISO/IEC 27000:2018, Information technology — Security techniques — Information security management systems — Overview and vocabulary, ISO 27000:2018, Geneva.
4. A.L. Porter (2010), "Technology foresight: types and methods," *International Journal Foresight and Innovation Policy* 6, No. 1/2/3 (2010): 36–45.
5. E. J. Mishan and Euston Quah, *Cost-Benefit Analysis* (London: Routledge, 2007), 4.
6. Michael D. Makowsky and Richard E. Wagner, "From Scholarly Idea to Budgetary Institution: The Emergence of Cost-Benefit Analysis," *Constitutional Political Economy* 20, no. 1 (2009): 62, https://doi.org/10.1007/s10602-008-9051-7; Pamela Misuraca, "The Effectiveness of a Costs and Benefits Analysis in Making Federal Government Decisions: A Literature Review," *Igarss 2014*, no. 1 (2014): 1, https://doi.org/10.1007/s13398-014-0173-7.2.
7. Mishan and Quah, *Cost-Benefit Analysis*.
8. Robert H. Frank, "Why Is Cost-Benefit Analysis so Controversial?," *The Journal of Legal Studies* 29, no. S2 (2000): 913–30, https://doi.org/10.1086/468099.
9. Marilyn M. Helms and Judy Nixon, "Exploring SWOT Analysis – Where Are We Now?," *Journal of Strategy and Management* 3, no. 3 (2010): 215–51, https://doi.org/10.1108/17554251011064837.
10. Jay B. Barney, 'Looking inside for Competitive Advantage', *Academy of Management Executive* 9, no. 4 (1995): 49–61.
11. John V. Richardson, "A Brief Intellectual History of the STEPE Model or Framework (i.e., the Social, Technical, Economic, Political, and Ecological)" (Los Angeles, 2016).
12. UNESCO, 'Environmental Assessment Method', http://www.unesco.org/new/fileadmin/MULTIMEDIA/HQ/CLT/pdf/ucha_Environmental_Assessment_Method_Southampton.pdf.
13. Ibid.
14. R. Mourik and Rob Raven, *A Practioner's View on Strategic Niche Management Towards a*
15. *Future Research Outline* (Energy research Centre of the Netherlands, 2006), https://publicaties.ecn.nl/PdfFetch.aspx?nr=ECN-E--06-039.
16. Marjolein C.J. Caniëls and Henny A Romijn, "Strategic Niche Management: Towards a Policy Tool for Sustainable Development," *Technology Analysis & Strategic Management* 20, no. 2 (2008): 245–66, https://doi.org/10.1080/09537320701711264.
17. David Wright and Paul Hert, "Privacy Impact Assessment," in *Privacy Impact Assessment* (Dordrecht: Springer, 2012), 3–32, https://doi.org/10.1007/978-94-007-2543-0.
18. Paul De Hert, Dariusz Kloza, and David Wright, "Recommendations for a Privacy Impact Assessment Framework for the European Union" (Brussels – London, 2012), https://researchportal.vub.be/files/14231615/PIAF_D3_final.pdf.
19. Björn Hofmann, "On Value-Judgements and Ethics in Health Technology Assessment," *Poiesis & Praxis* 3, no. 4 (2005): 277-95, https://doi.org/10.1007/s10202-005-0073-1.
20. Wessel Reijers et. al (2016), 'A Common Framework for Ethical Impact Assessment', Stakeholders Acting Together on the Ethical Impact Assessment of Research and Innovation – SATORI project https://satoriproject.eu/media/D4.1_Annex_1_EIA_Proposal.pdf.
21. Wessel Reijers et al., "Methods for Practising Ethics in Research and Innovation: A Literature Review, Critical Analysis and Recommendations," *Science and Engineering Ethics* 24, no. 5 (2018): 1437–81, https://doi.org/10.1007/s11948-017-9961-8.

22. Helen Nissenbaum, "How Computer Systems Embody Values," *Computer* 34, no. 3 (2001): 117–19, https://doi.org/10.1109/2.910905.
23. Aimee van Wynsberghe, "Designing Robots with Care" (University of Twente, 2012), 10, https://doi.org/10.3990/1.9789036533911.
24. Aimee van Wynsberghe, "A Method for Integrating Ethics into the Design of Robots," *Industrial Robot: An International Journal* 40, no. 5 (2013): 433–40, https://doi.org/10.1108/IR-12-2012-451.
25. René von Schomberg, ed., *Towards Responsible Research and Innovation in the Information and Communication Technologies and Security Technologies Fields* (Luxembourg: Publications Office of the European Union, 2011), 9.
26. Mirjam Burget, Emanuele Bardone, and Margus Pedaste, "Definitions and Conceptual Dimensions of Responsible Research and Innovation: A Literature Review," *Science and Engineering Ethics* 23, no. 1 (February 2017): 9, https://doi.org/10.1007/s11948-016-9782-1.
27. cf. Rome Declaration on Responsible Research and Innovation in Europe, 21 November 2014; https://ec.europa.eu/research/swafs/pdf/rome_declaration_RRI_final_21_November.pdf; Regulation (EU) No 1290/2013 of the European Parliament and of the Council of 11 December 2013 laying down the rules for participation and dissemination in "Horizon 2020 – the Framework Programme for Research and Innovation (2014-2020)" and repealing Regulation (EC) No 1906/2006, OJ L 347, 20.12.2013, pp. 81-103; Regulation (EU) No 1291/2013 of the European Parliament and of the Council of 11 December 2013 establishing Horizon 2020 – the Framework Programme for Research and Innovation (2014-2020) and repealing Decision No 1982/2006/EC, OJ L 347, 20.12.2013, pp. 104-173. cf. also https://www.rri-tools.eu.
28. Raluca Antonie, "Social Impact Assessment Models," *Transylvanian Review of Administrative Sciences* 29E (2010), https://rtsa.ro/tras/index.php/tras/article/view/39.
29. Joseph F. Coates, "Technology Assessment – A Tool Kit," *Chemtech* (1976): 372-383.
30. Rinie van Est, "The Rathenau Institute's approach to participatory Technology Assessment," *TA-Datenbank Nachrichten* 9, no. 3 (2000): 13-20, https://research.tue.nl/en/publications/the-rathenau-institutes-approach-to-participatory-technology-asse.
31. *Surveillance: Ethical Issues, Legal Limitations, and Efficiency*, 2012-15, https://cordis.europa.eu/project/id/284725.
32. *Detection Technologies, Terrorism, Ethics and Human Rights*, 2008-12, https://cordis.europa.eu/project/id/217862.
33. *Harmonized Evaluation, Certification and Testing of Security Products*, 2014-18, https://cordis.europa.eu/project/id/606861, http://hectos-fp7.eu/.

Annex 4: Inventory of relevant EU legal and regulatory instruments for border management[1]

Alessandra CALVI
Vrije Universiteit Brussel. E-mail: alessandra.calvi@vub.be.

4.1 Primary law

- Treaty on the European Union[2]
  - in particular: Article 3(2)
- Treaty on the Functioning of the European Union[3]
  - in particular: Title V Area of Freedom, Security and Justice
  - Protocol (No. 19) on the Schengen acquis integrated into the framework of the European Union
  - Protocol (No. 21) on the position of the United Kingdom and Ireland in respect of the area of freedom, security and justice
  - Protocol (No. 22) on the position of Denmark
  - Protocol (No. 23) on external relations of the Member States with regard to the crossing of external borders
  - Protocol (No. 24) on asylum for nationals of Member States of the European Union
  - Declaration (36) on Article 218 of the Treaty on the Functioning of the European Union concerning the negotiation and conclusion of international agreements by Member States relating to the area of freedom, security and justice
- Charter of Fundamental Rights of the European Union[4]

4.2 Secondary law

Schengen and Schengen Information System (SIS)
- Agreement between the Governments of the States of the Benelux Economic Union, the Federal Republic of Germany and the French Republic on the gradual abolition of checks at their common borders (14 June 1985)[5]
- Convention Implementing the Schengen Agreement of 14 June 1985 between the Governments of the States of the Benelux Economic Union, the Federal Republic of Germany and the French Republic, on the gradual abolition of checks at their common borders (19 June 1990)[6]
- Regulation (EC) No. 1986/2006 of the European Parliament and of the Council of 20 December 2006 regarding access to the second-generation Schengen Information System (SIS II) by the services in the Member States responsible for issuing vehicle registration certificates (cooperation on vehicle registration)[7]
- Regulation (EC) No. 1987/2006 of the European Parliament and of the Council of 20 December 2006 on the establishment, operation and use of the second-generation Schengen Information System (SIS II) (border control cooperation)[8]
- Annex to the Commission Recommendation establishing a common "Practical Handbook for Border Guards" to be used by Member States' competent authorities when carrying out the border control of persons and replacing Commission Recommendation C(2006) 5186 of 6 November 2006 [C(2019) 7131 final]
- Council Decision 2007/533/JHA of 12 June 2007 on the establishment, operation and use of the second-generation Schengen Information System (SIS II) (law enforcement cooperation)[9]
- Commission Decision 2010/261/EU of 4 May 2010 on the Security Plan for Central SIS II and the Communication Infrastructure[10]
- Regulation (EU) 2016/399 of the European Parliament and of the Council of 9 March 2016 on a Union Code on the rules governing the movement of persons across borders (Schengen Borders Code)[11]
- Commission Implementing Decision 2013/115/EU of 26 February 2013 on the Sirene Manual and other implementing measures for the second generation Schengen Information System (SIS II)[12]
- Commission Implementing Decision (EU) 2017/1528 of 31 August 2017 replacing the Annex to Implementing Decision 2013/115/EU on the SIRENE Manual and other implementing measures for the second generation Schengen Information System (SIS II)[13] [C(2017) 5893]
- Regulation (EU) 2018/1860 of the European Parliament and of the Council of 28 November 2018 on the use of the Schengen Information System for the return of illegally staying third-country nationals[14]

- Regulation (EU) 2018/1861 of the European Parliament and of the Council of 28 November 2018 on the establishment, operation and use of the Schengen Information System (SIS) in the field of border checks, and amending the Convention implementing the Schengen Agreement, and amending and repealing Regulation (EC) No. 1987/2006[15]
- Regulation (EU) 2018/1862 of the European Parliament and of the Council of 28 November 2018 on the establishment, operation and use of the Schengen Information System (SIS) in the field of police cooperation and judicial cooperation in criminal matters, amending and repealing Council Decision 2007/533/JHA, and repealing Regulation (EC) No. 1986/2006 of the European Parliament and of the Council and Commission Decision 2010/261/EU[16]
- Proposal COM(2020) 791 final [2020/0350(COD)] for a Regulation of the European Parliament and of the Council amending Regulation (EU) 2018/1862 on the establishment, operation and use of the Schengen Information System (SIS) in the field of police cooperation and judicial cooperation in criminal matters as regards the entry of alerts by Europol

Visa Information System (VIS)
- Council Decision 2004/512/EC of 8 June 2004 establishing the Visa Information System (VIS)[17]
- Regulation (EC) No. 767/2008 of the European Parliament and of the Council of 9 July 2008 concerning the Visa Information System (VIS) and the exchange of data between Member States on short-stay visas (VIS Regulation)[18]
- Council Decision 2008/633/JHA of 23 June 2008 concerning access for consultation of the Visa Information System (VIS) by designated authorities of Member States and by Europol for the purposes of the prevention, detection and investigation of terrorist offences and of other serious criminal offences[19]
- Regulation (EC) No. 810/2009 of the European Parliament and of the Council of 13 July 2009 establishing a Community Code on Visas[20]
- Commission Decision 2006/648/EC of 22 September 2006 laying down the technical specifications on the standards for biometric features related to the development of the Visa Information System[21] [C(2006) 3699]
- Commission Implementing Decision amending Commission Decision No. C(2010) 1620 final of 19 March 2010 establishing the Handbook for the processing of visa applications and the modification of issued visa ("Visa Handbook") [C(2019) 3464 final]
- Proposal COM(2018) 302 final [2018/0152(COD)] Proposal for a Regulation of the European Parliament and of the Council amending Regulation (EC) No. 767/2008, Regulation (EC) No. 810/2009, Regulation (EU) 2017/2226, Regulation (EU) 2016/399, Regulation XX/2018 [Interoperability Regulation], and Decision 2004/512/EC and repealing Council Decision 2008/633/JHA

European Dactyloscopy (Eurodac)
- Regulation (EU) No. 604/2013 of the European Parliament and of the Council of 26 June 2013 establishing the criteria and mechanisms for determining the Member State responsible for examining an application for international protection lodged in one of the Member States by a third-country national or a stateless person (recast)[22]
- Regulation (EU) No. 603/2013 of the European Parliament and of the Council of 26 June 2013 on the establishment of 'Eurodac' for the comparison of fingerprints for the effective application of Regulation (EU) No. 604/2013 establishing the criteria and mechanisms for determining the Member State responsible for examining an application for international protection lodged in one of the Member States by a third-country national or a stateless person and on requests for the comparison with Eurodac data by Member States' law enforcement authorities and Europol for law enforcement purposes, and amending Regulation (EU) No. 1077/2011 establishing a European Agency for the operational management of large-scale IT systems in the area of freedom, security and justice[23]
- Commission Regulation (EC) No. 1560/2003 of 2 September 2003 laying down detailed rules for the application of Council Regulation (EC) No. 343/2003 establishing the criteria and mechanisms for determining the Member State responsible for examining an asylum application lodged in one of the Member States by a third-country national[24]
- Proposal COM(2016)0272 final [2016/0132 (COD)] for a Regulation of the European Parliament and of the Council for a on the establishment of 'Eurodac' for the comparison of fingerprints for the effective application of [Regulation (EU) No. 604/2013 establishing the criteria and mechanisms for determining the Member State responsible for examining an application for international protection lodged in one of the Member States by a third-country national or a stateless person] , for identifying an illegally staying third-country national or stateless person and on requests for the comparison with Eurodac data by Member States' law enforcement authorities and Europol for law enforcement purposes (recast)
- Amended proposal COM(2020) 614 final [2016/0132(COD)] for a Regulation of the European Parliament and of the Council on the establishment of 'Eurodac' for the comparison of biometric data for the effective application of Regulation (EU) XXX/XXX [Regulation on Asylum and Migration Management] and of Regulation (EU) XXX/XXX [Resettlement Regulation], for identifying an illegally staying third-country national or stateless person and on requests for the comparison with Eurodac data by Member States' law enforcement authorities and Europol for law enforcement purposes and amending Regulations (EU) 2018/1240 and (EU) 2019/818
- Proposal COM(2020) 612 final [2020/0278(COD)] for a Regulation of the European Parliament and of the Council introducing a screening of third country nationals at the external borders and amending Regulations (EC) No. 767/2008, (EU) 2017/2226, (EU) 2018/1240 and (EU) 2019/817

Entry-Exit System (EES)
- Regulation (EU) 2017/2225 of the European Parliament and of the Council of 30 November 2017 amending Regulation (EU) 2016/399 as regards the use of the Entry/Exit System[25]
- Regulation (EU) 2017/2226 of the European Parliament and of the Council of 30 November 2017 establishing an Entry/Exit System (EES) to register entry and exit data and refusal of entry data of third-country nationals crossing the external borders of the Member States and determining the conditions for access to the EES for law enforcement purposes, and amending the Convention implementing the Schengen Agreement and Regulations (EC) No. 767/2008 and (EU) No. 1077/2011[26]
- Commission Implementing Decision (EU) 2018/1547 of 15 October 2018 laying down the specifications for the connection of the central access points to the Entry/Exit System (EES) and for a technical solution to facilitate the collection of data by Member States for the purpose of generating statistics on the access to the EES data for law enforcement purposes[27]
- Commission Implementing Decision (EU) 2019/326 of 25 February 2019 laying down measures for entering the data in the Entry/Exit System (EES)[28]
- Commission Implementing Decision (EU) 2019/329 of 25 February 2019 laying down the specifications for the quality, resolution and use of fingerprints and facial image for biometric verification and identification in the Entry/Exit System (EES)[29]

European Travel Information and Authorization System (ETIAS)
- Regulation (EU) 2018/1240 of the European Parliament and of the Council of 12 September 2018 establishing a European Travel Information and Authorization System (ETIAS) and amending Regulations (EU) No. 1077/2011, (EU) No. 515/2014, (EU) 2016/399, (EU) 2016/1624 and (EU) 2017/2226[30]
- Regulation (EU) 2018/1241 of the European Parliament and of the Council of 12 September 2018 amending Regulation (EU) 2016/794 for the purpose of establishing a European Travel Information and Authorization System (ETIAS)[31]

European Criminal Records Information System for Third Country Nationals (ECRIS-TCN)
- Council Framework Decision 2009/315/JHA of 26 February 2009 on the organisation and content of the exchange of information extracted from the criminal record between Member States[32]
- Council Decision 2009/316/JHA of 6 April 2009 on the establishment of the European Criminal Records Information System (ECRIS) in application of Article 11 of Framework Decision 2009/315/JHA[33]
- Regulation (EU) 2019/816 of the European Parliament and of the Council of 17 April 2019 establishing a centralised system for the identification of Member States holding conviction information on third-country nationals and stateless persons

(ECRIS-TCN) to supplement the European Criminal Records Information System and amending Regulation (EU) 2018/1726[34]
- Directive (EU) 2019/884 of the European Parliament and of the Council of 17 April 2019 amending Council Framework Decision 2009/315/JHA, as regards the exchange of information on third-country nationals and as regards the European Criminal Records Information System (ECRIS), and replacing Council Decision 2009/316/JHA[35]

Interoperability
- Regulation (EU) 2019/817 of the European Parliament and of the Council of 20 May 2019 on establishing a framework for interoperability between EU information systems in the field of borders and visa and amending Regulations (EC) No. 767/2008, (EU) 2016/399, (EU) 2017/2226, (EU) 2018/1240, (EU) 2018/1726 and (EU) 2018/1861 of the European Parliament and of the Council and Council Decisions 2004/512/EC and 2008/633/JHA[36]
- Regulation (EU) 2019/818 of the European Parliament and of the Council of 20 May 2019 on establishing a framework for interoperability between EU information systems in the field of police and judicial cooperation, asylum and migration and amending Regulations (EU) 2018/1726, (EU) 2018/1862 and (EU) 2019/816[37]

Prüm Convention
- Council Decision 2008/615/JHA of 23 June 2008 on the stepping up of cross-border cooperation, particularly in combating terrorism and cross-border crime[38]
- Council Decision 2008/616/JHA of 23 June 2008 on the implementation of Decision 2008/615/JHA on the stepping up of cross-border cooperation, particularly in combating terrorism and cross-border crime[39]

European Border Surveillance System (Eurosur)
- Regulation (EU) No. 1052/2013 of the European Parliament and of the council of 22 October 2013 establishing the European Border Surveillance System (Eurosur)[40]
- Regulation (EU) 2019/1896 of the European Parliament and of the Council of 13 November 2019 on the European Border and Coast Guard and repealing Regulations (EU) No. 1052/2013 and (EU) 2016/1624[41]

Passenger Name Records (PNR)
- Directive (EU) 2016/681 of the European Parliament and of the Council of 27 April 2016 on the use of passenger name record (PNR) data for the prevention, detection, investigation and prosecution of terrorist offences and serious crime[42]
- Passenger name records (PNR) Updated list of Member States who have decided the application of the PNR Directive to intra-EU flights as referred to in Article 2 of Directive (EU) 2016/681 of the European Parliament and of the Council on the use of

Annex 4

passenger name record (PNR) data for the prevention, detection, investigation and prosecution of terrorist offences and serious crime[43]
- Passenger name records (PNR) — Passenger Information Units — List of the Passenger Information Units referred to in Article 4 of Directive (EU) 2016/681 of the European Parliament and of the Council on the use of passenger name record (PNR) data for the prevention, detection, investigation and prosecution of terrorist offences and serious crime[44]
- Agreement between the European Union and Australia on the processing and transfer of Passenger Name Record (PNR) data by air carriers to the Australian Customs and Border Protection Service[45]
- Agreement between the United States of America and the European Union on the use and transfer of passenger name records to the United States Department of Homeland Security[46]

API
- Council Directive 2004/82/EC of 29 April 2004 on the obligation of carriers to communicate passenger data[47]

Dual-use
- Regulation (EC) No. 428/2009 of 5 May 2009 setting up a Community regime for the control of exports, transfer, brokering and transit of dual-use items[48]

Unmanned aircraft systems
- Commission Delegated Regulation (EU) 2019/945 of 12 March 2019 on unmanned aircraft systems and on third-country operators of unmanned aircraft systems[49]
- Commission Implementing Regulation (EU) 2019/947 of 24 May 2019 on the rules and procedures for the operation of unmanned aircraft[50]

Passports
- Council Regulation (EC) No. 2252/2004 of 13 December 2004 on standards for security features and biometrics in passports and travel documents issued by Member States
- International Civil Aviation Organization (ICAO) Doc 9303 Machine Readable Travel Documents, 7th edition, 2015[51]

Identity cards
- Regulation (EU) 2019/1157 of the European Parliament and of the Council of 20 June 2019 on strengthening the security of identity cards of Union citizens and of residence documents issued to Union citizens and their family members exercising their right of free movement[52] applicable from 2 August 2021
- ICAO Doc 9303 Machine Readable Travel Documents, 7th edition, 2015

EU bodies and agencies
- Regulation (EU) 2018/1726 of the European Parliament and of the Council of 14 November 2018 on the European Union Agency for the Operational Management of Large-Scale IT Systems in the Area of Freedom, Security and Justice (eu-LISA), and amending Regulation (EC) No. 1987/2006 and Council Decision 2007/533/JHA and repealing Regulation (EU) No. 1077/2011[53]
- Regulation (EU) 2019/1896 of the European Parliament and of the Council of 13 November 2019 on the European Border and Coast Guard and repealing Regulations (EU) No. 1052/2013 and (EU) 2016/1624[54]
- Regulation (EU) No. 439/2010 of the European Parliament and of the Council of 19 May 2010 establishing a European Asylum Support Office[55]
- Regulation (EU) 2016/794 of the European Parliament and of the Council of 11 May 2016 on the European Union Agency for Law Enforcement Cooperation (Europol) and replacing and repealing Council Decisions 2009/371/JHA, 2009/934/JHA, 2009/935/JHA, 2009/936/JHA and 2009/968/JHA[56]
- Proposal COM(2020)796 final [2020/0349(COD)] for a Regulation of the European Parliament and of the Council amending Regulation (EU) 2016/794, as regards Europol's cooperation with private parties, the processing of personal data by Europol in support of criminal investigations, and Europol's role on research and innovation
- Regulation (EU) 2018/1727 of the European Parliament and of the Council of 14 November 2018 on the European Union Agency for Criminal Justice Cooperation (Eurojust), and replacing and repealing Council Decision 2002/187/JHA[57]

Endnotes

1. The list also contains non-legally binding proposals aimed at updating current instruments.
2. OJ C 326, 26.10.2012, pp. 13–390.
3. OJ C 326, 26.10.2012, pp. 47–390.
4. OJ C 326, 26.10.2012, pp. 391–407.
5. OJ L 239, 22.9.2000, pp. 13–18.
6. OJ L 239, 22.9.2000, pp. 19–62.
7. OJ L 381, 28.12.2006, pp. 1–3.
8. OJ L 381, 28.12.2006, pp. 4–23.
9. OJ L 205, 7.8.2007, pp. 63–84.
10. OJ L 112, 5.5.2010, pp. 31–37.
11. OJ L 77, 23.3.2016, pp. 1–52.
12. OJ L 71, 14.3.2013, pp. 1–36.
13. OJ L 231, 7.9.2017, pp. 6–51.
14. OJ L 312, 7.12.2018, pp. 1–13.
15. OJ L 312, 7.12.2018, pp. 14–55.
16. OJ L 312, 7.12.2018, pp. 56–106.
17. OJ L 213, 15.6.2004, pp. 5–7.

18. OJ L 218, 13.8.2008, pp. 60–81.
19. OJ L 218, 13.8.2008, pp. 129–136.
20. OJ L 243, 15.9.2009, pp. 1–58.
21. OJ L 267, 27.9.2006, pp. 41–43.
22. OJ L 180, 29.6.2013, pp. 31–59.
23. OJ L 180, 29.6.2013, pp. 1–30.
24. OJ L 222, 5.9.2003, pp. 3–23.
25. OJ L 327, 9.12.2017, pp. 1–19.
26. OJ L 327, 9.12.2017, pp. 20–82.
27. OJ L 259, 16.10.2018, pp. 35–38.
28. OJ L 57, 26.2.2019, pp. 5–9.
29. OJ L 57, 26.2.2019, pp. 18–28.
30. OJ L 236, 19.9.2018, pp. 1–71.
31. OJ L 236, 19.9.2018, pp. 72–73.
32. OJ L 93, 7.4.2009, pp. 23–32.
33. OJ L 93, 7.4.2009, pp. 33–48.
34. OJ L 135, 22.5.2019, pp. 1–26.
35. OJ L 151, 7.6.2019, pp. 143–150.
36. OJ L 135, 22.5.2019, pp. 27–84
37. OJ L 135, 22.5.2019, pp. 85–135.
38. OJ L 210, 6.8.2008, pp. 1–11.
39. OJ L 210, 6.8.2008, pp. 12–72.
40. OJ L 295, 6.11.2013, pp. 11–26.
41. See in particular Chapter II Section 3 and Article 89; OJ L 295, 14.11.2019, pp. 1–131.
42. OJ L 119, 4.5.2016, pp. 132–14.
43. OJ C 358, 26.10.2020, p. 7.
44. OJ C 230, 2.7.2018, p. 6.
45. OJ L 186, 14.7.2012, pp. 4–16.
46. OJ L 215, 11.8.2012, pp. 5–14.
47. OJ L 261, 6.8.2004, pp. 24–27.
48. OJ L 134, 29.5.2009, pp. 1–269.
49. OJ L 152, 11.6.2019, pp. 1–40.
50. OJ L 152, 11.6.2019, pp. 45–71.
51. Cf. https://www.icao.int/publications/pages/publication.aspx?docnum=9303.
52. OJ L 188, 12.7.2019, pp. 67–78.
53. OJ L 295, 21.11.2018, pp. 99–137.
54. OJ L 295, 14.11.2019, pp. 1–131.
55. OJ L 132, 29.5.2010, pp. 11–28.
56. OJ L 135, 24.5.2016, pp. 53–114.
57. OJ L 295, 21.11.2018, pp. 138–183.